Grassroots Philosophy

and Real People

Best wishes

Leonard Friesen

By
Leonard Friesen
Author of the books
Cows, Cowboys, Cattlemen & Characters
Round-Up of Memories
Cattle Call

National Library of Canada Cataloguing in Publication Data

Friesen, Leonard, 1926-
 Grassroots Philosophy and Real People

 ISBN 1-55056-853-1

 I. Title.
PS8561.R49586G72 2001   081   C2001-911214-9
PR9199.3.F765G72 2001

Cover design by
Dorothea Schaab

Published by Friesen Cattle Company
Box 3511
Airdrie, Alberta, Canada
T4B 2B7

Printed and bound in Canada by Friesens Corporation

TABLE OF CONTENTS

ACKNOWLEDGEMENTS

Writing a book is a huge task. Like anything else in this life, other people are involved in such a venture.

In this particular book, I was pretty much on my own. However, many of the stories, anecdotes and incidents involve other people and, without their input and consent, some stories would not be told.

The Bible verses, which I quote, are from the King James translation. I am also grateful to the "Bard", William Shakespeare, for his wisdom, as well as other sages whom I quote and give credit to.

I want to thank Will, Ann and Shamus Verboven for word processing some chapters. Another person who deciphered some of the manuscript and helped put it into print was Darrel Stonehouse. I appreciated the encouragement I received from Lee Gunderson. I also thank Garth McLintock and the staff at *Alberta Beef* for permitting me to reprint some of the columns which I wrote for that magazine.

A special thank you to Dorothea Schaab and her assistants Angie Bellavance and Sandi Heath, for doing an excellent job of getting this book print-ready. It was a pleasure working with Dorothea, just as it was a number of years ago when she was editor of *World of Beef.*

I must not forget to thank my wife, Edna, for her patience while I was scribbling away for hours at a time. I would often read some of my writings to her for her to critique. I must admit I did not always take her advice on changes, but a few times at her suggestion, I did change some things which I had written.

Thanks to the rest of our family and also to some of my friends for your moral support.

As with all my previous books, I have received no assistance in the form of grants, funds or loans. Maybe it is false pride on my part, but I like to be financially independent when I write a book.

INTRODUCTION

I have written several books about the cattle industry and the people involved in it. These books have been well received. In this book, I decided to write about various areas of life which everyone experiences. Life is full of positive things, but we also encounter situations which cause us heartache and pain.

The secret is how we overcome adversity and carry on. As the old saying goes, if life hands you a lemon, make lemonade or, when the going gets tough, the tough get going.

The Bible contains a lot of wisdom. Whether or not we believe in God and the Bible, the fact remains, there is no other book which has more good advice and encouragement on how to live our daily lives. I quote a few scriptures in some chapters. Those who are not familiar nor interested in the Bible may be surprised at how our lives parallel the lives of people from thousands of years ago.

My goal, when I wrote this book, was to portray a mosaic of everyday life. I have only scratched the surface. There are hundreds of other forces and subjects which impact us every day.

I like philosophy. I am not an expert on the subject, but I have always appreciated the wisdom that many ancient philosophers put down on paper. We still enjoy reading their writings centuries later.

It may be presumptuous on my part to proclaim myself a grassroots philosopher, but you be the judge.

Most people have a philosophy about what life is all about. Few are bold enough, or maybe dumb enough, to put it on paper where it will undergo the scrutiny of other people.

What I like about philosophy is that it is someone else's ideas about various things. We may ponder that person's thoughts and views on life. It is our privilege to agree or disagree. I think that those who read this book will agree with most of the content. A few may disagree but, like I said, that is their privilege.

The historical accounts in this book are accurate, as are ninety-five percent of the incidents and stories about people. I seldom reveal their identity for obvious reasons. I received great satisfaction and pleasure writing the manuscript. I hope you experience the same when you read it.

CHAPTER ONE

READING AND WRITING

Reading and writing and arithmetic, taught to the rule of a hickory stick. You were my bashful, barefoot boy, I was your girl in calico, when we were a couple of kids.

This little ditty pretty well sums up what it was like in little country schools from the 1880s to 1950. I can relate to this. The little country school, which I went to was just like that. We learned reading, writing and arithmetic, plus language (grammar), history and geography. As for the hickory stick, it was absent. A leather strap took its place. I was bashful, but not barefoot, although some kids were barefoot. I was never a student of women's or girl's apparel, but I do think calico is still around, along with cotton and organdie.

Our education system does not put high enough emphasis on grade school (grades one to six). But there are a lot of dedicated teachers who help kids build a foundation that will propel them through junior and senior high school and then on to post-secondary education in colleges, universities and technical schools.

A young child's mind is completely open to new ideas and the fundamentals of life. Good parents, along with good teachers, are the catapult which launches children along life's journey. A child's mind is somewhat like a seed that is planted in the ground. If the weather and moisture conditions are right, the seed will sprout and grow. However, if it turns dry, the new plant may not develop very well, if at all.

Unfortunately, we are not all born with the same mental capacities. But even some slow learners will do well if they have a good teacher. Two young men that I know had a tough time in grades one and two. Because of good teaching, things kept improving until both became top students. Today, they are in university and both are doing well. One is studying to become a teacher; the other, an engineer.

The point which I am trying to make is that good teaching at the lower level has a tremendous impact on how well we do later in life.

Spenst School, five miles north of Waldeck, Saskatchewan. This was a typical one-room school, which dotted the prairie's landscape from the turn of the 20ᵗʰ Century until after the Second World War. Some of my cousins (the Nick Friesen family) attended this school. I went to several dances there in the early 'Forties.

Reading has always been the basis for attaining knowledge. It has been with us from the beginning of time. Hieroglyphics in ancient Egyptian tombs and in other areas of the world tell us stories from thousands of years ago. Some people have spent a lifetime deciphering those ancient writings and pictures, many from caves in Europe. The scholars in the Old Testament were called scribes. The large masses of people could not read nor write. After the invention of the printing press by Johann Gutenberg in Germany in 1440, reading became more widespread.

Although many people could not read, that did not stop philosophers and other wise men, starting from about 400 BC, through the middle ages to the present, from putting their thoughts on paper. It has had a profound influence on society. Without the written records of the Bible and other historical writings from past civilizations like China, our information of world history would be meager. Archeological diggings reveal some of this ancient history and activity but the written records do not need the imagination and interpretation archeology does.

A few years ago, some scholars researched the spelling in a Webster dictionary. They discovered there were three hundred and fifty-two spelling errors. I found that rather interesting. It made me feel a little better about my spelling mistakes. Some of those mistakes may have included words which may be spelled several different ways such as, meagre or meager, centre or center, cheque or check. In fact, Canadians and Americans often spell words differently. So we will give the dictionary the benefit of the doubt.

Some modern writers use words that ninety percent of the population do not understand. Many people also like to use big words when they speak or write to the general public. They might as well use Greek or Latin. That kind of writing or speaking is okay between academics or people anticipating writing a thesis for a doctorate. I am not inferring everyone is ignorant if he or she does not understand many seldom-used big words. Many of our young, and older, well-educated people do know the meaning of those words. I have the feeling some folks think it is avant-garde when they use words and phrases that few people understand. This is especially true of people who use those kinds of words along with a phony-practised accent.

Following are some words that folks use in their speech or writing: phenomenalism, zeugma, acephalous, pseudepigraphy, infelicicitous, abstemious, lurdane, protozoal, williewaught, dichotomy, iconographer, abalone, expurgate, acquiesce, incommunicado, quintessential, hypothesis, solfatarg, polygyny, epitomize, provenance and oxymoron.

In my lifetime, I have read hundreds of books and magazines. For over fifty years, I have read a daily newspaper nearly every day, which is approximately eighteen thousand issues. I have written four books. In spite of all my reading, I must confess that of the twenty-two words above, I only knew the meaning of four or five. How many did you know without looking in a dictionary? The reason I do not know the meaning of many words is because when I read a book or an article with difficult words, I skim over it. Rarely, do I pick up a dictionary to see what a word means, although occasionally I do.

I am sure my little tirade about people using words that few people know the meaning of will not change their habits but it gives me a good feeling when I write about some of the little glitches in our society.

Most people who use big words know what they mean even though those to whom they are talking or writing about may not. One of the ironies about this subject is when people, who are not well read or academic, start using words in the wrong context because they have heard them but do not really know what they mean. This sometimes happens when people have immigrated to North America and are still struggling with the English language. Sometimes when they learn the meaning of a word, they use it over and over, maybe ten times in one short conversation.

My grandmother, who was a teenager when she came from Europe with her parents, had a rather sketchy grasp of the English language. After she grew up and married, she and her husband continued to speak their own language at home. One day, she was talking to one of her English neighbors. The subject of meat came up. She told the neighbor that they had just butchered a pig. Her comment was, "We have a lot of pig beef." She though all meat was called beef.

In the past one hundred years, and especially in the past fifty, we have had an explosion of knowledge, ideas and inventions. Why? Because of reading. When people discover or have some good ideas, they write them down in books or articles. Often people read them and apply their own ideas to someone else's original thoughts. Then those added ideas are published and some more people begin expanding on that idea. The end result is an explosion of ideas and inventions around the world.

The Internet is a good example. In 1990, few had heard of the Internet concept. Today, it is so widely used and abused that it seems like it has been around forever.

Reading has unshackled millions of people from drudgery. Reading expands the mind. It makes people feel good about themselves. It also promotes tolerance. A well-read person understands where other people are coming from.

Unread, ignorant people are often filled with prejudice. Sometimes, they also feel inferior because of their lack of knowledge.

Book learning, either self-taught or in institutions of higher learning like universities, is important. However, this knowledge must be applied in real life. Head knowledge is not enough. We must act on it. Some people take seminars and courses all their lives, never really putting the things they learn into practice.

Writing is another kettle of fish. It is much easier to read than it is to write. Without writers, people would have nothing to read. At this moment in history, there appears to be no shortage of writers. Libraries and bookstores have millions of books on every conceivable subject. We also have hundreds of magazines and newspapers that grind out a prodigious amount of information. When one considers radio, TV and the Internet, the amount of material on every subject under the sun is staggering. It is important that we become judicious as to what we read.

Writers can only exist if there are people who will read their material. Over the years, I have read some mediocre books. Of course, I have also read some good ones. Reading tastes vary greatly. As the old saying goes, one man's junk is another man's treasure. That is how reading is. What some may love, others hate. If you have a story to tell, write it down. Someday you may wish to publish it.

Thousands of people have written stories about themselves and their families. Many never get published, at least not at the commercial level. But that's okay. I am sure future generations will appreciate this information about their ancestors. I wish one of my grandparents had recorded stories about their life.

In my humble opinion, reading and writing are two of the greatest gifts we have in our society. Hopefully, they will survive the computer and Internet era, which is in full swing. Good books, starting with the Bible, have been around for many generations. I sure hope they will be around for many more generations to come.

CHAPTER TWO

COURTSHIP AND MARRIAGE

Nearly every country and nationality of people in this world practices courtship before marriage. In some cultures, it is a brief period of time, including arranged marriages where there is no courtship. The nature of all females (including the animal kingdom) is the need to be courted before they give their bodies to the male for mating.

Courtship, if properly conducted, is a period of time where individuals get to know each other. It can lead to long, happy marriages. On the other hand, I have known people who dated for five years, got married and, a few years later, split up. Once in a while, a couple will have a brief courtship before marriage and they stay married for fifty years.

On average, I believe a couple should court at least a year before they get hitched. That is my opinion since my wife and I went together for a year before we got married. So far, our marriage has lasted fifty-four years.

Courtship has changed dramatically in the last one hundred years, at least in the western world. In the old days, young men and women had to be discreet. Often there was a chaperone present to ensure there was no hanky-panky. When a young man arrived at the doorstep of the home of the girl in whom he was interested, he politely asked if he could come in to visit "Sarah", or whatever her name was. If the parents knew him, or thought he looked okay, he would be invited in. During the first half hour or so, it was a family affair. Then, in the more liberated homes, the young man and the apple-of-his-eye would sit alone in the parlour and visit, providing the door was left open. Holding hands was as far as things ever went. This courtship could go on for a number of months.

When the couple found it hard to wait any longer, and both decided they were meant for each other, the marriage proposal took place.

There was one more hurdle. The young man had to ask the parents for their daughter's hand in marriage. In most cases, permission was granted. However, once in a while, parents refused to give up their daughter for marriage. When that was the case, one of two things happened. Either the romance was off (most young people obeyed their parents even into their early twenties, although most marriages in those days took place before the twentieth birthday), or, if the couple was madly in love, they would bide their time, then elope when the chance presented itself. This was a social disgrace, but usually after several years of marriage, the couple was accepted back into the family.

When it comes to daughters, fathers are sticklers. In their mind, their little girl, even if she is nineteen-years-old, is much too nice for some questionable suitor to claim for his own.

I had one father tell me that when his daughter grew up, he would not allow anyone to marry her unless he completely approved of the young man. When he told me what was required in order for a man to qualify for his daughter, I said to myself that only about one percent (of the single male population) could meet his standards. To my knowledge, that girl never married.

In my opinion, instead of protecting his daughter, he ruined her life. Do not misunderstand me. There are a lot of well-adjusted happy, older, single women. But they should be given the freedom of choice, not bullied by a father who is overprotective concerning her personal life.

Let's take a little tour around the world to see how different cultures conduct courtship and marriage.

In several countries in Africa, the young man wishing to marry a certain girl gave her father a number of cattle, goats or whatever animals are owned in those tribes. When the deal was agreed upon, the marriage was on. It called for a huge feast with lots of dancing (not much different from America). In some cases, the bride was examined to ensure she was a virgin (I am not sure what happened if she wasn't). The young couple often moved in with his parents until such time as the babies started to arrive. Then, they usually found a place of their own.

The North American Indians had their own rituals as to how a couple came together. Often a discreet courtship was going on. The young man and the girl of his choice would manage to meet in a secluded place in some trees or by a stream. The girl always slept in her parents' tepee, or wigwam. So, quite often, the young couple would agree to elope on a certain night. On the agreed-upon night, the girl would wait until her parents were asleep, then she would silently creep out of the tent and her lover would be waiting with two horses, one for himself and one for her. Sometimes he could only muster one horse and, in that case, they would ride double. They would ride to the place of his abode, which was often quite close, although sometimes he would be from another tribe some distance away.

When the parents awoke, they could be quite distraught, although in most cases, they had a good idea with whom their daughter had left. They also probably remembered what they did when they were young.

The Indians also had a barter system for brides. The trade in stock was always horses. If the girl was beautiful, she might have several potential suitors. If that was the case, her value in horses went fairly high, maybe up to twenty or thirty horses. However, in most cases, the price would be from one to six horses.

With the aboriginals of Australia, it was common for two men to exchange sisters, kind of a handy arrangement.

In parts of India, hypergamy is practised. A marriage is allowed within a tribe or caste. Some men are allowed to marry a woman from a lower caste. In India, all castes practice the dowry system. This simply means the father of the bride pays money to the groom. The amount may be large depending on how rich the father is.

It is hard to believe, but in some parts of the world, incest is practised on a regular basis. Those marriages may consist of cousins, nieces and nephews, brothers and sisters, even mothers and sons, and fathers and daughters. To those of us who live in western Christian countries this practice is repulsive. It sure does keep the family under one roof.

The offspring from these marriages are mixed, but a surprising number of them have normal intelligence and health. These marriages occur in places like Java, New Caledonia, parts of Burma and some of the Islands of Oceania. At times, the Eskimos also practice this custom. But within these various groups and cultures, there are also many that do not marry relatives. They marry unrelated people, even from other tribes and areas. Within the Jewish religion, cousins sometimes marry. It was a common custom in the Old Testament.

One type of marriage, or should we say marriages, is polygamy. This entails having more than one wife. It is widespread in many countries. Some who practice polygamy are Muslims, but there are others as well. At one time, North American Natives practised it.

In the early Mormon church, polygamy was part of their doctrine. There are still pockets of it today. It is reported that Brigham Young had twenty-eight wives. I am not sure how he managed all those women. He sure did a good job laying out the structure of Salt Lake City with its nice wide streets. He was also a pioneer in the field of irrigation.

I think the Mormons, and many other people, used Solomon in the Bible as a role model. Solomon had seven hundred wives and three hundred concubines. Can you imagine how wise he was. He was the CEO of a system that involved one thousand women. The Bible says that many of those women led Solomon astray because they worshipped other gods. This did not please God so, in the end, Solomon lost out and declared that all life is vanity.

Another practice is polyandry. This is where one woman has a number of husbands at the same time. It takes place in a few areas of India and also in isolated parts of Africa and, to a small extent, among the Eskimos.

My wife finds this hard to understand. She claims I am quite sufficient for her. What woman, in her right mind, would enjoy cleaning up after a half dozen husbands? Besides, it might be a little difficult to determine which one was the father of her children.

Monogamy is one man, one woman. It is the most common type of marriage. In this society, marrying a second wife or husband is called bigamy, which is punishable by law.

I mentioned that in some tribes in Africa, the young married couple moves in with the groom's parents. Actually this happens quite often in any society. We did not move in with my parents but, for two years, we lived in a little house in my parents' yard.

One funny incident that happened over sixty years ago took place at some people's home not too far from our place. It so happened that the son of some immigrants married an English-speaking lady. He could speak English well, but his mother could not. This young couple moved in with his parents in a two-storey house. The newlyweds slept upstairs.

Approximately one week after the wedding, the bride slept in, while her husband was out working in the field with his dad. When the young lady came downstairs for breakfast she said to her mother-in-law, "Would you give me a clean sheet for our bed?" The mother could neither speak nor understand English except for a few words so the daughter-in-law emphasized the fact that the sheet was for son George. The older lady became upset and excited so she blurted out in her native tongue with a little English mixed in: "I don't believe what you say. My George would never mess the bed." At this point, the young woman realized that her mother-in-law thought she had said that her husband, George, had relieved himself in bed. So, after the daughter-in-law got her composure back, she gestured and shook her head, no, no. Finally the older lady caught on to what she wanted. In her language sheet was the word for feces. When she heard the word sheet and George she jumped to the wrong conclusion.

I think this little incident helped bond the daughter-in-law with her mother-in-law. In time, the older lady learned a little more English. This is a true story.

Historically, and even today, many people marry a person of their own social status and wealth. This is especially true in England where there is still a lot of class distinction. There are a few Cinderella marriages where a poor girl marries a prince charming, but not many.

Another common thing that happens quite frequently is the May-December marriage. This simply means that women marry men who are twenty to fifty years older than they are. You can bet your bottom dollar that ninety-nine percent of these men are either celebrities or wealthy and, in most cases, both.

The percentage of these younger women who will do this is small. But, if only five percent of women do this, it still amounts to a large number of such marriages.

The most extreme case of such a marriage happened in the United States a few years ago. It involved a twenty-eight-year-old model marrying an eighty-nine-year-old billionaire. According to the paper I read, she is quoted as saying that she was madly in love with him. She wanted to bear his baby. I never heard whether she had that baby. If she did, I suspect she may have had some help from one of her younger male friends. These days, a DNA test would determine if the eighty-nine-year-old still had what it takes to make a baby. I suspect the reason she wanted to have a baby was to solidify her hold on his estate.

Just recently, there was a similar case. This involved a gold digger in Texas who was twenty-six-years-old. She married a billionaire who was also eighty-nine-years-old. She was a topless dancer. He died about a year-and-a-half later. She claimed he had promised her half of his estate which was valued at $1.6 billion. However, the will revealed otherwise. She was entitled to receive four hundred and fifty million dollars. She insisted that she should receive half which amounts to eight hundred million dollars. Her lawyer says she is not a gold digger that she dearly loved him and that the billionaire had said she was the love of his life and he wanted to take care of her. At the time of writing, this case is still before the courts.

Why work in a strip joint or pan for gold in the mountains, when a sick old man can be conned out of that kind of loot?

I personally know of a case where a woman married an older man. He was also very well off. It so happened that she had one daughter and he had five children, all grown up. After several years of marriage, he passed away. Would you believe that when his will was probated, he had left three-quarters of his estate to her and the other quarter to his five children. That was bad, but it gets worse. A few years later she passed away. When her will was probated, it revealed that she had left everything to her daughter, and nothing to her husband's children.

I know one of the five children real well. In fact, I did a lot of business with him. He is the one who told me the story. I know it is true, he was not one to tell fairy tales.

Nowadays, when older men remarry they usually sign nuptial agreements and that is the way it should be. This way his family will inherit a large portion of his estate.

I have also observed that many men who are successful in business are not happily married. They often decide to stay married because divorce costs money and it also hurts the children. So the couple stay together. But because the husband is so unhappy at home he expends all his energy at his place of business. Long hours do not matter to him. He likes business better than home.

The wealth accumulated over a period of years is a hollow victory. Once the children are grown up, the marriage usually ends in divorce and half of the estate goes to his wife. I have known several bitter men who had this experience. Even though they have taken up with another woman, the bitterness remains.

I had one man tell me he hopes the judge who awarded his ex-wife a huge divorce settlement, fries in hell! How much better it would have been if that couple would have settled their differences years ago and forgiven one another's shortcomings. They would have been happy with even a fraction of the wealth. This gentleman died shortly after he made that statement to me.

And now, back to courtship among younger people. These days, courtship is quite different from the old days. I personally think the courtship by horse and buggy which my parents had was much more romantic than courtship is these days.

In fact, courtship today is almost nonexistent. Many couples move in together after three or four dates. Of course, there are some young people with high moral standards who do court a while and do not live together until they get married.

It is a tragedy of our times that today almost half the marriages end in divorce. God blesses good marriages. They are the backbone of our families and society. Maybe in the 21st Century, more couples will stay married, "til death do us part."

Like I mentioned, opposites attract. But just recently, I read where researchers said that marriages where the man and woman come from the same background have a fifty percent better survival rate than marriages where a couple has different backgrounds. By backgrounds, they were referring to nationality, cultural, religious and even regional origin.

As in all other areas of life, there are exceptions to the rule. I know of a number of cross-cultural marriages that have worked out well. I think that of the four differences mentioned, religion is the biggest problem. If a couple

Our grandson, Ryan, kisses his bride, Kate, after making their vows "til death do us part."

are both orthodox in their own separate religious beliefs, problems can arise especially if there are children involved. Whose religion is taught to the children? Many couples switch to the other partner's religion, before they get married. That's a pretty good idea, providing they are sincere to what they are switching to. Very few couples change their religious beliefs after they are married. Some do.

I know of numerous marriages where the wife faithfully attends church while her husband stays home. Usually he has no belief. If he does, he keeps it to himself. I give credit those men who don't object to their wife taking their children to church.

CHAPTER THREE

WOMEN

An ancient Greek philosopher posed the question, What does woman want?

No man has figured out what a woman really wants. We guess at what she wants and it is usually wrong.

Over half of the world's population is female. We know that, without women, this would be a mighty dull world. Not as sex objects (although sex enters into the equation) but rather as equal partners. Men and women are totally equal, but different.

The Bible says that in marriage, man and woman become one. However, in the past three decades a large percentage of marriages have split up. Why?

There is no simple answer, but we do know that men have, to a large degree, abdicated their responsibilities as husbands and fathers. On the other hand, so have women abdicated their role as nurturers of the family. We know women who have left their husbands and young children. These days, single parents are both male and female. This is a sad state of affairs. Statistics indicate that a large portion of juvenile delinquents come from single-parent homes. Children need both fathers and mothers. That's how God intended it!

Women are full of surprises. I know of women who have rotten husbands, often womanizers and drunks, and yet these wives remain loyal to their husbands. I witnessed an unbelievable scene once when I happened to drop in on some folks one evening. The couple had just concluded a huge fight during which the husband had beaten his wife. She had managed to get to the phone to call the police. About three minutes after I got there, the police arrived. The officers asked her what her complaint was and she told them that her husband had beaten her. Their response was, "We cannot do anything unless you lay charges." She refused to lay charges against her husband. At this point, the husband taunted his wife by saying, "Go ahead, honey, lay charges against me." Even with his cruel physical and mental treatment, she refused to lay charges. This happened thirty years ago. Today, the law has been changed and the police can lay charges without the complainant's consent. That couple divorced.

A woman's heart often overrules her head, especially when there are children involved. My heart goes out to women who are married to ruthless, cold-hearted men. Of course, there are also some cold-hearted, ruthless women who think only about themselves. Quite often, this kind of woman is married to a gentle, decent man.

I have read a number of cases where intelligent, professional women have fallen in love with convicts - a murderer and, in several cases, mass murderers. They get married while the man is incarcerated for life. In a few cases, the man has been paroled and almost every one of those marriages has broken up. Several years ago, there was a mass murderer named Ted Bundy (he was rather a handsome chap). It was reported that he had thirteen marriage proposals from women while he was on death row. I guess there was safety in those proposals, since the women knew that if they did marry him, the marriage would never be consummated.

Some women like suspense and power, even if that power is totally misdirected like it is in sex slayings, ruthless business dealings and crooked politics. As long as the man has charisma and lots of money, they seem to tune out what a rascal he really is. Before I get into too much hot water, let me assure you that the percentage of women attracted to these types of men is relatively small. Most women prefer honest, decent, caring men, who will make good husbands and fathers. Occasionally, a caring woman and a caring man get married and become what is called soul mates — literally one flesh as the Bible calls it. This kind of marriage usually produces great children who are a credit to society and who, hopefully, will some day marry. They and their spouse will usually have the same good relationship their parents had. The molding factor in children is the home, school, community and church. Of the four, home is the most influential. In Proverbs

22:6, the Bible says, train up a child in the way he should go and when he is old he will not depart from it.

In the workplace, women are more inclined to work-to-rule than men. I think this is a direct result of women proving to the world they can be as tough as men. It is also a safe haven since the law is on their side. Rules must be obeyed. Common sense dictates that once in a while rules may be bent or broken without doing anyone harm. My experience with female Royal Canadian Mounted Police (RCMP) officers has not been good. I am not a habitual speeder but, like many people, I sometimes exceed the speed limit by a few miles an hour. This translates into eight to ten kilometres over the limit. This is usually on a good divided highway. Would you believe that if a lady Mountie catches me, there is no leeway or choice. She writes me a ticket, I broke the rules. On several occasions male Mounties either ignored my slight infraction of the speed limit, or gave me a mild warning to slow down, but no ticket. It does three times more good to slow me down than to issue me a ticket.

We cross the United States / Canada border at least ten times a year. About the only hassle we ever encounter is when a woman is on duty. This has happened on a number of occasions, and almost without exception, they cause us delay and frustration for no apparent reason. Just recently, one of those ladies confiscated seven oranges because they had not originated in the United States. The excuse was that Americans were tired of Canadians importing all kinds of junk and then taking it into the United States. They were good oranges, but she claimed they came from South Africa. Maybe they did; and maybe they didn't; I don't know. A minor incident, but annoying.

By now, I must have all the ladies, who are reading this, angry with me. Women have strong qualities which most men do not possess. My wife has a ton of compassion for all children and young people, especially underprivileged ones.

I definitely prefer female nurses to male nurses. I speak from experience. Again, it boils down to the fact that women have more compassion.

Women also have a lot more intuition than men. They seem to have a sixth sense that many of us men don't have. My wife can spot a phony a hundred feet away. It is pretty hard to fool her. I always say she would have made a good detective. She has never had a speeding ticket in her life. Frankly speaking, she speeds more than I do. Even without a radar detector, she senses when there is a police car half a mile away.

The world's oldest profession is going as strong as ever, despite many jurisdictions passing tough sex trade laws. Worldwide, there are millions of prostitutes. Of course, they would not exist were it not for the low morals of a lot of men.

The most despicable of these men are the pimps. They lure young girls into the sex trade by seducing them and getting them hooked on drugs. They also beat up the girls and take most of their money. I think it is about time these pimps were handed much stiffer sentences. It probably wouldn't stamp out prostitution, but it sure would slow it down. The Old Testament mentions harlots in a number of places, so it really is one of the world's oldest profession.

A man I used to work with told me a little story that pretty much sums up the low moral values of some men. When my friend was thirteen- or fourteen-years-old, he had a weekend job delivering telegrams on a bicycle in a city of approximately one hundred thousand people. One day he delivered a telegram to a seedy part of the city. When he rang the doorbell, a lady in a scanty nightgown answered the door. He handed her the telegram and told her there was a two-dollar charge for delivering it. She said she did not have two dollars. Instead, she said she would let him take it out in trade and, with that, she slipped off her scanty gown. She was stark naked and as she reached out for him, he was terrified and bolted from the house to his bike. Furiously he peddled back to the telegram office. He told his boss what had happened. The boss patted him on the head and said, "It's okay, I will deliver that telegram myself."

A woman enjoys sex with a man she loves. She abhors sex with a man she does not love. I guess that is why rape is such a horrible crime - even if the rapist is not real violent. It always puzzles me how a prostitute can give her body to any sleezebag that comes along for a few dollars, or even big money for high-priced call girls. No decent, self-respecting woman will stoop that low. To me, a rapist and a pimp are in the same category as a murderer.

Women have many other interesting aspects, such as shopping and knowing what clothes every other woman wore at a social gathering. They are also aware of their own appearance, especially their hair. Most women have a jealous nature (and so do men). If the man in their life happens to pay a little too much attention to another woman, he will receive the silent treatment. Or worse, the marriage bed suddenly turns to ice.

Women will stand by their children no matter what rascals they may be. Many are the tears shed by a mother whose son has stolen, raped or killed. He will always be her son. She may not defend the crime he committed. In his case, it was the circumstances that made him do it. She forgives him. A prime example of how they view their children is the old story of the mother who watched her son in the military marching on parade. As she watched, she commented on how everyone was out of step, "but my son, John."

One day a friend asked another friend, "How come single women are usually slimmer than married women?" "Oh," said his friend, "there is an easy explanation for that. When a single woman comes home she looks in the fridge then goes to bed. When a married woman comes home, she sees what's in bed, then goes to the fridge."

There are dozens of other traits, habits and abilities that define the modern woman. I will not touch on the subject of women's liberation. I happen to be on both sides of the fence on that issue For too long women were denied things that we take for granted today. On the other hand, extreme feminists have caused a lot of trouble in our society, not only for husbands and men, but also for women. Women are not shown the respect these days that I think they deserve.

Statistics reveal that women outlive men by six to seven years. I have no idea why that is We just have to conclude that women are tougher. It is estimated there are approximately ten million widows in the United States. Canada has about one million. A large percentage of them are under sixty-five years of age.

I never knew either of my grandmothers. They had passed on before I was born. I had a wonderful mother. She was intelligent, kind and loving. Imagine her patience raising thirteen children with no modern conveniences. I was the youngest child - number thirteen. I also had three good sisters who, my wife says, spoiled me. Of course, I deny that. My wife, too, is a wonderful woman who is partially liberated. She is an outstanding mother. We raised two great daughters who, though liberated, are not fanatical. Now we have seven beautiful granddaughters.

Yes, women have had a great influence on my life - not only the women in my family, but others as well. I like women, not in the sense of being a ladies' man, but as fellow human beings with whom we share this planet. They brighten our lives. God knew what he was doing when he created male and female. My wife and I have been married for fifty-four years.

CHAPTER FOUR

MONEY

We all know the old saying, money is the root of all evil, but give me more roots. Another saying is, you never miss money until you have none.

Money is a medium of exchange that is needed every day. We use it to transact our purchases of goods and services. It is a measuring device.

In the past five millenniums, it is amazing what has been used for money. There are hundreds of objects that various countries and societies have used for money. I will only mention a few of the most unusual ones: a pig's jawbones in parts of southern Asia; money made from stone in a few of the South Pacific islands; or how about feathers from a certain bird in the New Hebrides. Salt was also used in some parts of the world, including Ethiopia. Other materials were iron bars (you needed strong pockets), sea shells, elephant tusks, bear teeth, bear claws, beads and human skulls in Borneo. We must not forget that beaver pelts were used in Canada as currency three hundred years ago.

But by far, the most common item used as money was metal. Bronze, copper, silver and gold. The Bible mentions coins such as the talent, dinero and shekel. They also used silver, as noted when Judas betrayed Jesus for thirty pieces of silver.

As society evolved, all countries of the world adopted metal for coins and paper for currency. For years, the value of a country's currency was based on the amount of gold reserves it possessed. These days, many countries have gone off the gold standard.

It may be hard for proud Canadians, and the rest of the world, to admit but, today, the American dollar is more or less the benchmark by which all other currencies are measured. Germany and Japan also have strong currencies and, to a lesser degree, so do Great Britain and

France. Just recently, the eleven countries that belong to the European Common Market created the euro dollar. This is supposed to rival the American dollar. I personally doubt that it will.

Money, as we know it today, will soon be history itself. We are well on our way to a one-world cashless society. Soon all money transactions will be done electronically. Already, a large portion of our business is conducted with debit and credit cards. Every day, more and more financial deals are made on the Internet. Even cheques may become obsolete. No paper, just computers. A hundred years from now, today's money will be as outdated as pigs' jaws, nose rings or human skulls are today.

Money does strange things to people. It causes all kinds of problems, even for normal people. A person often does not know the character of someone until there is money on the line. Some people are incredible cheapskates. Jack Benny, the comedian, made a career of playing the cheapskate. He also fiddled around on the violin

A friend of mine said a certain individual was so cheap he "would skin a louse for its tallow." Some people are so cheap they would not pay a dime to see Janet Reno or Sheila Copps ride a Brahma bull for a charity event where the proceeds were earmarked to go to sick children.

Others use money like water, consequently, they are always broke. It is surprising how few people know how to manage their money. Many wait for a lottery win, or a rich relative to die. Usually neither happens. Often, when a rich relative dies, their money is left to charity or other people. I know several cases like that.

Why do people gamble? A simple answer is, "Maybe, just maybe, I will be lucky today and win big." You don't have to be a genius to figure out where all the money came from to build those huge hotels in Las Vegas.

Of course, governments are into gambling big time. I think it is a disgrace for governments to take all that gambling money from people who can least afford to lose. There are a few rich people who get addicted and, when that is the case, they will not be rich for long. Gambling when the odds are fifty-fifty is a little more tolerable.

Despite what the casinos say, the odds, in most instances, are about nine-to-one and higher than that on lotteries.

One story I must tell is about gambling in Las Vegas. About twenty years ago, a chap that I know well went to Nevada on some business. He took his son-in-law with him for company on that long trip. After his business was conducted, the two men stopped at Las Vegas for the night before their long trip home. Like most Las Vegas hotels, there was a casino downstairs, which was open twenty-four hours a day. After dinner, the son-in-law went down to the casino while his father-in-law stayed in the room reading a book. About ten o'clock that evening, the son-in-law came up to the room and flashed a big wad of bills. He told his father-in-law that he had won three thousand dollars. "Good," said his father-in-law. "Now, let's go to bed, because we are leaving in the morning." "Oh, no," said the young man, "I am going back down to win some more." About six o'clock in the morning, he came back to the room flat broke. He did not have enough money to buy a pack of cigarettes. He asked his father-in-law for money to buy cigarettes. The father-in-law now told him, "I will not give you one cent. You can suffer the consequences of your stupidity."

Money is also used for social status. Do you believe that Jackie Kennedy was in love with Aristotle Onasis? He was a billionaire who gave her a multi-million-dollar-a-year clothing allowance. In the end, she inherited very little of his estate. Worldwide, the super rich belong to many of the exclusive clubs where only the so-called elite may join. The exceptions may be a few famous actors or royalty, sometimes from long disappeared kingdoms and empires, but the descendants still use titles like Count, Prince or they are throne pretenders.

In England, which has a raft of exclusive male clubs, there are some members who may or may not be rich but through heredity have the right pedigree.

In North America, we are not quite as stuffy or class conscious as the British. But don't kid yourself, we also have huge class distinctions based solely on money. Much of that money was inherited from previous generations. These millionaires are owners of companies, or

CEOs of large corporations, some holding directorships in a number of other companies.

The older the money, the more prestige a person has. The new rich sometimes have a problem making the inner circle. If they have joined a lodge or two, it helps. Another thing that may hasten their acceptance is if a man marries a beautiful woman whose parents are part of the establishment, he has arrived as an elite via his wife. This happens quite often.

I have never been involved much with so-called upper-crust people. I have had a few small glimpses at that part of society and, quite frankly, I was not impressed. When I was cutting a fairly big swath in the business world, I was invited to several bankers' luncheons. The conversation centred on high finance, with a few stories thrown in about exotic vacations. I also held some bank shares, but I only ever went to one annual shareholder meeting. I doubt if I will ever attend another one. Everything was cut and dried. Very little opportunity was given for grassroots input.

Approximately seventy percent of bank directors are CEOs of large corporations. They also include a few women on the board to make it look a little more politically and socially correct. I would not be surprised if the women were better directors than the men. Many of those men are so consumed with their own companies that the bank gets second priority. This may be one reason that some of the top brass in the banks feather their own nests with high salaries, share options and other perks.

Recently, a CEO of a major bank parted company. His package amounted to twenty-two million dollars. He then went to work for a bank in England where his annual salary was reported to be six million dollars. Meanwhile, he is entitled to a large Canadian pension from the bank with which he parted company. If the directors were on the ball such a thing would never happen. In large corporations, the company policy seems to be directed by the management at the top, rather than by the directors or shareholders.

I have also been invited by business associates to several fairly exclusive clubs in Calgary - the Ranchman's Club and the Petroleum

Club. The Ranchman's sounds like my kind of club, but the two times I was there, bonafide cattlemen were as rare as hen's teeth. There were a few grandsons of original ranchers, but these guys were lawyers and oilmen and long removed from the ranching scene.

I have had some brushes with rich people. I must say, many of them were down-to earth people, not as stuffy as the folks in Britain or even in Canada. These were not eastern Americans. They were from the western United States. Some of them were excellent people. A very close friend of mine from Kansas was one of them. He was first-generation rich. He made the money himself but he never forgot his roots.

I was invited to an exclusive club in Texas once. It was an interesting evening; the talk that night was not about pocket change. They were all cattlemen/oilmen types. Nearly every conversation involved multi-millions of dollars. No small deals there. I was feeding quite a few cattle in Texas at the time. I was also contemplating buying a small shopping center in Amarillo, Texas.

I am quite a talkative person, as some of you may know. That night I said very little. The deals and amounts of money discussed were out of my league. I think the reason the super rich withdraw from the so-called common man is twofold. Number one, they think they are superior to ordinary people, even if they did not make the money themselves but inherited it. Secondly, they do not want to get too friendly with average people. Many people try to put the touch on them for funds - either outright loans or some business venture in which they hope the rich person will get involved.

I am a long way from being rich. But even I have had dozens of proposals for investing money in some cockeyed venture by someone with no money.

Another aspect of money is a loan. Today, the majority of people in North America have loans, even if they have a fair amount of wealth. Much of this wealth is tied up in properties and other investments so they use loans to operate their business. Another term for a loan is a mortgage.

Loans and mortgages cover a number of things such as houses, cars, land, livestock, student loans or any other consumer goods which people think they need but do not have the cash to purchase. Usually these loans come from banks or credit unions. Sometimes they are from private individuals. Bank and credit unions take some kind of security. It is pretty hard to get a loan if you have no collateral. The government often backs housing and student loans.

Memories are short when it comes to money. The day people get a loan they are so happy. However, when it comes time to repay it, the story is quite different. As I said, lending institutions have the loan secured, money loaned by a relative or friend is usually unsecured. I know of dozens of situations where people have borrowed money from someone and never paid it back. It has happened to me several times. The older a loan is, the less inclined they are to repay it. I know of a few cases where the person who had borrowed the money was outright angry because the person who had loaned the money had asked for repayment of the loan. Consequently, there are millions of dollars that never get repaid. We know the old saying: the quickest way to lose a friend is to loan them money.

In Canada, in 1999, there was over one hundred million dollars outstanding in overdue student loans, which were guaranteed by the government. When the banks asked the government to back that guarantee, there was a big outcry that the banks were ripping off the public. What the public forgot was that the banks paid the government several billion dollars in taxes in 1999. I do not exactly feel sorry for the banks. But a loan is a loan and should be paid back.

The whole world needs money. Our phone never quits ringing with people asking for donations for worthy causes. My wife donates to nearly forty charitable organizations. I donate to a few as well. I hope that money goes to the intended people and not to the middlemen running the charity. It sounds like my wife and I have separate accounts. Actually, we have joint accounts. The reason I say she donates to all those causes is because it is her idea to give the money, especially if there are children involved.

Then there is the government. They are constantly looking for funds. I think our tax rate bears that out. Much of that money is squandered. Just recently, they said on the TV news that the Human Resources Department paid out over one billion dollars in grants and other money-sucking projects. There was no proper accounting of the taxpayers' money. I am sure the same thing happens in Washington.

The social safety net also costs a fortune. Some spending of money is necessary but a lot of money is paid to people who work the system. Sometimes there are three generations on welfare and all have perfectly healthy bodies. I read a while ago that in some large American inner cities, up to five generations have been on the dole. Poverty feeds on poverty.

A socialist once confronted a wealthy industrialist in the United States and asked, "Why don't you share your wealth with everybody?" The industrialist did some figuring on a piece of paper, pulled out a cheque book and wrote a cheque for sixteen cents to the socialist. "Here is your share of my wealth," he said. The industrialist then lectured the socialist. "I am rich. I employ a lot of people. If I give all my money away then all my employees would lose their jobs and we would all be poor."

This story is almost one hundred years old. The industrialist was either Dale Carnegie or J.P. Morgan. If every citizen in the United States at that time, got an equal amount of his money, the amount would have been sixteen cents. After that encounter, the socialist left. He probably went for a coffee to calm his nerves. In those days a cup of coffee only cost ten cents. It is hard to say what he squandered, the other six cents on.

There is a book out called *The Money Changers*. It tells about fortunes made and sometimes lost on world money markets. All the major countries' currencies are listed on commodity exchanges. A smart trader can make a lot of money by figuring out which currency will go up and which one will go down. They can either go long or short. They trade in high volumes, so even if a currency only has slight fluctuations, they can clear a big profit if they are on the right side.

I dabbled in money markets a few times - not big, just kind of testing out how it works. I traded mainly in United States currency and also in German marks and French francs. I am a little ahead over all, but nothing earth shaking!

We used to buy cattle for United States packing plants on commission. From the time we invoiced the cattle out until they wrote a cheque to us took four or five days. In that intervening time, the United States dollar against the Canadian dollar would go up a little, or down a bit. When we received their commission cheque for the cattle, we either washed out or it was doubled, depending on which way the exchange rate had gone. I understand these days the rate is pegged on the day of shipment.

Gold has always mesmerized men. The gold rush in California in 1849 opened up the area for settlement. Until 1848, California belonged to Mexico. It was a sleepy outpost inhabited by Mexicans who owned some ranches. There were also some Roman Catholic priests who had established a number of missions. The rough, ragtag men and con artists who flocked to the gold fields overwhelmed them. California was ceded to the United States in 1848, one year before the gold rush.

In 1898, gold was discovered on the Klondike in the Yukon, a Canadian territory. Thousands of men made their way there. They came from all over the world. The biggest percentage were Americans. They sailed from Seattle to Skagway, Alaska. From there, they trekked across formidable mountain passes; then rafted or walked up the river to the gold fields. That was tough winter country. The hardship these men endured was incredible. Many died. A few got rich. Of the ones who did, nearly all died broke. They either lost it gambling or by making bad investments.

The lure of gold has decimated good men. The romance of searching for gold is much greater than the reality of finding the mother lode which is elusive. To be honest, I got caught up in a few gold ventures that turned into disasters. But I was not involved in BreX. I smelled a rat long before the hoax was revealed. Maybe it was once bitten, twice shy. We should always remember that, not all that glitters is gold.

Bribery is alive and well in this world. A large portion of the world operates on bribes. Recently, a business institute in Germany did a survey and report on business bribes and kickbacks. This involved the nineteen countries in the world with the biggest economies. The results were shocking. Every one of those countries, including the United States and Canada, were guilty of this practice. Canada fared slightly better than the United States. The bribes involved large corporations, as well as governments. Without these bribes, sometimes referred to as grease, the wheels of industry and the flow of goods slow down. It came across that, if you wanted to stay in business, you had to go along with the bribe system.

A good example was the bidding tactics for the 2002 Olympic Games at Salt Lake City, Utah. It was a scandal.

Many third world countries are riddled with bribes. One excuse given is that people receive such poor pay, they are forced to take bribes. A big portion of those bribe-takers are government officials. I had a little experience with bribes when I was in Colombia, South America. I mention this in another book that I wrote, *Round-up of Memories*.

Bribes can be subtle, almost impossible to prove. The most common one is money - cash. Sometimes it is other favors, such as goods and other services - including sex. We know stories about girls of the night being made available to businessmen, including politicians, during business negotiations that may last several days. I will mention a few specific instances where bribes were given and accepted.

I know of a wholesale food supplier owned by a man at a west coast seaport. What he did when a ship docked, was to board the ship, seek out the captain, and tell the captain about all the items he could supply for provisioning the ship. Then slyly, he would invite the captain to dinner that night. The captain usually accepted. They would meet at a fancy restaurant where they visited and, of course, had several drinks. At this point, no order had been placed. Before they parted ways, the man would slip the captain an envelope with a substantial amount of money in it and bid him good night The next day they met again, this time to do business. Almost without fail, the ship's captain would give him the whole order. Once a bribe is accepted there is little choice but to go through with the deal. The above scenario may not be quite the way it was done, but it's pretty close as it was relayed to me by a close associate of the man.

My brother and his wife were on their honeymoon in Mexico. They decided to travel across Mexico by train - sounds kind of unusual but this was years ago. In those days, you needed an exit visa to leave Mexico. As the train was getting close to the United States border, my brother discovered he had lost their exit visa. He almost panicked. He did not look forward to spending time in jail. Suddenly, an idea came to him, and it worked. When the man asked him for his visa, he said, "Sorry, sir, I have lost it, but maybe this will do." He handed him an envelope stuffed with pesos. The man eagerly accepted it and away they went into the good old United States.

I pride myself in the fact that the cattle business is relatively clean and free of bribes. However, I know of a number of instances where bribes have been given and some still are. A few have been exposed, but most of them have not been proven true. A bribe is almost impossible to detect. It is dangerous to make specific accusations of bribery. If it turns out to be false, the accuser is in trouble.

Bribes come in all sizes. Often a bribe is given in the form of an exotic holiday or cruise; sometimes vehicles are given, which the person giving the bribe may write off as an expense as though still owning the vehicle.

The most common bribe is cash. Many stores and businesses are vulnerable for employees taking bribes. For instance if a person is in charge of making large purchases, for a major corporation, he or she can give the purchase order to someone in business for themselves who is willing to give them a bribe. Often, this kind of activity is detected by other suppliers who offer as good if not a better product at a lower or competitive price. Despite this, the purchaser stays with the company that gives the bribe. Products may range from services to lumber, cattle and other commodities, and other consumer goods.

I personally think a clear conscience is worth far more than any bribe that may be received from a dishonest party.

Sometimes, bribes are confused with embezzlement. There is a difference. Embezzlers steal directly from their employer. Embezzlers are much easier to detect and convict than the person accepting bribes.

It usually involves "cooking the books." They get away with it for awhile, then get greedy and take larger and larger amounts. After a while the new-found wealth starts to manifest itself. The person buys a large house, drives a fancy car and takes expensive vacations. At this point, they come under suspicion. How can they afford this lifestyle on a modest salary? Upon investigation, the embezzler is exposed.

Some people who embezzle end up with no money. They keep on stealing money to feed their gambling habit or to pay some other debt which they incurred. In the end, when they get caught, they are disgraced and find out that, like all crime, it does not pay.

Just recently (October 2000), I read where a woman who had worked for a bank for ten years got caught embezzling one hundred and twenty-one thousand dollars. She got lucky and appeared before a bleeding-heart judge, who gave her a two-year-less-a-day house arrest. There is no jail time for her. I don't know what you think, but I think that could encourage other employees to try for a little free money even though it might mean hanging around the house for two years. That's a nice change from having to get up early every morning to go to work.

"Ripping off" is too kind a term for those people. The best description for those crooks who are involved in bribes, embezzlement and other petty theft is, low-life thieves.

Guess who pays for this theft? The consumer. Companies have little choice but to include the cost of theft, embezzlement and bribes into the cost of goods.

There are a few more parasites who swindle people out of their money. They are dishonest financial planners and people granted power of attorney. These thefts are usually perpetrated against older people. There are many documented incidents where old people lost all their money and assets to these thugs. I must add there are many honest financial planners as well as people who do not abuse their power of attorney.

Yes, money controls men instead of men controlling money. You do not have to be rich to be a materialist. I know some poor people who are just as obsessed with money as rich people. The difference is the poor man is constantly thinking of how he can get some money, while the rich man is constantly thinking of how he can protect and keep his money.

This day and age, we have all kinds of electronic gadgets, including such things at the Internet, e-mail and telephone answering machines. Often, when we phone someone, the answering service comes on. The usual message is something like this: "Hello, this is the Smith residence. We are not able to come to the phone right now but, if you leave a message, we will get back to you."

One young man decided he did not like such a mundane message so he devised one slightly different than usual. This is what he put on the recorder:

"Hello, this is John. If this is the phone company, I sent your money yesterday. If this is my brother Jake calling for a loan, I have no money. If this is one of my parents calling, could you please send some money. If this is the bank calling, you did not loan me enough money. If this is a good looking single girl calling, I have lots of money."

I like the old Jewish saying which comes from the Bible. *Cast your bread upon the waters and it shall come back to you twofold.*

What it is saying is if you are generous with other people your own wealth will double.

The difference between a bribe and a gift is this: a bribe is before the fact. It is given to gain favor or financial gain. A gift is given after the fact. It is given in appreciation, although sometimes it is given for past favors and future favors, so the bribe and gift are really bedfellows.

The queen was in the kitchen eating milk and honey.

The king was in the parlour, counting all his money.

Not much has changed since that nursery rhyme was written. Men and women are still obsessed with money. Many will not admit it, but it is a fact. In the end, it is like chaff. I know people who were misers all their life and never stopped to smell the flowers. That is what money is meant to do for us. Let's start today.

39

CHAPTER FIVE

MUSIC AND SINGING

Music is a universal language. It crosses all borders known to mankind - ethnic, cultural and religious. There is a wide variety of music. It has touched the minds, hearts and souls of billions of people. It is appreciated from the most primitive to the most sophisticated levels of society.

From the earliest time in human history, music was played in one form or another. The Bible mentions music in a number of places. Some of the instruments were harps, trumpets, psaltery, viol, timbre and other stringed instruments. In a number of African cultures drums are the dominant instrument. Drums also rated high with the Natives of North America as well as in the Caribbean, especially Trinidad. There is something about a drum beat that stirs the emotions of the inner soul in people.

Music is widely used in churches, not only Christian, but also every religion in the world. It is a call to worship. Many people enjoy the Mormon Tabernacle Choir from Salt Lake City, Utah. There are thousands of other choirs that have inspired people for centuries. In our western culture, we have a wide range of music which includes opera, classical, symphony, orchestral, pop music, bluegrass, rock and hard rock, hillbilly rock, rap, country and western, folk songs, jazz, modern, Christian choruses, Cajun music to name a few. There are also a wide variety of bands, including brass bands.

A large range of instruments produce this music - accordions, pianos, organs, violins, guitars, trumpets, and a number of other brass instruments. There are also banjos, ukuleles, harps and a variety of drums and cymbals.

The most unusual instruments are saws, bells and glasses. I have heard all three of them. They can produce enjoyable music. Oh, we must not forget the harmonica, often called the mouthorgan.

A glimpse of the past. Making music on the grass behind our house circa 1935. From left are: two unknown Alberta men; Ralph Powley, Pete Friesen, Nick Friesen, Fred Miller, Leonard Friesen, George and Sylvia Harder.

Over the centuries, history records some talented composers whose music lives on and does not get outdated. Music is an international language. You may visit a foreign country where you cannot understand the language, but when the music starts the language is the same. The singing sounds nice, but we may not know the words which are sung.

In some cultures, they sing acappella. In other words, no instrumental accompaniment, just singing. One country where this happens is Fiji. They have instruments but they often sing acappella. It is such beautiful harmony that even if you don't understand the words, you will enjoy it.

Few people enjoy the whole range of music. Speaking for myself, I do not like rap, rock or hard rock. Beyond that, I like most singing and music. My favorites are old-fashioned hymns, country gospel, some of the old country and western, blue grass, as well as marching bands. I do not like the high volume of noise that young people seem to enjoy. Except for the Mormon Choir, I did not mention the names of composers, singers, soloists, choirs and people playing instruments. The list of high quality musicians numbers into the thousands, even millions.

Music is sometimes used as social status. I know folks who go to symphony concerts and operas to be seen there by other highbrow people. Some of those people really do not enjoy that type of music but it is socially correct to attend. I know of several couples where the husband would just as soon stay home, but to please his socially-conscious wife he goes with her and suffers through the performance.

When I was twenty-four-years old, I took music lessons for about one year from a gentleman by the name of Dr. Banke. He was eighty-years-old. Believe it or not, when he was younger he was a conductor with the Chicago Symphony Orchestra for a number of years. Sometime in the dirty 'Thirties, the orchestra encountered some financial difficulties and owed him quite a bit of money which was in short supply. The result was they gave him a bunch of instruments for payment. He took me downstairs in his residence one day and showed me his collection of instruments. It seemed there were several hundred instruments, including every type of horn in existence, plus many stringed ones as well. He was not a master of each one of these instruments, but he said he could play them all. I asked him if there was any instrument that he did not like. He replied, "There is one that I am not fond of." "Oh," I said, "Which one is that?" Without hesitation, he replied, "The banjo." I was surprised. I have always enjoyed good banjo music. I guess he was not enough of a hillbilly.

Incidentally, the two instruments on which I took lessons were the trumpet and the bass horn. In the end, I learned to play the trumpet, not well, but good enough that some of my buddies and I had some pretty good sessions. I gave up the bass horn; it disturbed our neighbors too much while I was practising. My musical career lasted about five years. I have not played a trumpet for over forty years. I am breaking my self-imposed rule about not mentioning names. The men with whom I played include Tom Hewitt, Harry Hewitt, Johnny Gertz, Jim Landeryou, Art Gertzen and Jim Webster. They were a good group. We had a great time with a million laughs when an amateur like me missed some keynotes.

My wife and I enjoy good music, however, as a family, we are not real musical. Our eldest son, Lee, plays the guitar very well. Our second son, Ward, played the trumpet quite well. Our two daughters, Melody and Dee, both took piano lessons. Dee has her Grade Nine piano. As for Graham, and Trent, they also took some lessons, but I guess they followed me too closely and never really kept up on their musical skills. However, they enjoy good music. (Trent and Lee are no longer with us.)

Back to the important role music has played in history. Armies have been inspired by music on and off the battlefield. Some military bands are outstanding. They are well disciplined. Not many "blue notes" escape their instruments. The Natives also used music, mainly drums, to inspire and sometimes celebrate a victory over an enemy. What would a parade be without marching bands, including the Salvation Army which specializes in marching band music?

Churches rely on good music and singing. It can get quite tricky if the church happens to have a number of good singers and musicians. Who gets to perform? That is up to the music committee. I do not envy their task. I know of several cases where people departed a church because they felt they had been overlooked when people were selected to sing or play. But on the whole, most people are good sports when it comes to those kind of issues.

Today, we have many electronic gadgets and we can select exactly what music we wish to play in our homes and in our vehicles. Many stores also play music to soothe customers' nerves. I like soft dinner or background music. I hope you agree that the music of our choice brightens our lives.

I have barely touched on the role that music plays in our lives. Over the years, great musicals have won wide acclaim on stage and in movies. What would sporting events or other social functions be without national anthems? When Canadians and Americans hear their national anthems like *O Canada* and *The Star Spangled Banner,* respectively, pride swells up in our hearts.

CHAPTER SIX

TAXES

The old cliché that the only two things in this life that are sure are death and taxes rings true. The Bible attests to this, *It is appointed unto man once to die.* (Hebrews 9:27).

Before Jesus was born, Joseph and Mary went to Bethlehem to be taxed ... (Luke 2:1-5).

These days we can prolong life but, ultimately, we will die. As for taxes, they will also remain for as long as we shall live. But today, they are out of whack. Politicians talk about lowering taxes but, in fact, they have been steadily rising for the last fifty years.

In 2000, the average Canadian or American worked approximately six months of the year to pay their total tax bill for the year. It seems like everything is taxed. There are property taxes, business taxes, income tax (which was a temporary tax levied during the First World War), provincial or state taxes, gasoline tax, hotel room tax, airport tax, capital gains tax, and the hated Goods and Services Tax in Canada.

Besides all of the above taxes, there still are a number of other hidden taxes.

All this taxing might be acceptable if the tax money was used wisely. About half of it goes for good causes. The rest is squandered, especially in Canada. They include such things as high pensions for washed-up politicians and bureaucrats; welfare which is widely abused (some welfare cases are valid); transfer payments; a two-million-dollar painting that consists of three stripes, which, in my opinion, any Grade Three student could have done; plus all kinds of failed business ventures that the government tried to operate. It's enough to bring on nausea. The tax department can be cruel. We all know of situations where Revenue Canada or the Internal Revenue Service (IRS) in the United States have been unreasonable. I speak from experience. Once, in the United States, we got nicked for nine thousand dollars. This happened when, through an oversight or neglect, a nine-thousand-dollar tax bill had gone unpaid for one year. Would you believe that the interest and penalties were the same amount as the original bill? In one year it ballooned from nine thousand dollars to eighteen thousand dollars. We paid it.

I know of a much sadder tax story that took place in Western Canada. There was a farmer who worked hard all his life. He and his wife raised seven children. When he was in his mid-sixties, his wife passed away. By this time, all his children had moved away and were raising families of their own.

At that point, he decided to sell the farm. When he received the money for the farm, he gave a large portion of it to his seven children. He kept enough money to last him for the rest of his life. A few years later, loneliness overtook him and he married a women somewhat younger than himself. Shortly after, Revenue Canada started to hassle him for a huge tax bill they claimed he owed from the land sale. He battled them for close to a year. By this time, the bill had substantially increased with interest and penalties. The amount they were assessing him took all the money he had. He had no recourse, so he paid it to them. It cleaned him out. (I am sure no Ottawa bureaucrat lost sleep over that.)

His wife said they would be okay, that she would get a job and, along with his pension, they would get by. She got a job but, in spite of this, he remained depressed. When she came home from work after the first day on the job, she found him dead. He had committed suicide. What a tragedy. There are many other cases similar to that one. In the United States, there have been a large number of tough calls made by the IRS. One was the boxing heavyweight champion of the world, Joe Louis. He owed a three-million-dollar tax bill. He died with a large portion of that unpaid. Another was Willie Nelson, the singer. He's still with us. I think he's doing okay.

No taxes are pleasant. Some are worse than others. The one that I detest the most is the capital gains tax. If you purchase a piece of property or a blue chip stock for, say $100,000 and, ten years later you sell it for $200,000, you will be taxed on the profit of $100,000. The problem is inflation during that ten-year period pretty well wiped out the profit, yet you are taxed on it.

Governments love to wipe out initiative. If an employee works long, hard hours and does a good job, the company often rewards them with a bonus. Along comes the tax department and takes away almost half that bonus. They have already taxed the company on any profits that it made. The employee has also had high amounts taxed from his paycheque. The government comes out the big winner.

All the government has done is collect the taxes. Then they squander at least half the money on totally unnecessary programs and distribute it to numerous social agencies and phoney make-work projects. A large majority of those have-nots are allergic to work.

On the lighter side, the story is told of two IRS agents who went to a remote mountain ranch to check on the tax situation of the ranch owner. It so happened that the ranch belonged to an attractive forty-five-year-old widow with no children. Her husband had passed away several years ago. She employed six or seven men and a housekeeper. She invited the tax men into her beautiful ranch house. They told her who they were and why they were there. She took them into her office and told them to go ahead and check things out.

After working on the audit several hours, she invited them into the dining room for dinner. When the prime rib meal was finished, they went back to her office for another session. Around ten o'clock that night they realized they could not finish their work (it was a big ranch). They were about to leave for town some distance away and stay the night in a motel and come back in the morning to finish their audit.

"Oh," said the lady, "There is no need to do that. I have plenty of room in the house. You guys can stay the night."

They accepted her offer. She showed each of them to separate rooms upstairs. The next morning they were served a hearty breakfast, then back to the books. About mid-afternoon they finished up. Everything seemed to be in order. They thanked her and bid her farewell. The two tax agents did not work out of the same office. Every once in awhile they were assigned to the same project.

About three months went by and again the two men were assigned to work together for a day or two.

One of the men asked the other, "Do you remember the widow lady who owned the beautiful ranch that we audited three months ago?"

The other man responded, "I most certainly do."

The first man said, "After she took us to our separate rooms, did you get up and go to her room?"

The second man was flustered and embarrassed, but being an honest taxman (if there is such a thing) he sheepishly admitted he had gone to her room.

The first man then looked the guilty man right in the eye and asked, "Did you give her my name instead of your own name?"

This really shook him up. He stammered, "As a matter of fact, I did."

At this point the womanizer got curious as to how his partner knew about his shenanigans. So he asked how he found out. "We made a pact not to tell anyone about our little tryst," he said.

"Well," the first man replied, "She died two months ago and left me the ranch."

Here's another quote from the Bible : *Be sure your sins will find you out.* (Numbers 32:23)

If you don't believe this, ask Bill Clinton. David and Bathsheba are another good example.

Yes, taxes are here to stay. But it is a pity that hard-working middle-class people have to pay almost half their salary to the income tax department. Those people also pay all the other taxes. So their tax freedom day arrives about the middle of July.

CHAPTER SEVEN

BACHELORS

In the area of southwestern Saskatchewan, where I was raised, there were a number of bachelors. When western Canada and the western United States were opened for homesteading, many single men came west from the east and also from Europe to file for homesteads of one hundred and sixty acres. A number of them were remittance men from England.

A bachelor's homestead shack at Beechy, Saskatchewan. There were hundreds of these dwellings in Western Canada and the United States from 1880 to 1930 and later. Some were a little bigger than this one. Photo courtesy Jake Braun.

I am sure when those single men settled on their homesteads, they had every intention of marrying someday. Women were scarce in the early west. As time went by they became confirmed bachelors. Some of them were excellent housekeepers, but the majority were not meticulous when it came to household chores.

As time went by, they withdrew more and more from the community in which they lived. You rarely saw them in church or at country dances, ballgames or any other social event. Many of them lived in little houses, actually shacks is a better description. Since there were no women or children in their life, they saw no need to build a decent house. I have been in a few of their houses, when I was young, as well as in more recent times.

One day I heard about an old bachelor who had brome grass seed for sale. I drove over to his place to purchase some seed. When I entered his yard, I noticed the whole place was covered in three-foot-tall brome grass. Only the top of his old horse-drawn machinery was sticking out above the grass. In a little pasture close to the house there were four or five big draft horses as fat as bears ready for winter hibernation. I am sure neither the machinery nor horses had been used for the past ten years.

I knocked on the door and a grizzled old man peeked out from the partially opened door. When he saw it was a man at the door, he opened up the door and invited me in. It was like stepping into a fairyland, provided you did not look at the mess at ground level. The open-beamed ceiling and the upper walls were beautiful. There were a million intricate cobwebs. On those cobwebs was a layer of dust. At first glance it looked like some fancy crocheting. There was a strong wind that day and that old house was not airtight. So these cobwebs kind of shimmered as they swayed back and forth.

The rest of the house was a total mess. In one corner was a big pile of tin cans, cereal boxes and bread wrappers. The table was loaded with dirty dishes. On the south side of the room, at the bottom of the wall, was a hole approximately ten inches square. Through this opening his friends – stray cats, skunks, an odd rabbit and other little furry creatures, made their entrance for a daily handout. He threw them scraps from the table, which was often just plain bread. He said that he enjoyed their company. It was an early version of today's food bank for the needy. This was in 1951. I visited with him for awhile, then I paid him for the grass seed and left. (Incidentally that seed grew some good grass.)

Several months later I met one of his neighbors. I asked him about the old gentleman bachelor. Here is the story he told me.

Shortly after the turn of the century, this man and his brother homesteaded together. Both were young, single men. They hired a young lady for cooking and housekeeping. Nature took its course and, in due time, the young man, who was the bachelor I met, fell in love with the young woman. They set a wedding date. About two weeks before the nuptials were to take place, the young man came home and discovered that his loved one had eloped with his brother. She had been two-timing him right along.

That day he swore off all women and, for the rest of his life, he never spoke to another woman. He made sure when he went for groceries a man waited on him. (These days it would be difficult to find such a store.) He did not attend any social function unless it was men only. When he was old and very ill (not too long after I met him) he fought like a wildcat when his neighbors insisted on taking him to the hospital. He died shortly thereafter.

The moral of the story is we should forgive and forget past wrongs that have been inflicted on us. In the end we only hurt ourselves by being bitter the rest of our lives. I am sure that young man could have found another woman and lived happily ever after.

The above story reminds me of another incident I read about. A middle-aged bachelor married a young woman and, after a year or two, a son was born. When the boy was about two-years-old, his wife ran off with another man. She left the young son with his father. The man was devastated, so he built himself a little cabin in a mountain wilderness. He took his son with him and became a recluse and, more or less, lived off the land. Occasionally, he would sneak off to town and pick up a few essentials such as flour, sugar, salt, and a few canned goods. He always left his son at home. The boy grew up learning how to live off the land, although his education was almost nil. He only knew what his father taught him.

When the lad was sixteen-years-old, the father decided that it was time to show his son a little about the outside world. This took place in the western United States where every county has an annual fair. What better place to take his son than to one of those fairs. When they arrived in town, the boy's eyes got as big as saucers. Everything was new to him. He asked his dad dozens of questions. What is this? What is that? Pretty soon a couple of pretty girls strolled by. (He had never seen a woman since he was two-years-old.) "What are those?" he asked his dad. His dad glanced at the girls and said they were a strain of geese. The boy pondered that answer but never said anything. After a few hours, the father decided it was time to go home. On their way home, the father said, "Son, you saw a lot of new things today. If you could choose what you liked best, what would you choose?" After only a brief pause, he replied, "I would sure like to have one of those geese."

In spite of all the father's shielding his son from the opposite sex, it did not quench the young man's desire for female companionship.

I bought quite a few cattle from two old bachelor brothers. Their place was interesting. They cowboyed all their cattle on foot. They owned about six to seven hundred head. In the yard approximately fifty feet from the house was a pile of tin cans and other debris the size of a straw shack.

Another old bachelor where I grew up was filthy. Although he was a white man, he was so grimy that he looked like a man of color. My oldest brother rented his land for several years.

One other bachelor that I know well, lived in a little house with no running water. He had an outside biffy and was worth at least a million dollars with only a few distant relatives to lay claim to his estate.

A bachelor who lived about four miles from our place in southwestern Saskatchewan kept his house perfectly clean. I think he even baked his own bread. I never ate there, but a few of his neighbors said he was a good cook.

I believe what the Bible says: *It is good for a man to marry.* There is a big difference between men and women. Every woman I have known who did not marry kept an immaculate house.

CHAPTER EIGHT

TRUTH IS STRANGER THAN FICTION

Life is interesting. Some things that happen are indeed stranger than fiction. In fact much of fiction is what happens in real life. Authors often take the privilege of embellishing incidents and making it as dramatic as possible.

The following are some incidents that I have either witnessed, or was closely associated with, or happened to someone I knew. I will only mention a few names, most of the people involved will remain anonymous but the stories are true. I'll try not to embellish them too much.

One day, a rather heavy-set farmer's wife decided to take her own life. She walked over to a well on their farm. It was what they called a bored well. It was a round hole two-and-a-half to three feet in circumference. The well was approximately sixty feet deep, with about twenty feet of water in it. She removed the cover and slid down the hole. Just before she was to hit the water she had second thoughts about what she was doing. She quickly spread out her legs and arms against the sides which stopped her just before she plunged into the water. She began to yell for help. Luckily her husband and a few of the older children heard her cries. They rushed over to the well and dropped her a rope and pulled her up. It was no easy task since she was quite hefty. I am sure she must have felt sheepish when her head appeared at the top. It must have taken half a day to pull out all the slivers from her arms, legs and posterior. She lived for many more years after that episode.

One wet, rainy night, my brother Dave, who was driving a car came upon a truck that was stuck in the mud. It was a three-ton truck with dual wheels. Several cars pulled up behind Dave as well. It was a narrow, dirt country road. No one could pass the truck.

So four men proceeded to push the truck. They rocked it back and forth. Suddenly, Dave slipped and fell. Just at that point, the driver was able to back the truck up and ran over Dave with both dual wheels. Then the truck lurched forward and ran over him a second time. He lay there, pressed into the mud. The truck driver was not aware that he had run over him. That lurch forward got him out of the mud puddle and away he went.

The other three men pulled Dave out of the mud and loaded him into his car and headed for the nearest hospital, about twenty-five miles away.

The truck that ran over Dave was empty, which helped save Dave's life. It passed over him right in the stomach area slightly below the rib cage. The weight pressed everything he had eaten or drank for the past twenty-four hours through his rectum into his pants along with some blood. This hombre was both tough and lucky. Few people could live through that. But he did.

This was on a weekend. The hospital was small and under staffed. He lay there for hours with virtually no attention, certainly no cleanup or treatment. There was no doctor on duty. One of the other men had driven Dave's car to the hospital and parked it close to the door then he left with the other two men. After several hours when there was no staff around which was most of the time, he staggered out of bed, full pants and all, got into his car and drove to a bigger hospital a hundred miles away where he got the attention and treatment he needed.

When I met him two weeks later, he still looked peaked. He was one tough dude, a few cracked ribs, plus bruised insides. Just another day at the office. It was not the first time he suffered serious injury. He lived to be ninety-years-old.

My nephew, Bob Friesen, had a serious accident about twenty-five years ago. He was operating a crane on a steep mountain slope where they had a logging operation. Suddenly the crane tipped over. Bob was pinned underneath. The huge machine was laying across his body on the lower abdomen and pelvic area. His circulation was cut off to his legs and feet. It took them three hours to move in some equipment to lift the crane up.

They rushed him to the hospital. The prognosis was not good, they said he would never walk again. He told me after they worked on him for awhile, the blood started to flow back into his legs and feet. At that point the pain was so severe that it was unbearable. His legs had literally been dead. He was in the hospital for months. But he finally recovered. After about two years of therapy, he was able to go back to work. He has been operating big cranes ever since. Every week he flies up to northern British Columbia or Alaska, loading logs into ships. The human spirit and body can overcome big odds.

There was a couple who had four sets of twins in a row. On top of this, the husband was a playboy. I have no documented proof, but rumour had it that a number of women went for car rides in the country with this gentleman in the hope that they too would conceive twins. I never heard if any of them ever had twins. This took place over fifty years ago, before the so-called sexual revolution. These people did not live too far from our place, but were not close neighbors.

One day, a lanky young man (our neighbor) was pounding a post with a sledgehammer. In order to make it a little easier, he stood on a five-gallon pail with the bottom up. As he was about to pound a post into the ground, he took a mighty swing; he missed the post and hit the pail knocking it out from underneath him. He did a complete somersault. Luckily he did not hit one of his shins with that big post maul. Several other things happened to this chap which could have cost him his life, but he always lived to tell the tale.

I called in at a place one day to chat about some cattle these people owned. They told me that one of their good steers had died awhile ago. He was bloated up. They cut him open and discovered that he had some balled-up twine in his stomach. They reckoned that's what killed him. They added the meat seemed to be okay. I did not say anything but I left in a hurry because I was feeling a little queasy at that point. I love beef but not from an animal that dies on its own and not even bled. Hope I did not spoil the roast beef dinner that you are about to consume.

Every so often we read or hear about people getting sick or dying from food poisoning. I vividly remember having food poisoning when I was six-years-old in 1932. There were approximately twenty-five people staying at our place. They consisted of our family including my oldest brother and his wife and their three children. There were also some visitors from Manitoba, plus several hired men. I do not remember where we all slept. Some in the house, some in the bunkhouse and, I think, some in a tent.

Mother had a tough time rustling up enough food for that mob of people. There was a short fall in the meat supply. Our weekly meat allotment from the beef ring was not sufficient for all those people. Dad decided to butcher a suckling calf weighing about three hundred and fifty pounds live weight. There was no refrigeration in those days. Whatever could not be consumed in three or four days, mother canned.

We enjoyed several good meals, which included this veal. On the third day we finished eating the veal, that mother had not canned. Several hours after going to bed, I woke up with terrible stomach cramps. I got up and headed for the outside biffy. When I got there I was surprised to see a line up of people waiting their turn (something like you see these days at women's public restrooms). It did not take long till all those people waiting their turn could wait no longer. Off we went in every direction, each one groaning in agony, as we squatted down to relieve ourselves. It was a bright moonlit night. People were scattered all over the place. There were no close neighbors so there was plenty of open space which, including the ladies, gave each person a measure of privacy. In spite of this, I think everyone was somewhat embarrassed.

This went on all night. I must have gone about five times. Some people were really sick, literally rolling on the ground in pain. It was in the middle of the night. The closest hospital or doctor was twenty-eight miles away. Miraculously, nobody died. There were a lot of pale, listless people in the morning, but all were thankful to be alive. I think about that incident nearly every time I order veal cutlets in a restaurant. What surprises me is that more people did not die from food poisoning in the days before refrigeration.

Please do not think that my mother was a bad cook. She did an excellent job feeding her family. That is the only incident of food poisoning in our home. Over the years, I heard about a number of cases of food poisoning. Sometimes the food was served at reputable restaurants but, more often, at social gatherings such as birthday parties or wedding receptions.

Animals sometimes die from the same cause. Which reminds me of a story I once heard about a wealthy high society lady who loved putting on parties and entertaining people, usually for other rich or famous folks such as the mayor of their city. She had lots of servants but she liked to supervise everything to make sure everything was okay. The menus always consisted of a wide variety of exotic foods, including the lowly mushroom.

One day, when they were preparing to host an elite group of people, she was extra careful that nothing would go wrong. For some reason, she mistrusted the safety of mushrooms. She called over one of her maids and told her to test the mushrooms on her pet dog. It was about three o'clock, four hours before their guests were to arrive. The maid fed the mushrooms with some brown gravy to the dog. If the dog did not get sick, then the mushrooms should be safe to eat.

Three and a half hours after the dog had consumed the mushrooms, he seemed to be okay. So she concluded the mushrooms were safe. When the guest arrived there was the usual chitchat. After hors d'oeuvres were served, the guests sat down to partake of the fine food that had been prepared. Everyone enjoyed the dinner and most of them ate too much, except for the few ladies who were diet-conscious.

Just before the dessert was served, the maid, who had tested the mushrooms, called the hostess into the kitchen. She told the host lady that the dog had just died. The lady of the house was horrified. It was embarrassing, but she had no choice. She called the local hospital. They told her to sit tight, they would come right over. In five minutes, the paramedics were there with about half a dozen stomach pumps. They asked all the guests to lay down on the floor. Then they went to work pumping out their stomachs, which was a messy job. The last person to have their stomach pumped out was the hostess. She staggered off into the kitchen and asked the maid where the dead dog was. "Oh," replied the maid, "he is on the street in front of the house where the car hit him." Better safe than sorry.

My mother told me a story about a person who passed away. This happened over a hundred years ago. In those days there was no embalming and in the country there were no paramedics or doctors to pronounce a person dead. It was customary to bury a person the same day they died or the next day. (Jewish folks still follow this practice.) In the incident my mother told me about, the family quickly built a crude coffin then wrapped the corpse in a blanket. They took the body to a church for a funeral service. After the service they loaded the coffin in a wagon for a short trip to the cemetery.

The horses hitched to that wagon were rather skittish and suddenly the team bolted. The driver tumbled off his perch and away went the horses. After about a three hundred yard dash the team of horses veered off sharply. This caused the coffin to depart from the wagon. As it hit the ground the lid flew off. You can imagine the surprise of the people watching some distance away, when the body showed signs of life. Some people left in a hurry, others ran over to the former dead man. By the time they got there, he was sitting up. As far as I know he lived to a ripe old age after that.

I have heard of other incidents where they buried a person who was just comatose, not dead. Some of those were discovered years later when, for some reason, they exhumed the body. There was ample evidence that the person had struggled and scratched themselves. Maybe embalming a body is a pretty good idea. I sure don't want to be buried alive, do you? I don't remember what my mother said about the runaway team, as to where they ended up or who caught them.

Human nature is interesting, which reminds me of a lady I knew when I was a young boy. They lived some distance from our place but we met her and her husband quite frequently. She got married at age eighteen. Up to that point, she had always spoken the language her parents spoke; she could also speak English. After she got married she stopped speaking the other language. She only spoke English. Consequently, her children could only understand and speak English. When she was in her mid-eighties and in a nursing home, she got Alzheimer's.

Here is where truth is stranger than fiction kicks in. When her children came to visit her they could not understand what she was saying. After speaking only English for almost sixty years, she suddenly lapsed back to the language she had spoken when she was a child and a young girl. Kind of funny but sad.

My dad was a gun person. He literally had an arsenal of guns. He also liked to experiment. One day he concocted his own bullets. When he created these bullets he put a lot of gunpowder into them so they would have a high velocity. He put up a target behind the house about fifty yards away. He used the corner of the house to steady his hands as he aimed at the target. When he pulled the trigger, the gun exploded, taking a fair chunk out of the house with it. The amazing thing is that dad did not get injured very much. He flew back about eight feet and sustained a sore arm and some powder burns on his face.

Another time he saw a badger run into his hole or, should I say, he was in the process of digging a hole for himself. Badgers find a gopher hole, then dig down to the gopher's living room then feast on the whole family of gophers. At any rate, dad did not like badgers so he rushed over with his high powered gun. The badger was about three feet down. Dad stuck the gun into the hole and fired. The resulting concussion caused dad to fly back about ten feet. This time, he was injured slightly more than before from the home-made powder episode. But nothing life threatening. The gun was toast. I am not sure what happened to the badger.

One day dad was driving a team of horses. It was in winter so the rig he was pulling was a sleigh. Dad always had a gun with him. Suddenly a coyote jumped up and proceeded to cross the road in front of him. He quickly grabbed his high-powered rifle and shot at the coyote. He shot directly in front of him between the heads of the two horses. The loud explosion caused the horses to bolt. But dad managed to keep them under control. Would you believe one of those horses became partially deaf at least in one ear? A deaf horse is dangerous because he cannot hear you when you approach him especially if he has his head in the manger eating. If you touch him when he does not know you are there, he is likely to give you a swift kick.

Yes, dad was a bit of a daredevil and there were numerous other incidents, other than guns that could be life threatening, such as heating gas on a coal and wood stove. He used a five-gallon pail; his safety measures were that the pail was only half full. He reasoned it would not boil over onto the hot stove. How those fumes in that house did not blow up is a mystery to this day. The reason for heating that gas was that dad had the theory that in cold weather his stationary engine, which he used for sawing wood and other activities, would work better. One day my wife, with our one-year-old son, walked into my folks' house (we lived in the yard in another house). She beat a hasty retreat when she smelled all the gas fumes in the house.

Dad also was a bit of a firebug. I do not mean an arsonist. Just a little careless where he lit a fire. Every spring the fences around our yard would fill up with Russian thistles and tumbleweeds. Dad had an intense dislike for those old, traditional western weeds. He liked to burn them. Unfortunately some of the fence posts burned and some trees were scorched. It was always advisable to have a tank of water on a wagon nearby to douse the out-of-control flames. Mother always heaved a sigh of relief when dad finished his burning project.

In the old days, men often were in charge of most decisions made in the home and in a marital relationship. My dad was a sound example of that. I was born on June 20, 1926. However, dad did not get around to registering my birth until two months later. My parents named me Walter.

When dad arrived at the municipal office to register me, there were several people waiting in line to have their babies registered. Dad got into a casual conversation with another man who was waiting there and, as they visited, they discovered that they had a lot in common. Both had been homesteaders and they had about the same size families and they enjoyed the same things in life. Dad asked the man what they were going to name the baby. He told him, "Leonard". "Oh," my dad said, "I like that name." When it came to dad's turn to register me, the clerk asked him what my name was. "Leonard," dad said, without any hesitation. When he arrived home, he told mother the baby's name was no longer Walter, but was Leonard. Mother took it all in stride.

I find it difficult to think a thing like that would happen these days. For two months I was Walter and, for the past eight hundred and seventy-nine months, my name has been Leonard. I have often wondered what kind of man the other Leonard turned out to be.

My father, C.W. Friesen, circa 1920.

CHAPTER NINE

MEN

I hesitated to write about men. Since I am a man, I realize how short I and most other men fall in our character. I am not saying that all men are substandard in their behavioural patterns. But we do have flaws. One of my favorite clichés is men and women are equal, but different.

Sometimes I am ashamed of what some men do to women. It is a disgrace that it is not safe for a girl or woman to walk our streets at night. It is common knowledge that man is the aggressor when it comes to sex. That is no excuse for them to behave like an animal or worse. Men attacking women has always been a problem. But even in my lifetime, it has become increasingly worse.

Ninety-nine percent of men control their impulses and are decent citizens. When it comes to domestic skirmishes, it is more like fifty percent, although some of these marriage conflicts are as much the woman's fault as the man's. As the old saying goes, it takes two to tango.

A recent statistic stated that getting divorced affects a man more than it does a woman. I was surprised. I had always assumed it was more difficult for a woman. The article went on to state that women bond better with each other socially than men do. I have known several men who were totally devastated when their wives left them. On the other hand, a woman is often relieved when her husband leaves, as long as he keeps on supporting the family. There are always some exceptions. Some women are also devastated when the husband leaves. I know of a number of cases where the husband and father send no monetary support. Once again, it embarrasses me that there are men like that.

I am far from an expert on marital matters, so I will discontinue that subject and go into a trait that we men have, good and bad adventures. In the old days, men sailed the seven seas, often in leaky old sailing vessels. Their goal was to discover some new territory hoping for an Eldorado. A few did find great riches. For most though it was a tough life of scurvy, disease and mutiny. Often they were robbed by pirates, sometimes killed for the loot they had plundered in the New World.

After the whole world had been discovered and much of it colonized by European countries, a huge trading era came into existence. This world trade was led by Great Britain. Young British men wanted to become sailors. This meant months, sometimes even years, away from their wives, family or sweethearts. Quite a sacrifice for a little adventure on the high seas.

Men are more sexually aggressive than women. They are also more aggressive exploring the outer limits of society. They constantly seek to push back the frontiers of the status quo. If you analyze world history in the area of war, from Biblical days to the present, you will discover that ninety-nine percent of all the wars in the world were started by men. Sometimes it was a woman who caused a war, but the war was started by a jealous man. Throughout history, and even at the present time, there are evil men who think nothing about millions of innocent people dying because of their greed or lust for power.

I do not want this chapter to sound like a battle of the sexes. I am merely pointing out how men and women differ in their approach to life. I never cease to marvel at how opposites attract.

The percentage of women who are test pilots or astronauts is relatively small. This also applies to scaling the highest mountain peaks in the world. While I am not much on big game hunting, many men are. Few women hunt big game. In the high tech world, men also outnumber women in terms of inventing and pushing new ideas. By now every liberated woman may be angry at my analysis. Calm down. You are every bit as intelligent; it is just expressed in different areas than men. Speaking for myself, I confess that most women are ten times better at operating the latest electronic gadget than I am. So we men, just like you women, differ in our areas of expertise. Men and woman complement each other. Men and women have to learn to accept each other's strengths and weaknesses. I am sure every marriage counsellor will agree, if both sexes practised this understanding and tolerance, our divorce rate would take a drastic plunge.

In most areas of life we share many traits and similarities. We are of equal intelligence. As for health, we are subject to the same diseases, with slight variances. In women, it is breast cancer; in men, prostrate cancer. Women are tougher than we are; they outlive us by six to seven years. We appreciate the same music, our choice of reading may vary a little.

However, there are two areas where we are quite different - emotions and physical strength. It appears that men are less emotional. Maybe we men have been conditioned from a young age that boys and men do not cry or show outward emotions that might be considered weak. No boy on the school yard wants to be a sissy. I was never a sissy, but as an adult man, I have often cried and so have many other caring men. This crying usually happens when a loved one or dear friend has passed away or when someone near and dear is sick. But generally speaking, in those situations, women show more sentiment than men do. Millions of mothers have shed buckets of tears over their children, in life and death.

The other area where we are not the same is physical strength. Sure, there are strong women but on average, men are much stronger. If you question that, just think of how many women could play in a professional football league, or for that matter, a men's hockey or basketball team. A few tried out, but the physical aspect of playing with men jut overwhelmed them. Of course, they have their own hockey, baseball and basketball leagues, which provide great entertainment.

There are some women weightlifters, but at the present time they are not close to what the top male weightlifters can lift. Women excel in sports that do not require extreme physical strength such as tennis and golf.

I do not like to compare ourselves with the animal kingdom, but there is a parallel. Almost without exception, the male is the most muscled and much stronger than the female. However, when it comes to hunting or protecting the young, female animals are not to be trifled with. They can be dangerous, just like some of our human mothers.

I often feel sorry for teenage boys and young men. One example is car insurance. It costs a king's ransom for insurance if you are under twenty-five-years-of-age. Why? Because statistics reveal boys from age sixteen to twenty-five cause a large percentage of accidents. Most of those young men are good drivers. In fact, that is the problem. They are overconfident and take chances that sometimes end up in serious accidents.

Driving, along with sports, are areas where they can exhibit their skills and feel invincible.

The other sad statistic is eighty-five percent of all prisoners are male. This stems directly from the aggressive nature that men have. They are out to conquer the world, even if it means stealing, dealing in drugs and an assortment of other crimes including home invasions and burglaries. This crime pattern starts at an early age. By the time they are twenty-one-years-old, they are hardened criminals. These men are in the minority. Most young men are law-abiding citizens. They work off their aggressive impulses in sports, recreation and business ventures. It also helps if they marry the right woman. I have seen young men do a complete turnabout in their behaviour after they marry.

There are two common sayings that I do not like or appreciate. One is when some people apply the phrase to almost any older man and that is "dirty old man". What's the difference between a dirty old man or a dirty young man? As far as I am concerned there is only one difference and that is that the average old man is harmless. Unless he was a dirty young man when he was young (a leopard does not change its spots). On the other hand, a "dirty young man" can be dangerous as many women have found out over the years.

Whenever a sexual subject is discussed and an older man makes a comment, immediately young men and most women consider him a dirty old man. Whereas if a young man makes the same comment, he is considered well informed and worldly wise. Incidentally I have not heard myself being called a dirty old man. I am sure I may have been. But not to my face.

The other comment I do not like is when people say he's worse than an old woman. Those old women are our wives, mothers, grandmothers and sisters. I do not think that we should belittle the female gender like that. The saying comes from the fact that older women often are not active and approach life in a rather cautious manner. They have experienced a lot of life and hardships. So in older age they practise moderation. When a man has a timid and cautious nature, they refer to him as worse than an old woman.

If you are a person that uses either the "dirty old man" or "worse than an old woman" saying, it might be wise to eliminate them from your vocabulary.

None of us can help which sex we are born. I am proud to be a man. I must confess that sometimes I am slightly envious of some of the character traits that women possess. Come on, men, let us show the ladies that we can be macho and a gentleman at the same time.

CHAPTER TEN

TIME

Time is the most precious thing any human has. Years ago I made the casual remark, "I have more time than money."

The older gentleman with whom I was talking, rebuked me. He said never say that. Time is much more valuable than money. Once time passes, you cannot get it back.

I would venture to guess that most of us say the word time at least a dozen times every day. What time is it? Is it time to get up? What time do you have to be at your appointment? It's about time you smarten up. Did you have a good time last night? What time did you get home? I am running out of time. I was at the right place, at the right time. He is never on time. The list could go on and on, but I do not want to waste your time reading all this time business.

Most sports events such as football, hockey and basketball are based on time. In rodeo events, time is crucial. When you are riding a bronc or bull, eight seconds may seem like forever. In the timed events, every tenth of a second counts. In ladies barrel racing, they clock it to the hundredth of a second.

Offices, churches, schools, other services and events have a certain time when they start. If you are not on time you may miss something important. People get fired from their jobs for constantly being late for work. When I was in school, it was common for kids to stay in school for a half hour longer as punishment for being late in the morning for no valid reason.

Time is measured in split seconds, seconds, minutes, hours, days, weeks, months, years, decades, centuries, millennia and eternity – which is timeless.

We only have so much time on this earth. Less than a century for most of us. Our life span in Canada is seventy-four years for men and eighty-one years for women. In the United States, it is slightly less.

For that reason, we should make good use of our time. By that I do not mean we should work hard every moment. We should arrange our life so there is a time for work, time for play, time to do good for others and a time to rest.

For a new business venture to succeed, timing is important. There are thousands of stories of people going into a certain business at the right time and just as many people going into business at the wrong time. A few examples might be buying some high-priced cows at the top of the cattle cycle. Two years later, they might be worth only half of what was paid for them. On the other hand, timing was good if the cows were bought at the low cycle. These cows doubled in value in one or two years. This applies to all commodities and stocks. If timing is right, everything turns to roses. If it is wrong, it turns to thorns.

Sometimes, people start a business just before a recession sets in. Chances are the business will fail. It happened to me in several business ventures started in the early 1980s. By the mid-1980s we had a full-blown recession. It cost me millions of dollars because my timing was wrong. The three businesses were a food plant, a mini-storage facility and a sand and gravel business. Plus, I lost massive amounts of money on thousands of head of cattle. All those losses could be blamed on wrong timing. Seven years later all those ventures would have been winners.

In our daily lives, we must make time for things that are important to us, such as enjoying our families, reading good books, praying and worshipping God, not only at church, but at home as well.

We all have the same amount of time, twenty-four hours a day. Some days go fast, others slow, at least that is how it seems. If we are busy and enjoying ourselves, time flies by. When we are doing something we do not like, time drags by.

I often think that for prisoners, time must seem endless. That is what they call a jail sentence — doing time.

Whenever I contemplate writing a book, I always think how much time will it take to get it written, edited and published. Is it worth it? For me, it is time well spent. I enjoy reading and writing. I do not make much money from my writing but I like doing it. When I am writing at my desk, time flies by.

The whole world operates by time. There are twenty-four time zones. The four seasons are timed so that we know exactly how long we will have daylight every day of the year, from the longest day, June 21, to the shortest day, December 21. For those of us who are raised and live in the four seasons region of the world, we may find it difficult to realize that on the equator the days and nights are exactly the same twelve months of the year. You can set your clock or watch by the exact moment the sun rises or sets.

In developing countries, time is not as important on a daily basis as it is to those of us who live in the industrial world. I have spent a little time in a few of those third world countries. They are much more laid back than we are. Everything is not rush, rush.

When I was in Colombia it was not uncommon for an airline to be an hour or two late. Nobody was too concerned or upset over the delay. Those late arrivals and takeoffs had nothing to do with weather. Maybe the pilot slept in (at least he was well rested) or they were waiting for an important passenger to show up who had slept in. Another reason may be the old plane needed a few repairs. (I remember one flight where they wired the door shut with baling wire because the latch was broken.) In the end, we always arrived at our destination safe and sound.

An afternoon meeting or event that was to start at one o'clock may not get going until three o'clock. What is two hours here or there?

In most of those hot countries people take time for a nap during the heat of the day. Not a bad idea. I think, even in colder climates, a short nap can be refreshing. Recently, I read where some businesses and industries are considering making provisions for employees to have a short after-lunch siesta. Experts claim that this would improve the employees health and productivity.

In Ecclesiastes 3: 1-8, we read:

To everything there is a season and a time to every purpose under heaven. A time to be born and a time to die. A time to plant and a time to pluck up that which is planted. A time to break down and a time to build up. A time to kill and a time to heal. A time to weep and a time to laugh! A time to cast away stones and a time to gather stones together. A time to embrace and a time to refrain from embracing. A time to get and a time to lose. A time to keep and a time to cast away. A time to rend and a time to sew. A time to keep silence and a time to speak. A time to love and a time to hate. A time of war and a time of peace.

So you see, folks, not much has changed about time since Solomon wrote these words four thousand years ago.

I read once that Queen Victoria said on her deathbed, "I would give a fortune for a few more hours of life." (Life cannot be bought. She died minutes after that statement.)

CHAPTER ELEVEN

HAIR

Have you ever sat in an airport or shopping mall and watched people walk by? Most of us have. Isn't it fascinating the variety of people we have? Some are tall, some short, some skinny, some fat, some neither skinny nor fat. Some young, some middle-aged, some old. Some pretty, some ugly, most are somewhere in between.

But as the old saying goes, you can't judge a book by looking at the cover. Many of the less attractive people have a hidden talent and personality that does not show on the outside. They are intelligent, caring folks who just were not blessed with exterior looks. I am sure that Eleanor Roosevelt and Albert Einstein would not have won a beauty contest. There are millions more like them who have made this world a better and more interesting place to live, yet their appearance would not have indicated that.

What can we do to enhance our looks? The average person can do little to become one of the beautiful people. There are things like clothes, losing weight, gaining a little weight, plastic surgery – including face lifts and breast enhancements. These so-called improvements in our appearance are hard to attain and can be costly. Millions of dollars are spent on cosmetic surgery. How about our hair?

It seems to be the single most important asset we have to change our appearance, especially with women. From the beginning of time, hair has played a big role in the lives of people. The Bible mentions hair dozens of times. I will quote a few references:

And Solomon said, if he be a worthy man, not one of his hairs will fall to the ground, but if wickedness is found in him, he will die. I Kings 1:52

Grey hairs are here and upon him, yet he knoweth not. Hosea 7:9

But the very hairs of your head are numbered. St. Matthew 10:30

Neither shalt thou swear by thou head, because thou canst not make one hair white or black. St. Matthew 5:36 (That has changed with hair dye.)

Doth not even nature itself teach you, that if a man have long hair, it is a shame unto him? I Corinthians 11:14

But if a woman have long hair, it is a glory to her: for her hair is given her for covering. I Corinthians 11:15 (These days the reverse is often the case. Men with long hair, often worn in a ponytail, and women with short hair.)

It was Mary who anointed the Lord with ointment, then wiped his feet with her hair. St. John 11:2 (It is hard to imagine any woman wiping a man's feet with her hair in today's society, but then Jesus was no ordinary man.)

There is one story about King David's son, Absalom, who obviously had long hair. He rode his mule under the branches of a big oak tree. His hair got tangled in the branches and, as the Bible puts it, left him hanging between heaven and earth, while the mule under him kept going. As he was hanging there, one of his enemies thrust a spear through his heart. (His extra long hair didn't work for him that time.)

We are all familiar with the love story between Samson and Delilah. Delilah made him sleep on her knees, then cut off his hair. She had turned traitor. When he woke up, his strength had left him. Then the Philistines gouged out his eyes and made him a prisoner. An interesting story. If you have never read the story, turn in your Bible and read the Book of Judges, Chapter 16 for the complete story.

Hair comes in many colors such as black, dark brown, light brown, blond, auburn, red and many shades in between. There is fine hair, coarse hair and average hair. Hair also varies greatly in density. Some people have thick hair, some average, some thin and some no hair at all (mostly older men).

Through the centuries, hairstyles have constantly changed. In my lifetime I have witnessed many changes in hairstyles, in both men and women. Some of the names that come to mind are straight long hair, straight short hair (common with the ladies these days). One of my daughters had naturally curly hair when she was a young girl. She spent a fair bit of time trying to make it straight like her girlfriend's hair. Then there is braided hair, pig tails, pony tails, the beehive look, tight curls, loose curls, boyish bob, pompadour, a bun at the back of the head, the fluffed look, the fuzzy look, the pageboy, spiked, loose wavy hair, bangs, kiss curls, small tight braids (often worn by black women), extremely long (they can actually sit on it), and a number of other styles.

My mother had long hair, which she often put up in a bun. From the day she was born until she was eighty-years-old, a scissor never touched her head. I thought it was a pity that the nursing home she was in decided to cut her hair. She passed away at eighty-two-years of age. Hair, no matter what color, style or length, is precious to a girl or woman. Just recently one of our granddaughters, who had beautiful long dark hair, decided to shave it all off to raise funds for juvenile diabetes. A noble cause. She is fifteen-years-old. Fortunately hair is a renewable resource. I am sure a year from now she will once again have beautiful long hair.

Men and women spend billions of dollars on their hair every year. The ladies lead the parade. They think nothing of spending a hundred dollars or more to get their hair cut, permed and colored. When special occasions come along like weddings, graduations or any other social event, the first thing a woman thinks about is her hair (at least my wife does). Today, hairstyles come in tangled messes or real short or the wet look or any other look. In other words, women are more liberated as to how they wear their hair. Short, straight hair seems to be the choice of many career women. It sure cuts down on the upkeep. Those women want to be recognized for their brains, not their hair.

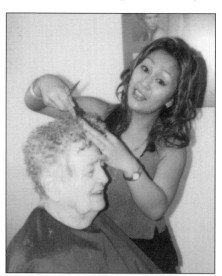

This is Tran Quach. She is busy beautifying my wife Edna's hair. While she does that she engages people in interesting conversation. Incidentally, she also cuts my hair. She operates in Airdrie, Alberta.

We men mess around with our hair as well. That is, if we have any hair left to mess with. In my life, I have had traditional haircuts, brush cuts and fairly long hair. These days, I am back to traditional. During the hippie era of the '60s and early-'70s, young men – and a few older ones – let their hair grow long and often wore it in a ponytail. However, few men washed their hair as often as women did. At least that is how it looked to me because their hair usually looked greasy and dirty. Hairstyles, especially in men, are often a protest against conventional society. In other words, they are making a statement of their rebellion against what they consider the establishment. In the last few years, I have seen a number of teenage boys with blue, green, purple or bright red hair. Sometimes they have a partly shaved head while others

Here is another perspective on how to utilize your hair. No this is not a mountain man. He is the author's nephew Wilf (Nipper) Friesen who lives in the Fraser Valley at Chilliwack, British Columbia. He is an intelligent business and family man. For recreation, he drives his own cars in drag races. As the saying goes, do not judge a book by its cover. We can be a regular person whether we have long, medium, short or no hair It's what's on the inside that counts. To me, Wilf looks like a philosopher from the Middle Ages.

have spiked hair. Most adults and parents do not appreciate these kinds of hairstyles. I guess if the young girls like those styles, that is all that matters to these young men.

Men have one advantage over women and that is they have facial hair (beards). Quite often a man who is basically bald will sport a huge beard. Men's beards, like women's hair, come in all shapes and sizes. In my humble opinion, most men who wear beards are making a statement. For one thing, they want to be noticed. Often a rather small diminutive man has a beard, sometimes partially shaved for extra effect. My great-grandfathers and grandfathers wore big beards. My dad was down to a moustache. Ninety-nine percent of my life I have been clean shaven. I grew a beard three times for brief periods. Some men have goatees.

Forty years ago, Bill Renard said to me, "Never trust a man with a moustache." He must have had a bad deal from a moustached man. If that is the case, virtually no men should be trusted these days, because nearly all have moustaches, including my sons and sons-in-law. Everyone of them is a trustworthy man.

In the old days, wigs were popular, especially with men. I have seen a number of pictures of high profile men from one hundred and fifty to two hundred years ago. They wore fancy powdered wigs.

When the Americans outmanoeuvred the British in 1846 concerning the Oregon territory, talks were held in London, England in panelled oak offices. Everyone sat around a huge oak table in a stuffy atmosphere with their powdered wigs. The United States came out the big winner, when the 49th parallel was established as the border between the British colony called the Dominion of Canada and the United States. The British negotiators were more concerned about their appearance than in trading away a large chunk of Canadian territory.

In later years, wigs became more popular with women. My wife even wore one occasionally. These days, wig stores are almost out of business. There are still a few diehards, like Dolly Parton, who still wear wigs.

Hairpieces are also widely used by men whom nature deprived of natural hair. If I lacked hair, I probably would wear a hairpiece as well. They look very authentic.

When people wear the same clothes and have the same haircut, they do resemble each other. That is one of the reasons the armed forces insists on crew cuts and uniforms. This puts everyone in the same category, at least in appearance. It helps with discipline.

We must not forget animals. They all have hair. Their hair is for protection against the weather. In cold climates, the animals' hair is thicker and usually longer. Grazing animals shed their winter coat of hair, which is already replaced underneath by shorter hair. Hair can make a big difference in the appearance of an animal. I have judged hundreds of cattle shows. At these shows, they have what they call a grooming class. People showing cattle spend hours clipping, washing and brushing the hair of their show animal. Some of those cows, steers, heifers and bulls are so spruced up they remind me of a girl all prettied up for her debutante ball. Some use haircreams and color as well. Often after a show, my hands are colored and greasy from touching those animals.

Remember the days when greasy hair was in? Young men slicked their hair down with various types of creams. I only remember brylcream.

Each generation changes styles from the previous generation. There are only so many things you can do with hair. So in a lifetime of, say, seven decades, old styles come back, such as moustaches or the length of hair or where a man's hair is parted. I notice a number of young women, the earthy type, have the same hairstyle our grannies did two generations ago.

Hair and nails are the only things that keep on growing until the day we die. Many of our middles and bums do as well, but that's different. It is dictated by genes, food and exercise, whereas hair and nails grow whether we eat a lot or a little, or exercise or not. The Lord knew what he was doing when he created our hair.

I like hair, except when I find it in my food.

CHAPTER TWELVE

SALT

In ancient times, salt played a huge role in society. The Bible and other history books recorded the importance of salt. Following are few quotes from the Bible concerning salt.

Salt is good; but if the salt have lost its saltness, wherewith will ye season it? Have salt in yourselves, and have peace one with another. Mark 9:50

Every oblation of thy meat offering shalt thou season with salt: neither shalt thou suffer the salt of the covenant of thy God to be lacking from thy meat offering. With all thine offerings thou shalt offer salt. Leviticus 2:13

Can that which is unsavoury be eaten without salt? Or is there any taste in the white of an egg? Job 6:6

Let your speech be always with grace, seasoned with salt, that ye may know how ye ought to answer every man. Colossians 4:6

None of us like people with acid tongues. Their statements come across too blunt, with no concern that they may hurt a person's feelings. But a speech seasoned with salt is good. It lets us express our feelings honestly. At the same time, it conveys a message to the person we are talking to in a non-sarcastic manner. I like to call it, tell it like it is, or no beating around the bush.

This world would be a mighty bland place without salt. Humans and animals require some salt in their daily diet. For the last number of years, salt has received a bum rap from the medical profession. People shun salt as being unhealthy. A number of people, including one of our daughters, put no salt shakers on the dinner table. These folks claim they put a modest amount of salt into the food while they are cooking it. I disagree with that concept.

Food salted at the table tastes every bit as good as food salted while it is being cooked. Some people disagree with that statement. I stand my ground on it. I have tried both methods. Believe me, there is absolutely no difference in the taste of the food. The main reason I don't like pre-salted food is how does the cook know how much salt the people eating it want. Some may want less and some may want more salt than was added to the food while being cooked. Why add any salt while cooking? Let people decide how much salt they want at the dinner table.

Incidentally, the medical profession has done an about-face on the amount of salt a person should ingest. Several doctors told me when I was in the hospital that I can eat as much salt as my body craves. They said the only exceptions are people with high blood pressure. I have low blood pressure, in spite of using lots of salt all my life. I also have low cholesterol.

I have often said I would not have fared well in a saltless society. A number of aboriginal people in many areas of the world had no salt available to them. We know that the food we eat contains a certain amount of salt, even without salting it. I am told if we have a completely saltless diet, our health would deteriorate fast.

Animals crave salt as well. Every year, millions of salt blocks and salt licks are put in pastures. Horses, cattle, sheep, elk, deer and other animals hang around those salt licks. On several occasions, I have been a little negligent in putting out salt blocks. When I do arrive with salt, the cows all crowd around them to replenish the lack of salt in their bodies.

Salt has a tendency to make man or beast thirsty. This is good. We are supposed to consume eight glasses of water a day. On real hot days, we need a little extra salt due to evaporation that takes place by profusely perspiring. Have I convinced you yet that salt is extremely important in our diet? I have not quite convinced my wife.

Before we had refrigeration, salt played a huge role in preserving meat at home, in butcher shops and packing plants. Even today, ham is cured in a salt brine. Fish are sometimes cured with salt. If it had not been for salt, millions of people would have died from food poisoning. It was salt that looked after the little bugs and bacteria that made people sick. I am not sure if they still do it, but when I worked for a packer years ago, thousands of cattle hides were salted to keep them from rotting before they shipped them to tanneries, often overseas.

How about all that salt that is mixed in with sand and gravel then spread on our roads in the winter? The salt causes ice and snow to melt even if it is below zero. It is hard on cars and trucks since it has a tendency to cause rust. But I dare say over the years thousands of accidents and deaths have been prevented by the use of salt on our roads and sidewalks.

Salt is one of the few things that is dirt cheap on our supermarket shelves. The reason is the world has more salt than any other commodity. A little further on, I will mention how much salt the world contains.

On the commodity exchanges things like sugar, tea, coffee, cocoa, orange juice, and all types of grains are traded. But I have never noticed salt on the list.

In our daily conversations, salt is frequently mentioned. He or she is the salt of the earth, meaning they are genuine, real people whom you can depend upon.

In rodeo, a tough bronc is often referred to as salty. Those salty broncs are tough to ride. They are out to buck you off.

Sometimes we hear the expression, he is not worth his salt. In other words, he does not amount to much.

When we get older and our hair starts turning grey, people call that salt-and-pepper hair. I am long past that stage − my hair is white. Maybe that is from eating all that salt. Yes, we need salt in our food and in our character.

Now, a brief history of salt. The scientific name for salt is sodium chloride. It dissolves quickly in either hot or cold water. In the old days, many parts of the world had no access to salt. There are parts of Africa where, until recent years, salt was only for the rich. There were also caravans of camels carrying salt from the salt oases in the Libyan Desert. Even today, some salt is still moved by caravan across the Sahara Desert. Worldwide, total annual production of salt is approximately fifty-five million tonnes. As the saying goes, that is only the tip of the iceberg.

The world has trillions of tons of salt reserves, not counting the oceans which are salt water. So the stores will not run out of salt any time soon. It is estimated that if the oceans dried up, they would yield four-and-one-half million cubic miles of rock salt. That is at least twice the bulk of all the mountain ranges in the world. That would salt a lot of roads – or eggs.

The Dead Sea (three hundred and ninety-four square miles) contains approximately 11-billion, 600-million tonnes of salt. The water is so salty that a human body floats on top – kind of handy for nonswimmers. There are some plants that separate sea water from the salt. This is not done for the salt it yields, but for the water needed in some parched areas for drinking and irrigation. Israel is one of those areas. The process is costly, consequently it has not been developed as fast as governments had hoped for.

Nature has an efficient way of distilling the salt out of sea water. It simply evaporates into the air, then returns to us in the form of rain or snow, which in turn flows back to its origin, the ocean. I must have quoted this one hundred times, there is no less water in the world than there was five thousand years ago.

This also applies to salt. Every year, billions of tonnes of salt flow into the oceans from the world's water sheds. They ensure the oceans will remain salty forever.

Let us be thankful for salt and enjoy it. But be careful you do not turn into a pillar of salt. That is what happened to Lot's wife when she longingly looked back at the sinful cities of Sodom and Gomorrah. Today, sin and corruption have almost caught up to those two ancient cities. If you're fleeing from sin, don't look back, you may also turn into a pillar of salt.

Chapter Thirteen

EXCUSES

Making excuses is almost a daily routine with many people, including myself. Just what is an excuse? According to the dictionary, it is when we try to remove guilt from ourselves for being careless; to free ourselves from obligations, a pretext. It does not say so, but it has been my observation, that most excuses are little white lies (sometimes not so little).

Often when people receive an invitation to someone's home or a larger social gathering on a given date, they immediately start looking for an excuse why they cannot attend. There is a long list of valid sounding excuses such as: I am not feeling well; we have a prior engagement on that day (sometimes true, sometimes not); Aunt Sadie may be coming over that day (even though she never said she would); my car is broke down and my son is using the pickup; we can't leave Granny home alone (even though she has stayed home alone many times when we went to something that interested us); We have to stay with my mother-in-law, she has the sniffles; or our favorite mare is due to foal that day. The list of excuses could fill a whole book.

The excuse we give for making those excuses is we do not want to hurt people's feelings. But I think when an excuse is transparent or flimsy, it would be better to level with people and tell them the real reason why we are not coming. In the past four years, I have had approximately one hundred autographing sessions in bookstores, conventions and places of business. I am there to sell the books that I wrote. I really enjoy visiting with people, so it's always a pleasure for me to go to those places. The host is always gracious to me and so are the folks who drop by my table. But there is always a small percentage of people who make excuses why they do not purchase a book. In fact, the excuses are quite interesting.

The one excuse I readily accept is that they are not particularly interested in the type of books I write. I understand that. If Stephen

King were autographing books at Chapters or anywhere else, I would have the same excuse. I am just not interested in what he writes. But for most of the others, the excuses are not that valid. For instance, a number of people have said to me, "I do not know any of the people in that book." My reply is that in my lifetime I have read several thousand books and only in about a dozen of those books did I know any of the characters the author writes about. And when it comes to fiction, nobody knows the people in the book because they don't exist.

Another excuse they often give is, I have no time to read. Pardon the expression, but what a crock that is. We have time for what we make time for. I bet those same people often waste a bunch of time looking at the television or other trivial pursuits. The truth is they just don't like reading. Or how about I can't read. This is really sad because that might be a valid excuse. I recently read where about fifteen percent of Canadians are illiterate even though it's claimed we are ninety-nine percent literate. Sometimes people tell me they can't afford a book. This may be true, but often the reason is they left most of their paycheque at the bar. Another excuse is I am too busy today to buy a book but I will be back. They seldom come back. One valid excuse that is real is when older folks say their sight is failing. That is so sad. I often think how devastated I would be if I could not see well enough to read anymore.

Some excuses are real, but the bulk of them are little white lies. Like I said earlier, ninety percent of the people I talk to, whether they buy a book or not, are genuinely good people. Forgive me if I stepped on some toes.

In courtrooms, judges hear dozens of reasons or excuses why the accused is in court. This is especially true in juvenile courts where young offenders blame some of their peers or their parents or the system or whatever for what made them do what they did. It really was not my fault, I did not know the gun was loaded, or I did not mean to stab him, he just kind of got in the way of my knife. I was just defending myself. It was my friend who broke into the store, I just happened to be with him.

Some of the most common excuses come from husbands who cheat on their wives, or vice-versa. I have heard some unbelievable stories concerning errant husbands. One that comes to mind was a man who told his wife he was going to Exshaw over the weekend to buy some hogs (he was a livestock dealer). The real facts are Exshaw has no hogs or anything else, except a cement plant. The truth was he was with another woman in Banff about thirty miles west of Exshaw. I doubt if his wife was naive enough to believe that story.

One of the most common excuses by husbands and wives is that they are working late at the office. I know of several cases where an irate wife took it upon herself to go to the office to check things out. What she found was a husband who was busy with his secretary but it was not doing books.

Out-of-town business trips are perfect for cheating spouses, both male and female. I have personally encountered men whom I knew that were five hundred miles or more away from home with another woman, while their wife was at home looking after their kids and holding down the fort for her loving husband. What a disgrace.

Another place where excuses are rampant is in the workplace. Many employees have a whole repertoire of excuses why they could not get the job done on time or properly. "I'm overworked. The person with me did not do their share of the work. The equipment I had to work with was faulty." When I was head cattle buyer for a packing company, I heard all kinds of excuses why the cattle that a certain buyer purchased were a disaster. He ran out of time so he looked at the cattle in the dark, that is why he misjudged them. Or he thought they had been on feed for five months instead of sixty days (this results in low yields). Sometimes a buyer would tell me, "You said we needed cattle, so I just bought the cattle for high money even if they did not measure up."

One day in Colorado, I invited a chap over to the ranch to show him some cows we had for sale. In due time, he and his sidekick showed up. We drove to the pasture to look at the cows. They liked the cows. Both the cows and the calves were in good shape.

When we got back to the buildings I invited them in for a coffee. They said they would love to come in for a coffee but they had to decline. They were in a hurry and had no time to stop for coffee. I told them I understood their situation.

When I went into the house I told my wife those men had to leave. They had no time for coffee. About ten minutes later we decided to go to town for a few supplies and the mail. After that, we decided to go to the local cafe for a coffee.

Lo and behold, when we walked in the restaurant, both men were sitting there quite contentedly sipping coffee. I tell you, those were two embarrassed hombres. They turned red and stuttered a few lame excuses. They got caught red-handed telling a little white lie.

A week later they sold those cows for us. We received a good price. Every once in a while we make bad choices. This happened to be one of those times for those gentlemen. They are still my friends. I have done a fair bit of business with them since that incident, but I have never asked them in for a coffee again.

In wars, there are many reasons and excuses why the battle was lost. Many wars are based on excuses. A good example was the destruction and bombing at Kosovo in 1998. NATO gave the excuse they were saving the Albanians from the Serbs when, in fact, they did ten times more killing and destroying than the Serbs had done. The truth of the matter is, if the Albanians had the upper hand, they would have been just as ruthless as the Serbs were to them. In fact, after the attacks, the Serbs suffered at the hands of the Albanians.

The real reason for the NATO bombing was that United States President Bill Clinton was trying to turn the spotlight off himself and Monica Lewinsky. Another reason was that NATO was wanting to try some new bombing techniques – some that they had not used in the Gulf War. Nothing like keeping up-to-date on how to develop equipment that will destroy the greatest number of people with relative safety to the aggressor. Yes, this world is full of excuses. It has been going on ever since God created man. The Bible is full of people making excuses for their actions. A classic example is when Adam blamed Eve for giving him the apple from the forbidden tree. He said to God, "The woman thou gavest me got me to eat that apple."

We have all heard the little saying, God made man, then rested, then he made woman. Since then, no one has rested.

Sorry ladies, I am only kidding. We men appreciate and need you.

CHAPTER FOURTEEN

POLICE

Police are important in our society. Without them there would be anarchy. If every person was a law-abiding citizen, we could pretty well eliminate the police. But human nature hasn't changed much in the last five thousand years. If anything, it is worse. Worldwide, there seems to be a wave of crime unequalled in history, murder, rape, kidnapping, stealing, fraud and terrorist attacks.

How do the police handle all this? In some cases, very well. In others, shoddily. Of course, it depends on which country we are talking about. Let's look at some of the police activities in various countries of the world.

During the seventy years of communist rule in Russia, the police force was the KGB. They operated largely as undercover spies and agents for the government. Their job was to keep people in line. This they did with brute force. They also operated as undercover spies in many other countries of the world, including the United States. In Russia, millions of people died at the hands of these brutal men, many of these people died while exiled to the labour camps in Siberia. Often their only crime was disagreeing with the government. A number of other Eastern European countries had similar police forces. In fact, the KGB trained many of them.

The story is told about two fishermen who went fishing on a large river nearly every day. It so happened that on the east side of the river the communists ruled the country. On the west side, the country was a democracy. These two fishermen had never met. They could see each other across the river that was almost a mile wide. The man on the west side sometimes used his binoculars to watch the other gentlemen casting his line. He noticed that this man caught few fish. On the west side, where he fished, he caught all kinds of fish. One day curiosity got the best of him so he took a rowboat and rowed across the river to the east side. When the two men met, they discussed their fishing success. The man from the west side asked his new found friend, "How come you catch so few fish?" "Oh," said the man from the east side, "the fish on this side of the river are afraid to open their mouths."

During Hitler's reign in Germany, the police force was the Gestapo, who were just as ruthless as the KGB in Russia. They rounded up millions of Jews and other people and sent them to death camps.

In many so-called third world developing countries, the police are corrupt. Most of them are on the take. In other words, bribery is rampant.

A good example is Colombia, South America. I spent a little time there. I heard a number of stories about how corrupt many of those policemen were. For instance, they make a pretence of catching drug dealers, but that is just a pretence. What they do is stretch a heavy rope across a highway to stop every car and truck. They search the vehicles. If they find drugs, the operator of the vehicle gives them a couple hundred or maybe a thousand pesos, depending on the amount of drugs. Away the dealer goes with his drug cache intact. The police pocket the money. They issue no tickets or receipts.

Similar things happen in other Latin American countries, including Mexico. One of my cousins was murdered in Mexico. This did not involve drugs. It was just plain robbery. The police did nothing to solve that crime.

England has their well-trained Bobbies. They also have Scotland Yard detectives who specialize in catching serial killers and other riffraff that inhabit the big cities of Britain.

The United States has four types of police. There are city police in the big cities. They also have sheriffs, who are elected in each county. The sheriff appoints whatever number of deputy sheriffs he requires. It could be one or it could be a dozen depending on the size and population of the county. Highway patrol policemen are employed by the state. At the top is the Federal Bureau of Investigation (FBI), a federal force. They investigate crimes for the federal government. The FBI has a good reputation. However, every once in awhile they botch up big time. Waco, Texas was a good example.

Those of you who like western history know what many of the sheriffs and marshalls were like a hundred years or more ago in the Wild West. Some of them were excellent lawmen whom the outlaws feared. However, a number of them were thugs as well. They hid behind their badge, which gave them some respect. The badge gave them good cover for their connection to the outlaws. They were so discreet that the local population never caught onto the fact that their sheriff was as crooked as a dog's hind leg. Some of the well-known lawmen of the old west were pretty suspect, yet they kept a semblance of law and order. A few names that come to mind are John Behan, William Bradley, Virgil Earp, Wyatt Earp, Wild Bill Hickock, Pat Garret, Bat Masterson, Roy Bean (the hanging judge), Bill Tilghman and many others. Most of these gentlemen had shady pasts themselves. I guess the old adage applied, it takes a thief to catch a thief.

When thieves broke into our house in Colorado, they stole a bunch of stuff. There was very little investigation. In fact, I am sure they never even tried to take fingerprints. We offered a thousand dollar reward for information about this crime. Nothing ever came of it.

In Canada, we also have several different police forces. There are the city police forces, provincial police forces and municipal police, which I call County Mounties. The most respected and widespread police force in Canada is the Royal Canadian Mounted Police (RCMP), often called the Mounties.

In my humble opinion, they are the best police force in the world. Even so, there are a few bad apples in their midst as well. I know of one former Mountie who said that quite often when they confiscated liquor from people, a few of the Mounties from his detachment would have a party with that illegal liquor. But I have heard of very little bribery. Most of the Mounties are proud to be a part of that force and do an excellent job policing.

I have a friend who used to be in a city police force for a number of years. Before he retired, he was a detective. He can tell some pretty gruesome stories about undercover work. The bulk of criminals are low-life individuals. Not too smart. However, there are some intelligent people who go wrong. They are the ones that give police lots of trouble. In the end, they usually find that crime does not pay.

The public does not hold the police in high esteem. One of the main reasons for that is traffic tickets. Policing costs a lot of money. Traffic tickets are the only income they have from the public. Murder or theft bring no income, only expense. The way I see it, traffic tickets are a huge subsidy. The problem is many of those tickets are given out to basically honest, decent citizens who have exceeded the speed limit by a few miles an hour.

The police have safety and saving lives on their side of the story. The problem is a little speeding on the roads isn't what kills people. What kills people is dangerous driving, weaving in and out of traffic, drunk driving or excessive speeding, as well as going through stop signs.

Off and on, Montana has no daytime speed limit. Whenever they had no speed limit, I always felt safe driving there. The reason is I knew I was on my own. That caused me to be more cautious than when there were all kinds of speed zones. When they had speed limits, often the posted speed was too fast for a certain stretch of road but because the speed limit was sixty miles an hour, one drove sixty miles an hour, even if you should only have been driving forty-five miles an hour. You were driving to rule, not using your own judgement.

The police there still handed out tickets for dangerous driving. So, in spite of no speed limits, there was still a restraint on people's driving habits.

Back to other jurisdictions. The police will deny the accusation that they have a quota of sorts. In other words, they must hand out a certain amount of tickets each day or their superiors will think they are not doing a good job. Those borderline infraction tickets are what infuriates the average citizen and turns them off on the police. In my opinion, the police should be there to protect us, not to hassle us with minor infractions, traffic or otherwise. With all the rules and regulations, plus gun laws that we have these days, it may only be a matter of time until we have a police state like they did in Russia and Germany in the past. Sound far-fetched? I think not.

CHAPTER FIFTEEN

TRAFFIC

We hear much about road rage. Sometimes it even results in shooting incidents. We condemn that kind of action and so we should. However, if we are honest with ourselves, we have to admit we have got rather hot under the collar when someone cuts us off.

There are several things in traffic that really annoy me. For instance, if there is road construction ahead on a busy thoroughfare and all the traffic funnels into one lane. Most people are courteous and allow you into the lane where the traffic merges into a single lane. The traffic at this point just sort of creeps along. Suddenly you notice someone speeding by you, passing everyone. His vehicle is half on the road and half on the shoulder of the road. He roars past fifty, sixty, maybe a hundred cars then muscles into the line where there is a slight gap between cars. I always wonder what kind of person that is. Does his conscience ever bother him that he has such ill manners, with no reason other than his small mind considers himself the most important person around. Those kinds of individuals have no respect for other people's rights or property. The sad part is it is not only one person that behaves that way. I would venture a guess about five percent of the public have the same kind of mental attitude.

Another thing that annoys me in traffic is excessive speeding. They often pass other traffic on a solid-line no-passing zone. On a freeway with two lanes going in each direction, I will exceed the speed limit by three to five miles an hour and along comes a vehicle tailgating me for half a mile until I have a chance to switch into the slightly slower-moving outside lane. As he roars by, it is not uncommon for him to vent his anger by honking his horn or giving me the finger. I could understand his frustration if I was driving ten or fifteen miles under the speed limit. This impatience boggles my mind.

Whenever I drive on a freeway with three lanes of traffic going the same direction, I usually drive in the center lane. I set my cruise control at whatever the speed limit is, plus maybe another three to five miles per hour more. The result is I have vehicles passing me on either side as though I am standing still. I will mention a few locations where this has happened: north of Denver, Colorado on Interstate 25; south of Phoenix, Arizona, on Interstate 10; and on Deerfoot Trail passing through Calgary, Alberta.

I like four-way stops but it really annoys me when people cheat and go before their turn.

Slow-moving traffic is also a menace. You catch up to them much faster than you realize, especially if they are going forty-miles-per-hour in a seventy-miles-per-hour zone. It is a good idea to drive defensively – not too fast, not too slow. You never know what you may encounter on the road. Countless injuries could be avoided and many lives saved.

I am glad they are cracking down on drunk drivers. Statistics tell us that approximately fifty percent of accidents involve drunk drivers. Actually the rate of accidents that drunk drivers are involved in are nineteen times that high. The reason is that less than five percent of drivers are drunk. In other words, five percent of drunk drivers cause fifty percent of the accidents, where ninety-five percent of sober drivers cause the other fifty percent of accidents. Seem confusing?

Incidentally, it was a drunk driver that killed both of my wife's parents. That same accident also severely injured my wife and our two daughters. Two of our other children escaped with only bruises. I was not in the car with them at the time. This same story has happened to millions of other people worldwide. I recently read where more people have been killed in motor vehicle accidents that have died in all the wars in the last one hundred years.

Some years ago two of our sons, Leland and Graham, were hitchhiking in New Zealand. A man stopped and picked them up. The boys sat in the back seat where they fell asleep. Suddenly there was an awful racket. They felt themselves tossed around like rag dolls. The car flipped end-over-end about six times. The car was a total wreck.

The driver and our sons only had a few bruises. Leland lost his wallet, which he never found. The reason for the crash was the driver had one too many drinks and fell asleep at the wheel. No charges were laid. Leland thinks maybe the driver stole his wallet.

My nephew, Loran Harder, told me what happened to one of his friends. This chap decided to go to Las Vegas to do a little gambling. It was dark as he was driving on a lonely stretch of road in Nevada. Suddenly, he came upon a car parked partially on the road with no lights on. He crashed into it. It turned out to be a young couple who were college students. The young man was instantly killed. Miraculously, the girl was not really hurt, only dazed. As she watched in her daze, a car stopped and went over the car where Loran's friend was laying unconscious. They rifled through his pockets and stole fifteen hundred dollars from his wallet. They even tried to remove a ring from his finger. Then they quickly jumped into their car and took off. The girl was too shook up and spaced out to even get the license number of those ruthless thugs.

After awhile, another car came by and its occupants phoned the police and ambulance. Loran's friend survived. It took him three years to heal from his injuries. Several years later Loran was in a car accident himself. He was hurt pretty bad. Both his legs were broken. The car was totalled. He, too, healed up after several years. Would you believe one of the paramedics stole Loran's Rolex watch and it was never recovered?

Our youngest son, Trent, died in a vehicular crash a mile-and-a-half from home. This time there was no alcohol involved, only speed. The person hit his pick-up truck broadside. The man denied he was speeding, but the horrific crash indicates otherwise. There were no eyewitnesses, so it was hard to prove.

Some die and some live, but I think it is about time as a civilized society we start operating our vehicles in a safe, civilized manner. If not, we may become a statistic ourselves. I like the slogan, the life you save may be your own.

A good organization to support is Mothers Against Drunk Driving (MADD).

Chapter Sixteen

GRASS

We take grass for granted. We see it nearly every day of our life. I think grass is the fourth most important thing on this planet. Only air, water and maybe fire are more important. These three things are closely connected to grass. All human, animal and plant life need air to live. Grass needs water for it to grow. Fire also plays a role in grass. Even in the old days there were many fires set by lightning. These days prairie fire can be devastating, but it cleans up and purifies the earth. A year after a fire, provided it rains, the grass is better than ever.

Grass grows on every continent of the world except the Antarctic. Grass, along with trees, does not have to be planted. Mother Nature (God) has planted both of them everywhere. Of course, these days both grass and trees are planted by humans as well.

All wildlife depends on grass for its survival. Huge herds of grazing animals depend completely on grass. The carnivores kill and eat the animals that graze. Even birds need grass. Dozens of bird species eat grass seeds. A number of them also build their nests in the grass. Our domestic animals such as cattle, horses, sheep and goats need grass – not only for grazing but for the hay it produces to be fed in the winter. Cereal grains are part of the grass family. So, directly or indirectly, grass produces meat, dairy products and all forms of pastry. About the only food that does not involve grass is seafood and fruit and vegetables. I suppose pure vegetarians could survive without grass.

Grass brightens up our lives. Think of what a park, even with trees, would be without grass to romp around on. Or how about the millions of lawns worldwide. These lawns give urbanites a little green space in a concrete jungle.

Grass also stabilizes the top soil. Without grass, erosion would become a major problem. It already is a big problem in some areas of the world because of over-grazing. Also, a lot of land has been broken up to plant other crops. Much of this land should never have been ploughed up.

In both Canada and the United States, millions of acres were broken up by homesteaders shortly after the turn of the century. They planted annual cereal crops such as wheat, barley, oats and corn. In some areas they were successful. However, large areas were much too arid for any consistent crops.

After trying to eke out a living for a few years, many abandoned their land and let it go back to grass. On our ranch in Colorado I know of at least ten abandoned homesteads. There may have been more since some of them were abandoned seventy to eighty years ago and all signs of human inhabitation have disappeared. None of those people planted tame grass. After a number of years, the native grass returned.

This is pretty good land but the rainfall is unpredictable so growing grain can be quite hazardous. These days the area has some very big grain farms. The difference between the old days and today is the farming methods. Agriculture has found out how to preserve moisture. Another difference is nobody is trying to make a living on half a section of land. The grain varieties have also improved. In spite of this, I still prefer the grass to farming. When a dry year comes along your grain crop is wiped out unless you get rain before the first of June or by the first of July further north. The native grass will grow any time of the year as long as it rains, even late in the growing season. Grass never dies from drought. This is very evident in Australia, where they will have three to five years with virtually no rain. Then, when the rains finally come, the grass grows stirrup high.

In ancient Biblical times, stockmen with their flocks or herds moved to wherever the best grass was located. This nomadic fashion of grazing is still going on today in parts of Asia and Africa. In a country like Mongolia, this is a way of life, as it is with Bedouin people in the Middle East.

Grass played a huge role in the settlement of the west in both Canada and the United States. Large ranches sprang up in Mexico, also in Texas and about sixteen other western states and three provinces in Canada. All were based strictly on grass. Those ranchers frowned or opposed the homesteaders who broke the ground for farming. This ranching activity spawned the working cowboy. The rodeo cowboy developed from the working cowboy. In other words, rodeo as we know it today, was a direct result of grass and not the farming activities that had gone on in the east for several hundred years.

Grass plays an important role in many sports, including lawn bowling, golf, soccer, football, baseball, polo, some horse racing and a number of other sports. In sport, grass is usually referred to as turf.

Grass is used in many manufactured projects such as baskets, mats, hats, grass skirts, ropes and several other items. A large

Edna Peters (my future wife) modeling grass skirts from Hawaii.

percentage of the world's population lives in grass huts. Sometimes the walls may be made from other materials like wood or stone, but the roof is always made of thatched grass.

The early homesteaders built sod houses (soddies). They cut square pieces of grass with dirt attached to the root system (sod). Those little abodes were quite warm, especially if they were built into a hillside.

In our daily language we use the word grass quite often. Some examples are: the grass is always greener on the other side of the fence; that kid is as green as grass; he (or she) does not let the grass grow under his (or her) feet; I am moving to where the grass is greener. When a loved one dies, we often say: They have gone where the grass is always lush and green.

I probably have not told you anything about grass that you did not already know. Sometimes it is good to reflect on how certain things we take for granted impact our lives. This would be a mighty dull world without grass. Think about that the next time you play with your kids on a lawn or at a park. Also when you enjoy a prime rib roast, which is grass converted to meat.

Bread is often called, the staff of life. Since wheat is part of the grass family, I think we should change that saying to: Grass is the staff of life.

CHAPTER SEVENTEEN

CATTLE

When I started to write this book, I decided not to write about cattle. I was like an actor looking for a new role rather than the character he portrayed in previous films. They are out to prove to the world that they are capable of playing a wide variety of roles other than the one they are noted for.

I have been deeply involved with cattle all my life. In spite of this, I have pursued other interests such as history, geography and philosophy. I consider myself a people person. Yet somehow the subject of cattle never left my mind. With that, I decided to write one chapter about cattle.

Cattle have played a huge role in the lives of people worldwide. The Bible mentions cattle a number of times. In Psalms, we read that God owns the cattle on a thousand hills. (Sounds like Alberta, Montana or Argentina.) There were many cattle and livestock. Men of note, such as Abraham, Lot, Laban, Jacob and others. Their livestock also included sheep, goats, donkeys and camels. They used them for food (meat and milk), clothes, blankets, tents and shoes.

One important function these animals provided, especially oxen, was for blood sacrifices in the temple. This was a forerunner of the supreme sacrifice that Jesus made on the cross. The Jewish people held to the belief that without the shedding of blood, there is no forgiveness of sins. Christians today believe the same thing, only it is by the blood of Jesus not that of an animal.

The various species of bovines include buffalo, bison, yak, gaur, benteng, zebu and all the domestic breeds which are present in every country and region of the world except the Arctic and Antarctic. There are almost one hundred different breeds of cattle. In North America, we have around fifty breeds. About thirty are well known and only fifteen have large numbers.

Worldwide, there are approximately one billion, four hundred million cattle. This old planet has over six billion people. That averages out at 3.7 people for every head of cattle. In Canada, there are 2.1 people for every head of cattle. In the United States, it is 2.6 people per animal. Australia is the lowest, at 1.2 people per head of cattle. Japan has the highest number of people per head of cattle at 24.8.

A large number of the world's cattle population are dairy cattle. The amount of milk, cheese, butter and other dairy products they produce staggers the imagination. How about the hides? If all the hides from those one billion, four hundred million cattle were laid side-by-side, they would circle the globe nearly three-and-one-half times. That represents a lot of leather. It always surprises me how expensive leather goods are. Only in luxury cars do you get leather seats. About eighty percent of our footwear is made from leather.

What would dining be without prime rib, t-bone steaks or even the lowly hamburger? Beef is premium food in our society. These days we have a number of vegetarians although percentage-wise they are only a tiny minority. But they sure make a lot of noise. In many countries a person's wealth is determined by the number of cattle they own. If you do not believe me, go to Texas and see for yourself. In Texas, the social elite are large ranchers. Owning a few oil wells also helps.

In India, cows are so sacred that the Hindus do not slaughter them. In China and in a number of third world countries, oxen are still used to pull farm machinery and wagons. In 1972, I saw a number of oxen pulling wagons in Italy.

Brahma cow with new baby on Friesen Ranch at Kit Carson, Colorado (1991). Photo courtesy Jeff Colvin

In a number of countries in Africa, cattle are used as a dowry to purchase a bride. I suppose those young men who own cattle have their pick of the most desirable girls for their wife. Those with goats probably get second cut wives.

In a chapter of this book called, 'The Mystique of the Cowboy', I mention the important role cattle played in the development of cowboy culture, both on the range and in the rodeo arena. The romance of the early west was steeped in the cattle industry. There were big and small ranches. They trailed big herds of cattle out of Texas to railheads in Kansas. Also many herds were trailed north to establish ranches in Colorado, Wyoming, Nebraska, the Dakotas, Montana and several other states. They came as far north as southern British Columbia, Alberta and Saskatchewan.

Cattle were not only important to ranchers. They also played a huge role in the life of the sodbusters. Without Bossy, who supplied their families with milk, butter and meat, many homesteaders could not have survived. Oxen were also used to break up some of the prairie. The radical environmentalists blame cattle for destroying vegetation and polluting streams. Now many scientists say that a moderate

A few of our Willow Creek cattle (ELF) on the ranch just east of Colorado Springs, Colorado. Photo courtesy of Steve Ptolemy.

amount of cattle is good for the grass they forage on. Their sharp hooves act like a stimulant to the soil. They do not recommend over-grazing. As for polluting water courses, it too is grossly exaggerated, although some water sources should be fenced with only a few designated watering areas. Manure is biodegradable. It comes from the grass and it goes back on the soil as fertilizer for the grass. They often blame cow manure and cow belching for the depletion of the ozone layer. I am a doubter of that theory. Some scientists say that the so-called hole has come and gone for centuries. Maybe it was because the number of buffalo and other animals inhabiting the earth went in cycles.

There is a special friendship that exists between cattle people. It goes deeper than just owning cattle. It is a certain unwritten code that binds us together regardless of religious beliefs. I have had good visits with hundreds of cattlemen in the United States and Canada – many of whom I had never met before. Two of our sons, Leland and Graham, are cattle buyers. In 2000, Leland purchased two hundred and ninety-five thousand head for Cargill Foods. Graham buys feeder cattle. I have been in the cattle business all my life and have enjoyed every bit of it. I have written a regular column on the cattle industry for twenty-seven years.

Chapter Eighteen

HORSES

There is no other animal on the face of this earth that has given mankind the kind of pleasure that horses have. From ancient times to the present, horses have played a huge role in people's lives. It is such a vast subject that to cover it properly would take a thousand volumes. Thousands of books have been written about horses, so why do I bother to put in my two cents worth? I hope to give you a condensed version of the importance of horses. When a person has a lot of wisdom, people say that person has a lot of horse sense.

Up until the First World War, horses were the main vehicles for armies. They still used some horses in the First World War.

In the 13th Century, Genghis Khan conquered much of Asia on horses. Alexander the Great conquered half the known world on horses. Other wars and battles that involved horses were as follows: Napoleonic Wars in Europe and Asia, the Boer War in South Africa, the Revolutionary War in the United States, the Civil War in the United States and the American-Mexican war. All the Spanish conquistadors used horses in the subjugation of the Indian tribes in South America, Central America and Mexico. The British and French also fought several wars. The United States Cavalry used horses almost exclusively to do battle with the Natives. The Indians were no slouches when it came to the use of horses in war. They rode them bareback and sometimes they rode them with a blanket on the backs of their horses.

English knights were all well mounted, they had to have sturdy horses to carry all that armour.

Some of the best horsemen in the business were the Cossacks in Russia. Another group of excellent horsemen were the Mongolians (they are to this day). There were countless other wars and battles over the centuries that were fought on horses.

We often read of the millions of soldiers that died in all those wars. The number of horses that died in those conflicts also numbered in the millions. The difference between men and horses in battle is simply this: when a man is wounded in battle, his comrades often drag him to safety for some medical treatment. When a horse was wounded, the owner often shot him to put him out of his misery.

It is interesting to note in the battle at Little Bighorn in Montana the Indians wiped out every one of Custer's men, and all the horses except for one, which lived to a ripe old age.

One horse that also survived a lot of action in a war, was Winchester. He was owned and ridden by General Philip Sheridan during the United States Civil War. He survived forty-seven battles. After the war, the General retired him and he lived for another fourteen years.

Now let's look at some of the more pleasant stories about horses, other than in the military. There are a huge variety of horses. They come in all sizes from miniature to big draft horses and all sizes in between. They also come in many different colors. As for breeds, there are dozens, maybe even hundreds of them. Each breed has unique characteristics.

A hundred or more years ago, when the western United States and Canada were opened up to homesteaders, horses were the key to success or failure in the operation of a farm or ranch. Millions of acres were ploughed up to plant crops. The land was broke up with horses – at least eighty percent of it was – the other twenty percent was broke up with oxen. The early west was totally dominated by horses, ranchers, farmers, cowhands, outlaws, lawmen and eastern dudes. All had to have a good horse to ride or drive. Horses were essential to those folks for their survival in that hostile environment.

Stagecoach horses had to have a lot of stamina. Those coach roads went over a lot of very rough terrain. Sometimes they had to outrun bandits that were trying to rob them. The pony express riders also had to have tough horses. And then there were the buffalo hunters. In this event, the buffalo, the horse and the rider were all at great risk. The buffalo usually lost out.

The role of saddle horses and horses pulling a buckboard was to provide fast transportation from point A to point B. If a man was riding alone and got bucked off or his horse stolen, his life was at risk. A man on foot in that vast open wilderness could easily die from thirst or from exposure to either heat or cold, depending on the time of year. That was the reason stealing horses was considered a crime equal to or worse than murder. Many is the man in the Old West who was hung from the nearest tree for stealing a horse or horses. Justice was swift. A horse thief's trial would only last three to five minutes. Then he would be ushered into the presence of his maker, dangling from a rope.

In the old days, and even the present time, ranches - both big and small - use horses for gathering, sorting or moving cattle from one pasture to another. They are also used for treating sick cattle and branding calves. These cow ponies can 'turn on a dime and give you some change'. It is a pleasure to ride them or watch someone else ride them. They can outsmart the most ornery old cow in the herd. Over the years, many a dude or would-be cowboy went sailing into space when his horse made a sharp turn. On the big ranches, the saddle horse herd was called a remuda. Early in the morning, several cowboys would bring them to the corrals. They call this 'jingling the horses'. The word wrangler was also used. This could apply to rounding up either horses or cattle. Once corraled, one cowboy (they took turns) would rope each individual horse and turn it over to whoever was to ride that horse that day. Once they were all mounted, they scattered all over the ranch to the area where the foreman had asked them to go.

Good horses are incredibly tough. They can be ridden at a fast pace all day. They may be tired but they will still give their best.

In various Indian tribes, horse stealing was considered okay. Their theory was that 'if we steal horses from one tribe, other tribes may steal from us'. One advantage the Indian folks had was there usually were a number of people in an encampment. There is safety in numbers. Very seldom did all the horses get stolen. This allowed a few brave young warriors to sneak into an enemy camp and steal some horses. Often those horses had belonged to them in the past. Sometimes they could sneak up on foot and steal a few horses. Horse ownership was like musical chairs. In a lifetime you might own the same horse three or four times. After branding became popular, it was not uncommon to see a horse with four or five different brands.

In the early west, in both Canada and the United States, there often were huge open areas where few domesticated animals, such as horses, cattle and sheep lived. Much of that unoccupied land was in semi-wilderness areas in the high foothills and mountains.

As the horse population on farms and ranches increased, a number of domesticated horses left their home ranges and escaped to this wilderness. As the years went by, large numbers of these horses became the wild horses often referred to as 'feral horses'. In Texas, they called them mustangs.

The image which most people have about wild horses is from pictures they have seen of a magnificent wild stallion, with its nostrils flaring, and mane and tail blowing in the wind. The stallion is usually standing on a high point of land surveying the countryside for potential enemies such as wolves or men on horseback. He is also standing guard watching out for other stallions that might want to steal some of his mares. In his band of mares (a harem), there is one head mare who helps keep the rest of the mares in a tight group as the young mares may take the notion to escape with a young stallion hanging around in their vicinity.

For a number of years, some cowboys have become proficient in capturing these wild horses. These horses have become wiley

This wild stallion leaped to its death rather than be captured by a cowboy who tried to rope him. My brother Nick claimed it was a true story. This painting depicts that event. By artist Nick Friesen.

and are difficult to corral. Once in a stout enclosure, they mill around looking for a weak spot in the corral through which they can make their escape.

At this point, the cowboys survey their catch. The quality of those horses is quite poor. Some have swaybacks; some have crooked legs, untrimmed hooves, a tangled mess of manes and tails; some are runty, and some have bad heads. There usually are few good specimens of what a horse should look like. The inferior quality of these horses is due to a lot in inbreeding. The bulk of them end up being slaughtered and the meat is shipped to Europe.

There are a few good wild horses, but the ones I have seen do not fall into that category.

For the past number of years, the governments in both the United States and Canada have encouraged people to buy these horses cheap. The government actually owns these horses since they graze on federal land, BLM and forest reserve in the United States. People who buy the wild horses are on a rescue mission. They want to prevent the slaughter of these horses.

There are wild horses in a number of states including Colorado, Idaho, Montana, New Mexico, Nevada and Wyoming. In Canada, the horses are found in Eastern British Columbia and Western Alberta. The British Government leases from the Alberta Government a large piece of land north of Medicine Hat at Suffield. Here, they train British Army soldiers. This is called the British Block. (Some of those British Military men have purchased some of the books I have written.)

This area became completely overrun with wild horses, to the detriment of other wild game. A few years ago, a large number of these horses were rounded up and sold to various people including rodeo stock contractors. However, the number of wild horses that became good bucking horses was relatively small. Just because they are wild does not mean they will make good bucking horses, but a few do.

I talked to Rex Logan, who is from Sundre, Alberta, about this article and he confirmed that what I wrote is fairly accurate. He has spent a lifetime capturing wild horses. Art Klassen and Bruce Sunstrom operate the Big Stone Rodeo Company. Just like Rex Logan, Art agreed with what I wrote. They bought a number of British Block horses and only a few turned out good although one was rank enough to go to the National Finals Rodeo.

Stewart Napper heading for the finish line with the Friesen Cattle Co. chuckwagon in the 1980 Calgary Stampede. Photo courtesy of Roger Dueck.

Horse racing is often referred to as the Sport of Kings. Over the centuries millions of people have derived much pleasure and, in some cases, big losses in the racing business. There are a variety of races, such as thoroughbred racing, quarter horse racing, sulky races, chariot races, relay races and in some rodeos, chuckwagon racing. Huge sums of money are wagered on these races (not chuckwagons). Few people, if any, get rich betting on horse races. It can become an addiction. Some race horse owners have done well, if the calibre of their horses is good enough to get into the big stake races. Most of those race horse owners are rich to begin with and more or less own race horses for social prestige and the challenge of coming up with a winner.

Then there is rodeo, the great western sport. Every single event, except bull riding, involves horses. There is saddle bronc riding, bareback riding, there are roping horses, steer wrestling horses, ladies barrel racing horses, pickup horses, wild horse race horses, wild cow milking, which requires a horse, team roping, steer roping (in seven states only), team penning horses, cutting horses, and trick riding horses. These horses are well trained. In fact, in every event it is the horse that helps the contestant win. No matter how good a horseman is, if the horse does not perform well, no money. Bucking horses are not really trained, but they are encouraged to buck by the flank strap and spurring action. An experienced bucking horse knows what is expected of him and he usually delivers. Incidentally, the spurs they use are quite dull so they do not injure the horse.

There are also horse pulls, gymkhanas, jumping horses, and polo (playing ball on horseback). In Great Britain, they love fox hunting on horseback, which is an endangered sport these days. They also have steeplechase contests on horseback. Not only is thoroughbred racing for the rich, you also have to be pretty wealthy to participate in polo, jumping horses and cutting horses. The other horse events are more for the masses of the people. Whether rich, poor or in-between, there is some sport involving horses that everyone can participate in, including trail riding or just plain pleasure riding.

I grew up with horses. My four older brothers, especially two of them, were horse nuts. They talked horses every day of their life. They

Above. Art and Albert Galarneau gathering horses on the Finnigan Ranch. Photo courtesy of Pete Jahnke.

At right: Some of the Friesen family horses on the home place at Beaver Flat, Saskatchewan.

knew all of the bloodlines for generations back. In their eyes, every horse they owned was a winner, even if he was not. Something like a mother feels about her children.

The horse business is alive and well despite all the mechanization and modern means of transportation. There are more horses in the world today than there were one hundred years ago. Many women love horses. A survey done by the American Veterinary Association a few years ago indicated that women own approximately seventy percent of all pleasure horses in the United States.

I have concrete evidence of how much some women like horses.

Recently, a young woman heard that we might have a two-year-old Quarterhorse filly for sale. When the woman dropped in at our place, I took her to the corral to show her the horse. The filly was halter-broke but still a little nervous when approached. This young lady sweet-talked her for about fifteen minutes. Lo and behold, at that point, she was able to catch the filly. For about half an hour, she quietly chatted to the horse and led it around.

Montgomery Lee Petty, age fifteen, from Trinity, North Carolina gives her hose "Those Eyes Adore You" an affectionate kiss, after her horse won reserve championship in Western Pleasure at the 2000 All American Quarter Horse Congress. Photo courtesy of America's Horse, Holly Clanahan and Montgomery Lee Petty.

She let the horse nuzzle her face. It seemed like they were meant for each other. She was totally in love with the horse.

After a while we retired to the house where I showed her the registration papers for the horse. I was almost one hundred percent sure that I was going to sell the horse. After discussing the filly's pedigree for a few minutes she said how much she liked the horse.

Suddenly she said to me, "I would like to buy the horse but I have a few problems." "Oh," I said, "what are they?" "Well," she said, "I have no money. Secondly, I have no place to keep her and thirdly, my husband doesn't like horses." Then almost as an afterthought, she said, "I have no way to haul her." I told her I could haul the filly for her, but the other three problems I could not solve. She said she would still like to buy the filly sometime in the future. She offered to come and work with her once in a while. She told me she would teach the filly to lunge. I said that was okay, but I did not want her to ride the filly unless she bought her.

That's where it stands now. By the time this book is published, she may own her, or maybe not. Only time will tell. This is rather a long-winded incident. I just wanted to back up the fact as to how much some women love horses. Although the odds are completely stacked against this woman, she still hopes to own that filly.

Yes, many women love horses. England's Prince Philip once said of his daughter, Princess Ann, whose whole life seems to center around horses: "If it doesn't fart and eat hay, she isn't interested." Rather crude language, but I am only quoting the Prince.

I never yet went wrong in sizing up a man by the kind of horse he rode. A good horse always packs a good man." Will James.

You can't say I lack courage when I have the nerve to publish a poem which I composed about an incident that actually happened on our ranch. This is my first attempt at western poetry and it will probably be my last.

We was fixing to gather cattle
For this job our horses we did saddle
The horses were only green broke
So which one of us would get bucked off was a standing joke.
A city gal was visiting the ranch
She was a teller at a major bank branch.
I asked her if she could ride
"Of course I can," all joking aside.

We saddled her a real well broke cow pony
He had a lot of cow sense and that was no baloney.

We gathered two hundred head out of the brush
I told the crew, "Take your time, there is no rush."

Things went well with the cattle all strung out.
When suddenly a steer took off, he was wild without a doubt.
Old Cheyenne took after him with the city girl on board.
I am sure she was breathing a prayer, "Please stop him, Lord!"

Cheyenne was quick as a cat
In trying to turn the critter back.
As the steer ducked, so did he,
He cut no slack.

The girl flew through the air and landed on her back.
We rushed over to her, thinking she was hurt.
To our surprise all that happened to her was
That she was covered with manure and dirt.

All the hands began to laugh; they thought
it was a great joke.
She started to cry because of all the fun we did at her poke.
We suddenly remembered our good old western ways.
So we sobered up and gave her a little praise.

We said it can happen to the best hand on the range
When Old Cheyenne turns on a dime and gives you some change.

True story by Leonard Friesen

In Europe and Asia, horse meat is consumed in large amounts. I personally could not and never will knowingly eat horse meat. I am glad that we in North America do not eat horse meat. Maybe a few people do, but I never hear them boast about it. A number of horses are slaughtered in North America and the meat is shipped to Europe, usually by airplane.

This world would seem mighty empty if there were no equestrian events. My hat is off to all the great horses and horsemen that have inhabited our planet for the past five thousand years. I think we should erect a monument for all the horses that have died in battle. The site could be alongside some war memorial honouring the soldiers who gave their lives.

A pause that refreshes. Herman Cornelson and grandson Todd at Swift Current Creek.
Photo courtesy of Herman Cornelson.

CHAPTER NINETEEN

MAN'S BEST FRIEND

Dog lovers often tell stories about their dogs or other people's dogs. A number of lives have been saved by wise and loyal dogs. There are several hundred different breeds of dogs. Each breed has its own area of expertise, just like people. They are used as watchdogs, police dogs for sniffing out drugs, hunting dogs, sleigh dogs, seeing-eye dogs, cattle and sheep dogs. Some are just plain pets with not too many virtues or skills, again, just like some people. Pets generate billions of dollars of business in pet food and supplies. Across North America there are hundreds of pet cemeteries. Some graves even have flowers on them. I have never noticed a dog pay much attention to flowers except to use them instead of a fire hydrant. A big, old beef bone on the grave would be more appropriate.

By now, I have all the dog owners angry with me. Calm down, I like dogs. They are more loyal than a best friend, but they are still only animals.

The downside to dog ownership is the folks who own huge dogs in the city. Some of these dogs have the disposition of a wounded water buffalo; one often reads of certain breeds of dogs attacking people, often children, sometimes killing them.

It is interesting to watch people walking their mutt. They stop at strategic places, usually a neighbor's shrub or fence where a dog lifts his leg to do you-know-what. Meanwhile the dog owner is casually looking the other way, pretending they do not notice that their dog is watering the neighbor's shrub. Sometimes, he makes a larger deposit as well. This helps fertilize the plants.

I knew an old Scotsman who owned several well-trained sheep dogs. They were a pleasure to watch at work. Behind the scenes their treatment was quite cruel. For the least little misdemeanour, they got a swift kick in the ribs. The dog would yelp in pain. Then almost immediately, the dog would come over to the owner, wagging his tail and trying to lick his hands or even the foot that just booted him.

One of the most touching dog stories that I ever heard was told to me by a friend of mine. The incident took place in a little cow town in southwestern Saskatchewan.

On the edge of town lived a bachelor in a little shack. He was a recluse and nobody knew much about him. He associated with no one. One cold winter day he passed away. Somehow, someone discovered he had died. (He was probably dead for several days.) They notified the Royal Canadian Mounted Police (RCMP) and, upon further investigation by the Mounties, they found no known relatives. They contacted a local minister to conduct a little graveside service. One problem that they had was there were no pallbearers. To solve this, the Mounties went to a local bar and recruited six men who had not yet indulged too much.

Away they went to the cemetery (the town had dug the grave). People present were two Mounties, six pallbearers and the minister. None of the people there really knew the gentleman they were laying to rest. The friend who told me this was one of those pallbearers.

He said there was one real mourner and that was the deceased's dog. The dog sat on the mound of dirt with a forlorn look, watching as they lowered his master into the grave. It was almost as though he had tears in his eyes. I hope the Mounties found a good home for that dog.

Why do some women say dogs are better than men?

1. A dog is much easier to train.
2. A dog misses you when you are gone.
3. A dog is not afraid to show affection in public.
4. A dog knows NO means NO.

Some men prefer dogs to women for the following reasons:

1. A dog's parents never come to visit you.
2. A dog does not care if your clothes are on the floor.
3. A dog does not care if you forget his birthday.

4. A dog is a lot happier to see you come home no matter how late it is.

Yes, dogs are loyal. The domesticated wolf has come a long way in the past five thousand years.

Author's sisters, Margaret and Susie Friesen, with family pet dog. (Before I was born.)

CHAPTER TWENTY

THE MYSTIQUE OF THE COWBOY

The West has always been known for its friendliness and hospitality. Picture by Susan Robertson. Courtesy of Ed and Pat Silbernagel.

One of the mysteries in life is why cowboys and cowboy culture holds such a fascination for millions of people. Hollywood has capitalized on this fascination by grinding out hundreds of western movies, some good, some not too bad, others come across as phoney as a three-dollar bill.

The cowboy tradition actually started in Spain. All over Europe and Asia, including the Middle East, people rode horses. Whole armies rode horses. Somehow the riding of a horse to gather or work cattle was something the Spaniards were proud of. The riders wore large sombreros to protect their head and eyes from the hot sun. It was the Spanish who introduced horses, along with cattle (from which the Texas Longhorns descended) to the New World (the Americas). Ever since, horses and cattle have been synonymous. You need horses to work cattle. It is interesting the word cowboy evolved rather than, say, horseboy. Cowboy has become a household word. The Mexican cowboys are called vaqueros and in Argentina they are called gauchos. Mexico, Texas, California, New Mexico, Arizona and southern Colorado were all part of Spanish land claims in the New World. When those territories, with the exception of Mexico, became part of the United States, the cowboy culture had already been firmly established, especially in Texas. A number of words pertaining to cowboy equipment and activities came from the Spanish language such as: rodeo, remuda, conchas, chaps (from the Spanish word chapperreras, and lariat from the Spanish word lareata, which means rope).

Over the years, the equipment that cowboys use has changed a lot. That includes hats, saddles and cowboy boots. The spurs in the old days had big sharp rowels. The ropes too are totally different from the ropes they used one hundred years ago.

In my lifetime, I have witnessed a dramatic change in cowboy gear and clothes. In spite of this change, the basic image of the cowboy has not changed much. They are perceived as macho, tough daredevils who can stand a lot of hard knocks without complaint. They also respect women and each other. In the old west, women were relatively safe from men molesting or raping them, even the outlaws did not hurt women often. If they did, their life was in great jeopardy, even from their other outlaw friends.

Today, we have ranch cowboys, feedlot cowboys, rodeo cowboys, dude ranch and trail ride cowboys. The cowboy culture blossomed west of the Mississippi from southern Texas clear into Canada. They worked for little pay – even today they are not high on the pay scale. They do it because they love the lifestyle. In the past they sometimes were called waddies, cowhands, cowpokes, line riders and in eastern Oregon, northwestern Nevada and southern Idaho, they are called buckaroos. Those buckaroos wear high crown hats and usually lace-up cowboy boots.

People are inspired to become cowboys because of the freedom there is in riding and living in the great outdoors.

In the last several years there has been a renewed interest in the cowboy way of life. One reason is that Hollywood has glamorized the lifestyle.

A few years ago a movie called *City Slickers* came out. It portrayed moving a herd of cattle from southern New Mexico to Colorado. In that group of riders there were several jaded businessmen from New York City. The lead characters were Billy Crystal and Jack Palance. The movie had a wide distribution, including overseas. The result was many city people and others suddenly had a great longing to be involved in taking part in a cattle drive.

I was told that dude ranches in Wyoming were completely booked every summer by would-be cowboys, a large number of them from Germany. I am sure this is also true for places like Colorado, Montana, British Columbia, Alberta and even southern Saskatchewan, plus any other states where there are dude ranches.

The book *Lonesome Dove,* which was later made into a movie and then a TV series, also had an impact on people who like the western way of life. The book is about a cattle drive from Texas to Montana. Then there was the Australian movie, *The Man from Snowy River.* This movie involved a major horse roundup in some of the mountainous country in Australia.

When I was young, I read western books written by Will James and Zane Grey as well as several other authors. In those books they often told about young men coming west, hoping to become cowboys. A number of them succeeded although many went back east after a short stint of trying to be a cowboy. In order to succeed, they had to take a lot of ribbing from the real cowboys. They also had to have a tremendous desire to master the art of riding a bronc, including many buck-offs. They had to learn how to rope and to tough out long days in the saddle.

Like I said, many made the grade. Some famous eastern greenhorns that history records making the grade include Charlie Russell, who became a horse wrangler and cowboy in Montana. Later, he became the best western artist ever, at least in my opinion. When you look at his paintings it is as if you were experiencing the action.

Then there was Teddy Roosevelt from New York City, who cowboyed for a few years in South and North Dakota. He later became president of the United States.

Guy Weadick was born in New York State. As a young man he moved to Wyoming, where he became a cowboy. In 1912, he came to Calgary, Alberta where he promoted and started the first Stampede. It was a success. Then, in 1919 he produced another Stampede and again in 1923. It has been held every year since. Some seventy-five years later it is called, The Greatest Outdoor Show on Earth. Cheyenne, Wyoming may dispute that claim. They call their rodeo, Frontier Days, the Daddy of Them All. However Calgary draws more people, over a million each year. There is more money up for the cowboys, including fifty thousand dollars in seven events for first place. Not bad for a show that had its origins from a boy growing up in New York hoping to be a cowboy some day, which he did in grand style.

There are thousands more who came west from the eastern United States and eastern Canada as well as from Europe who became cowboys and cattlemen of note.

I have attended the Calgary Stampede every year for the past fifty years, except for two years when we were in the United States. For ten years I was quite involved in that organization. I am still a shareholder.

I have also attended the Cheyenne Frontier Days several different years. In my opinion, it is the most western event in North America. The action is wild and woolly. Although on average the bucking broncs are not as rank as they are at Calgary or any number of the rodeos in Canada, including Innisfail, Alberta.

The desire to become a cowboy is not new. It has been going on for over one hundred years. In 1998, the mayor of the City of Calgary declared that the city would honor its heritage by making 1998, The Year of the Cowboy. The local media cooperated and told various stories about Alberta concerning cowboys and ranching. The strange thing was the rank-and-file Calgarians did not really join in. They do Stampede Week. I have worn cowboy boots and a hat all my life. Those of you who know me know that I grew up kind of a cowboy and I have spent a lifetime in the cattle business. The reason I say Calgary seemed to be lukewarm to the ideas was that whenever my wife and I go to a restaurant or mall, I often am the only person out of hundreds wearing a hat and cowboy boots. Maybe some folks have an interest in cowboy culture. It is just they do not want to look like a dude in a hat. After all, a hat and boots do not make a real cowboy (maybe a drugstore cowboy).

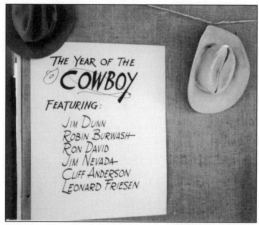

Board at Nose Creek Valley Museum (1998). The first five names are real rodeo cowboys. I was asked to join this elite group because of my lifetime of involvement with the cattle industry and writing about our western heritage.
Photo courtesy Mary Hickely.

The cowboy mystique has its roots in history. Hollywood has also helped to keep it alive, featuring people like Roy Rogers, Gene Autry, John Wayne, Slim Pickens and others. The freedom of the open range also intrigues people. Then there is modern day rodeo. Rodeo is a dangerous sport with relatively small financial rewards. Just like ranch cowboys, rodeo cowboys do it because they love it, even though it involves thousands of miles of travel each year. Not as relaxing as the confines of a big ranch.

Women like brave, daring men. At least fifty percent of rodeo fans are women. A number of them compete in ladies barrel racing.

Rodeo evolved from working cowboys. They had great pride in their riding and roping ability. A town in Texas (I forget the name) says that the first rodeo, or bucking contest as it was called, was held

Above: Trent Friesen at college rodeo in Claresholm, Alberta, 1989 on a Hugh Wilson horse called Jet.
        Photo courtesy Graham Friesen.

At right: Don Perrin on Kid Weir at the Calgary Stampede in the early 'Thirties.
        Sketch by Nick Friesen.

at that location. Colorado claims to have held the first rodeo, or so a sign along Interstate 70, at Deer Trail, proclaims. Wherever it was, the sport of rodeo grew slowly. It was sort of mixed in with what they called wild west shows. These were staged performances put on by folks like Buffalo Bill Cody and others. In the past fifty years rodeos have really taken off. Today there are thousands of rodeos, including Little Britches, High School, College, Old-Timers, Indian, Amateur and, of course, professional events. Most of them are in the western United States and Canada but more and more rodeos are held east of the Mississippi River in places like New Jersey, Florida and several other eastern states.

Of the ten or twelve events in rodeo, only about half relate to actual ranch work. They are saddle bronc riding, calf roping, team roping, team penning, cutting horse contests and steer roping, which is only allowed in seven states, and not in Canada. There is no other rodeo or equestrian event where as many dudes race around on horseback thinking they are cowboys or cowgirls than in team cattle penning. Now that every team penner is angry at me, I will modify the above statement. Approximately half of the penners are legitimate cowboys. The others may also attain real cowboy status some day, providing they do a number of other jobs on a farm or ranch over a period of several years that requires a person to be on horseback.

The other rodeo events are inventions to entertain people. They are bareback bronc riding, bull riding and even steer wrestling, which is often referred to as bull dogging and was not practised on the open range.

Like in any sport, rodeo has its followers of young women looking for a date with one of those brave heroes of the rodeo arena. The girls especially like bull riders. Those girls are called buckle bunnies.

I do not know if I solved the mystique of the cowboy but it appears their image is safe as we enter the 21st Century. People are searching for reality and I guess the cowboy fits that image. They are viewed as independent free spirits, be it ranch or rodeo, old days or modern era. These men and women are the true champions and pioneers of the west.

Pendelton Roundup, 1993.
Courtesy Duane Daines

Ty Murray on Internet at the Daines Ranch Rodeo, 1999.
Photo by Mike Copeman. Courtesy Jack Daines

Glen O'Neil spurring out a good bronc ride at Camrose, Alberta on a horse called Red Sky, owned by Bruce and Illoe Flewelling.

Photo courtesy Bruce Flewelling

Cheryl Daines running the barrels on her horse, Coyote, at Kelowna, British Columbia's Black Mountain Rodeo, 1995.

Courtesy Duane and Cheryl Daines

122

CHAPTER TWENTY-ONE

THE COYOTE

Coyotes are native to North America. They are present from Alaska to Central America. According to my research, they are not found in South America. (I always thought they were.) The coyote is part of the dog family. Their cousins are wolves and jackals. Those two are native in many countries. Coyotes are quite a bit smaller than wolves. The average adult coyote only weighs about thirty pounds, although the coyotes in Alaska, Canada and the Northern States are at least ten pounds heavier than those in the southern United States and Mexico.

They are survivors. Over the centuries, they have been ruthlessly hunted with guns, hounds, traps and even poison. In spite of this attempt of virtual extermination by man, they are more plentiful today than ever. A coyote is sneaky and wily.

Every place I have ever lived had coyotes. This includes Saskatchewan, Alberta, Colorado and Arizona. Many is the night I have listened to their yapping, barking and melancholy howl. I rather like it. I have read stories about how frightened many young wives of homesteaders were when their husband was away and the coyotes started to howl. They often equate them with wolves. Of course, in those days there were also wolves on the plains. The coyote yodel reminds me of another era, before civilization crowded out a number of animals including wolves. It drove them to the mountains and protected wilderness areas.

The coyote makes itself at home anywhere. I have read about how in the Hollywood Hills, coyotes have become a pest. People there live in multi-million dollar houses. Coyotes can run up to speeds of forty miles per hour when chasing fleet -footed prey like rabbits. They also hunt in relays. They chase the game in a big circle then another coyote takes up the chase. They are carnivores. Their food consists of rabbits, mice, birds, bird eggs or any other small rodent. I think they are a little wary of weasels. A weasel is the most vicious fighter, pound for pound, of any animal with the exception of the little shrew.

Coyotes also eat some berries including the prickly pear cactus fruit in Arizona or wherever cactus grow.

Like wolves, coyotes mate for life. I am not sure whether a coyote widow or widower finds a new mate. I know they do not divorce like we humans do. The pups are born in an underground den. They have anywhere from two to six pups in a litter. The parents teach them all about hunting for the first eight months. After that, they are on their own, although they remain a member of the pack, at least until they fall in love with a member of the opposite sex. At that point, they may leave home and join another pack.

When I was growing up in southwestern Saskatchewan, hunting and trapping coyotes was routinely done. Some people supplemented their income in the dirty 'Thirties and early 'Forties by trapping coyotes, skunks and weasels.

My dad hunted coyotes with a gun. I never really had a heart for it. I think I took a few shots at a coyote, but never even came close to hitting one.

One of our neighbors had a regular trap time line in the late fall and early winter when the coyote's fur was in prime condition. What he did was buy a few old horses, for little money. I think sometimes he got them for nothing. He would shoot a horse then cut the carcass into four quarters. He placed those pieces of meat about half a mile from each other. Then he set the traps close to the meat. He had to be careful how he handled those traps. They were buried shallow. They also could not contain the scent of a human. A coyote, like a dog, has a keen sense of smell. I think he used special gloves dipped in a little blood or whatever, to take away his scent. Even with all those precautions, it sometimes took days for a coyote to venture close enough to that meat to get caught in a trap. (There were several traps at each site.) Eventually, hunger got the best of the coyote and he approached the meat for a good meal. Instead, bingo, he was caught in the trap.

I saw a number of those trapped coyotes when I was riding to check our cattle. It really turned me off on trapping. Every once in awhile a coyote would actually chew off the leg caught in the trap and make his escape. I saw several three-legged coyotes the following summers.

I have a love/hate relationship with coyotes. I like to hear them howl at night. I also like the fact that they eat mice and gophers. What I do not like is when they kill all the rabbits, or even an odd fawn. I have not seen a rabbit around our place for years. (Maybe the Aussies should import a bunch of coyotes, they are overrun with rabbits.) Nor do I like it when they maim or kill domestic livestock such as chickens, sheep and baby calves.

Several years ago one of our cows was laying down trying to have a calf during the night. A coyote came along and ate a fair bit of the calf's head and neck, enough to kill the calf before it was born. When I found the cow in the morning, it turned me sick to my stomach to see this dead calf partly eaten and half of it still inside the cow. It was hip locked. I pulled the calf out. The cow was OK. Needless to say, after that little episode, my admiration for coyotes slipped a notch. We also lost a number of other newborn calves to coyotes. Some coyotes remind me of human urban criminals. The coyote has become

Two wily coyotes on our log-gate entrance.

so used to humans that it is getting bolder all the time. There are many stories about coyotes killing cats and small dogs. Sometimes, they come right onto porches and decks of houses to snatch cats and small dogs.

These days coyote pelts are worth very little so the sport (if you can call it that) of chasing them down with hounds has almost disappeared. I hope coyotes will always be with us in moderate numbers. They are part of nature.

We have a high log gate at our yard entrance. On top of this gate are two coyotes. They are cut out of sheet metal. We bought them in Arizona several years ago. To me, they are a symbol of the west. Phoenix even named their National Hockey League team the Coyotes. South Dakota is called the Coyote State.

CHAPTER TWENTY-TWO

DOCTORS

Medicine is a fascinating science. It touches every one of us. It has been around a long time. Ancient China practised medicine. So did many primitive cultures. The treatment usually consisted of plant and herbal extracts, although quite often healing was performed by a shaman or witch doctor. I think the herbs and plants were more effective.

Folks in Biblical times also practised medicine. In the New Testament, Luke was a physician. Jesus is sometimes called the Great Physician. He healed many people by just touching them. Later on, his disciples did the same, by praying for the sick in Jesus' name. Even today, thousands of people worldwide make the same claims. In spite of all the medicine and prayer people continue to die, although we have a much longer life span than they did a hundred years ago. The Bible says: *It is appointed unto man once to die, and after that judgment.*

Medicine in the old days was vastly different than today's highly specialized, computer operated clinics and hospitals.

One form of medicine that has survived for thousands of years is acupuncture. There are also thousands of chiropractors these days. I believe in both acupuncture and chiropractors, to some degree. However, I do not think they can heal every disease as some claim they can.

Back to the old days. My mother told me when she was a young girl they practised blood-letting when someone was sick. They would make a cut in a vein and drain a quart or two of blood from the patient. I am not sure if she said it ever cured any diseases, but maybe it has a psychological effect which made the person feel better.

In those days they also had a variety of poultices that they applied to wounds or boils. Some of the materials used were boiled flax or wheat, animal fat, even hot cow manure. Mustard plasters on the chest for severe colds or pneumonia were the standard treatment. My mother even did that for me (not the cow manure).

Today, it takes six to seven years to become a medical doctor. Ten years or more to become a specialist. After a doctor has practised a number of years, they often take courses to keep up with the latest medical advances. No wonder most of us hold doctors in high esteem. They have demanding, tough jobs. In spite of all the training, there is a big difference in the ability of doctors. They all have different personalities. Some just seem to go through the motions, not really too concerned about your health. They give you a quick check, prescribe some pills and off you go.

Some doctors do an excellent job. They get to the bottom of your problem. You feel they have a genuine interest in your well being. Most doctors are overworked. That is why patients (especially older people) just become a number to be shuffled through the system.

Remember the days when doctors made house calls? You have to be sixty years old or older to remember those days. When I was nine years old a doctor came to our house to remove my tonsils and adenoids on the dining room table. He arrived with a car. In the real old days they travelled with horse and buggy. In the winter (at least in high snowfall areas) they used horses and sleighs called cutters. They served the people well for the limited medical knowledge and technology available to them in those days.

I recently read a book by Dr. Cornish, who was a country doctor in the Claresholm district of southern Alberta. It was extremely interesting to read of the different situations he encountered when he left his office for a journey in the country. I cannot mention any of those stories since it is a copyright edition.

In the early west, many is the bullet that those country doctors dug out of some unfortunate soul who had stopped some lead in a gunfight. They were the lucky ones. Many died from those gunshot wounds, often referred to as lead poisoning.

There are a number of stories about doctors who risked their lives treating wounded soldiers in a war zone (the TV show MASH portrayed some of those situations).

Over the years, thousands of doctors have gone to mission fields where, for very little pay, they worked long hours to relieve the suffering of those poor folks.

Dr. David Livingstone was one of them. There are many other doctors who did the same thing but did not receive the publicity. My former doctor donates about six months a year of his time doing missionary doctor work in Indonesia. His name is Dr. Bill Bieber.

I read a book awhile ago about Dr. Viggo Olsen, who went to Bangladesh to practice medicine. Disease and sickness is rampant there. Also, once in awhile, horrendous typhoons hit, drowning and injuring thousands of people. Can you imagine the pressure on doctors and medical staff after a natural disaster like that?

Doctors, hospitals, nurses and other health professionals are not infallible. I read recently that annually in the United States more people die from medical mistakes than from traffic accidents. I found that hard to believe.

Several years ago I experienced something I will never forget. One day my heart was racing approximately double the normal beat. I was also light headed. We headed for the emergency room of a big hospital. They checked me over, then rushed me into the trauma room. They applied the electric shock treatment. When that two hundred volts of electricity hit me, I bounced about a foot off the stretcher. It felt like somebody had shot me in the chest with a double barrel shotgun.

What happened is the young anaesthetist thought I was out but I wasn't. They waited a few more minutes then applied three hundred volts, and then another two hundred volt jolt. At that point my heart decided to go back to its normal rhythm. This time I was out and did not feel it. In automobile and other accidents they often apply this treatment to bring the person back to life. Most of these people are unconscious when this shock is given. In an emergency like that minutes, even seconds, can mean the difference between life and death. The paramedics do a good job saving lives.

After I woke up, no less than three doctors came to my bed and apologized for what had just happened. One nurse told me I could sue the hospital. I would never do that. It was not done on purpose. I was glad to be alive.

A man said to me one day he knew an undertaker and a doctor who were in business together. I asked what the business was. He replied the undertaker buried the doctor's mistakes.

The amazing things these days are the successful organ transplants, as well as joint replacements. I have an artificial hip and knee. They both work perfectly. The pain in those joints has been completely relieved. The knee is especially good.

The more advanced and sophisticated medicine becomes, the more it stays the same in some areas. Take, for instance, heart problems, strokes and arthritis. Guess what the doctors main remedy is? Aspirin, which has been around for one hundred and seven years. Until twenty-five years ago it was mainly recommended for headaches and colds, taken with lots of water. But suddenly it has become the darling of the medical profession. I have first-hand experience. I have taken five fast trips to the medical emergency room. In each case, they gave me electric shock to bring my heart back to normal. The only medication they told me to take was an aspirin a day for the rest of my life.

When my wife had a mild stroke, they told her exactly the same thing. Aspirin is supposed to thin your blood.

I sometimes jokingly say that if I had a six-month crash course, I could be a GP or family practitioner. When you go to a doctor for a checkup, he (or she) takes your pulse, looks in your mouth and ears, listens to your heart with a stethoscope and takes blood samples. If there seems to be a serious problem you are referred to a specialist.

I sure hope my doctor does not read this. She may just cut me off. This is all tongue-in-cheek stuff. I would not want anyone with a six-month course to examine me.

Our medical system is not perfect, but I sure am glad we do not live in one of those so-called developing countries. In those nations doctors and medical facilities are almost nonexistent. My hat is off to all doctors and medical professionals even though they make mistakes because, like all of us, they're human.

How about dental doctors (dentists)? I think dentistry has made the largest strides of any medical profession in the past one hundred years. In the old days, their main occupation was pulling teeth, often with only a shot of whiskey as an anaesthetic. I know of people who pulled their own teeth with ordinary pliers. No freezing or painkillers whatsoever. A severe toothache can drive you to distraction. I know, I have had many of those gut-wrenching toothaches.

These days, dentists avoid pulling a tooth. I sometimes wonder if it is not a financial decision. Once a tooth is pulled, game over, no more dental work on that tooth.

Following are a few procedures that dentists perform: root canals, crowns, fillings, veneer, bridges, braces, partial plates and, as a last resort, pulling teeth, which results in a set of dentures (false teeth).

They also clean teeth, fluoride them, polish them, as well as bleach them. I have upper false teeth, which never bother me. I still have my own bottom teeth. Prices for the above procedures are astronomical, up to fifty thousand dollars in some cases.

CHAPTER TWENTY-THREE

WILLIAM SHAKESPEARE

William Shakespeare, 1564-1616, was born in Warwickshire, England. His life was checkered until 1592 when his name surfaced in London as a poet, actor and playwright. The first twenty-eight years of his life were not too shiny. It involved such things as poaching on other people's estates and excessive drinking. Those years are often referred to as the lost years.

After 1592 he became a prolific poet and playwright. He passed away at fifty-two years of age. From 1592 to 1616, during a twenty-four-year period, he wrote no less than forty-three plays and sonnets. The best known ones are: A Midsummer Night's Dream, Taming of the Shrew, Comedy of Errors, Richard III, Julius Caesar, Anthony and Cleopatra, Romeo and Juliet, MacBeth and Hamlet.

Of all the philosophers, poets, writers and playwrights in the past thousand years, none have enjoyed the worldwide acclaim that Shakespeare has. He is taught in schools, colleges and universities in numerous countries. Hundreds of movies and stage plays have used his material.

Was he a sinner or a saint? I think he was more of a sinner than a saint. He acknowledged the existence of God but very little, if any, of his writing referred to scripture from the Bible.

I do not profess to be an expert on Shakespeare, but I have in my possession every play and sonnet he ever wrote. For some people a little bit of Shakespeare goes a long way. So I am not going to quote too much of his writing in this book. His writing often contains substantial wisdom about life. It is written in old English grammar of four hundred years ago. This can make for tedious reading. Most of his plays are love stories.

Serve always with assured trust,
And in thy suit be humble true:
Unless thy lady proves unjust.

Press never thou to choose anew:
When times shall serve, be thou not slack
To proffer, though she put thee back.

-A Shakespeare Sonnet

My husband is on earth, my faith in heaven:
How shall that faith return again to
Earth, unless that husband send it me
From heaven, by leaving earth?

- Romeo and Juliet

Here's a knocking indeed! I a man were porter of hell's gate, he should have old turning the key. Knock, knock, knock. Who is there in the name of Beelzebub? Here's our farmer that hanged himself on the expectation of plenty. Come in time! Have napkins enow about you, here you'll sweat for it. Knock, knock, knock. Who is there i' in the other devil's name? Faith here's an equivocator that could swear in both the scales against either scale. Who committed treason enough for God's sake. Yet could not equivocate to heaven O come in equivocator. Knock, knock, knock, who is there for sealing out of a French hose. Come in tailor, here you may roast your goose. Knock, knock, knock. Never at quiet, what are you? But this place is too cold for hell. I'll devil-porter it no further: I had thought to have let in some of all professions, that go the Primrose way to the everlasting bonfire.

- MacBeth

The sun will set before I shall discharge what I must strive to do.

-The Tempest

Indeed the top of admiration; worth what's dearest to the world! Full many a time I have eyed with best regard! and many a time the harmony of their tongues hath into bondage brought my too diligent ear; For several virtues have I lik'd several women; Never any with so full soul, but some defect in her did quarrel with the noblest grace she owed, and put it to the foil; But you, O you, so perfect and so peerless, are created of every creature's best.

- The Tempest

The mistress which I serve quickens what's dead. And makes my labors pleasure; Oh, she is ten times more gentle than her father's crabbed;

- The Tempest

He that dies pays all debts.

- The Tempest

If you do love me you will find me out.

- The Merchant of Venice

Immortal gods, I crave no pelf.
I pray for no man, but myself.
Grant I may never prove so fond,
To trust a man on his oath or bond,
Or a harlot for her weeping,
Or a dog that seems asleeping,
Or a keeper with my freedom,
Or my friends, if I should need.

- Timon of Athens

There shall your master have a thousand loves,
A mother, and a mistress, and a friend.
A phoenix, captain, and an enemy.
A guide, a goddess and a sovereign.

A counsellor, a traitress, and a dear.
His humble ambition, proud humility
His jarring concord, and his discord dulcet,
His faith, his sweet disaster, with a world
Of pretty fond adoptious christendoms,
That blinking cupid gossips, now shall he –
I know not what he shall – God send him well.

- All's Well That Ends Well

(How many of you knew that All's Well That Ends Well was some of Shakespeare's writing?)

And out of all these to restore the king, He counsels a divorce, a loss of her, that like a jewel has hung twenty years about his neck, yet never lost her luster: Of her that loves him with that excellence that angels love good men with! Even of her that when the greatest stroke of fortune falls, will bless the king, and is not this course Pious?

- King Henry VIII

The unyok'd humor of your idleness! Yet herein will I imitate the sun, who doth permit the base contagious clouds, to smother up his beauty from the world, that, when he please again to be himself, Being wanted, he may be more wonder'd at, by breaking through the foul and ugly mists of vapors that did seem to strangle him. If all the years were playing holidays, to sport would be as tedious as to work.

- First Part of King Henry IV

For he will never follow anything that other men begin.

- Julius Caesar

A woman mov'd is like a fountain troubled – muddy ill-meaning, thick bereft of beauty.

- The Taming of the Shrew

Therefore thy earliness doth me assure thou art uprous'd by some distemperatures, or if not so, then here I hit it right. Our Romeo hath not been in bed tonight. That last is true: The sweeter rest was mine. God pardon sin! Wast thou with Rosaline?

-Romeo and Juliet

Bove the contentious: waves with his good arms in lusty stroke to shore, that o'er his wave worn basis bow'd, as stooping to relieve him: I not doubt he came alive to land.

-The Tempest

Visit the speechless sick, and still converse with groaning wretches; and your task shall be, with all the fierce endeavor of your wit to enforce the pained impotent smile. To move wild laughter in the throat of death: it is impossible: mirth cannot move a soul in agony. Why that's the way to choke a giving spirit.

Whose influence is begot of that loose grace, which sallow laughing hearers give fools! A jest's prosperity lies in the ear of him that makes it, then of sickly ears deaf'd with clamours of their own ear groans.

- Love's Labours Lost

Comforts in heaven, and we are on the earth.

- King Richard II

Come my sweet wife, my dearest mother, and my friends of noble touch: When I am forth. Bid me farewell, and smile I pray you come. While I remain above the ground, you shall hear from me still; and never of me aught, but what is like me formerly.

- Coriolanus

Pretty, witty, wild, and yet, too gentle there will we dine: this woman that I mean, my wife — but I protest, without desert — has often times upbraided me withal.

- Comedy of Errors

I pr'y thee daughter, do not make me mad! I will not trouble thee, my child: Farewell: We'll no more meet, no more see each other – But yet thou are my flesh, my blood, my daughter.

- King Lear

You are too indulgent, let us grant it is not amiss to tumble on the bid ptolemy; to give a kingdom for a mirth: to sit and keep the turn of tippling with a slave: to reel the streets at noon, and stand the buffet with knaves that smell of sweat: say this becomes him – as his composure must be rare indeed, who these things cannot blemish – yet must.

- Anthony and Cleopatra

Is that enough Shakespeare for now?

CHAPTER TWENTY-FOUR

INTERESTING INCIDENTS

The Bible states, *Be sure your sin will find you out.*

Truer words were never written. Sometimes it seems like people can get away with anything. In the end it always catches up to them. If in no other way, maybe in failing health from excessive boozing or womanizing – which often results in broken homes or sometimes social diseases like AIDS.

I remember as a child how one man's sins caught up to him. There was a store and post office a mile from our place in southwestern Saskatchewan. It sat all alone on the prairie. There was no town, only a little house behind the store.

Those days in the country no one locked their house, even if people went away for several days. Stealing was almost unheard of. One weekend the owners did go away. They decided to lock the store, even though their house remained unlocked. The store was located at a bit of a crossroad, a little south of the south Saskatchewan River. It was called Beaver Flat.

That weekend a thief broke into the store and stole a number of items, including a box or two of peaches which had been shipped in from British Columbia.

On Monday morning, when the owner opened his store, he noticed a broken window. Upon further inspection, he discovered there were a number of items missing, including the peaches. He called the Royal Canadian Mounted Police (RCMP). When the Mounties arrived from Swift Current, about twenty-seven miles away, they asked the store owner what articles had been stolen. He gave them a list of what he thought had been taken, including the peaches. The police had come by automobile. In the Dirty 'Thirties a lot of people were still driving horses hitched to buggies, democrats or wagons. The police scouted around and determined the culprit had used a democrat, which actually is a large buggy. The Mounties decided he had gone south on a dirt road. They followed the faint tracks. Suddenly one of them noticed a peach pit on the edge of the road. They slowly kept going and sure enough another five or six hundred feet, there was another peach pit. The thief must have been hungry. Maybe peaches were his favorite food. For several miles the Mounties found pits from five hundred to a thousand feet apart, some probably landed on the grass beside the road. The peach trail led right into a farmer's yard four or five miles from the store. He must have eaten half a box of peaches on his way home from his successful break-in (I am sure he had the runs that night).

Can you imagine the surprise on the farmer's face when the Mounties arrested him for theft? The culprit realized too late that he should have tossed those pits into the ditch, rather than onto the road. Better yet, he should have disciplined himself not to eat any peaches until he got home. These are the kind of cases that gave the Mounties the reputation that they always get their man.

The little white building at the top was the store from which the peaches were stolen. Bottom right is the new store which replaced it and was closed in the 1960s.

There was a chap who lived about fifteen miles from our place. This man was a real con artist. A whole book could be written about the fraud and stunts this gentleman pulled. He was usually well dressed (probably stolen clothes).

During the Second World War, the Canadian government made it mandatory for every Canadian to register and to carry that card with them. What an opportunity for this con artist. He got himself some kind of Commissioner's uniform, along with an official looking cap. He drove his car to a level part of Highway One between Swift Current and Moose Jaw. He parked his car beside the highway. (I guess you could call that an early version of a ghost car.)

The road was all gravel so nobody was really speeding. But he would flag motorists down. His question to them was could I see your registration card. If they could produce their card they were on their way. However, over half of the people did not carry the hated registration card with them. Those folks he fined five dollars on the spot. If there were three or four people in the car he got fifteen or twenty dollars. Not a bad haul in 1941. Traffic those days, with gas rationing in effect, was not heavy. His take for the day amounted to between one hundred and fifty dollars and two hundred dollars. In today's dollars that would be between fifteen hundred dollars and two thousand dollars. A cafe meal cost from thirty-five to fifty cents, sometimes only a quarter.

I can't remember exactly how long he got away with that racket, but I think it was the next day when the Mounties caught up with him. He had gone back for more loot. The Mounties arresting him did not concern him too much since it meant only three to six months in jail during the winter. This gave him a warm place to sleep and free board. He was incarcerated a number of times in his life. This gave him time to talk with other con artists and he devised new schemes for extracting money from unsuspecting people.

Once a family house burned down. Besides losing all their possessions, there was a loss of life. Several organizations started a fund for the survivors of this tragic event. Our con man was on the job immediately. He was collecting money for this worthy cause. The problem was he had no authority to collect money. Of course, the money all went into his pocket. Some people said he was a good fundraiser. He even cried crocodile tears. This caper was more lucrative than his registration scam.

One more little story about this man. One summer at a local rodeo he figured out how to give himself and a few other people a good deal. What he did was knock a dozen boards off on the far side of the rodeo grounds away from the front gate. A number of cars parked there at the back. He posed as a ticket taker. His carrot was they got in for half price. He kept all the money. This little scheme did not last long. Some customers knew there was something wrong so they reported it to the officials. Oh well, you can't win them all. Better luck next time.

Another gentleman that lived about ten miles from our place was a semiprofessional gambler. However, he was as crooked as a dog's hind leg. He hung around hotels in larger centers where he was not well known. In most cities, there are pockets of gambling. It was illegal but the police paid little attention to that activity. That was in the days of prohibition in the United States so the Canadian police were too busy trying to catch rum runners.

He would acquaint himself with people. This led to a meeting later on in back rooms or even quite openly for a friendly game of poker. The hotel, as well as the police, turned a blind eye on these games. The hotel profited from renting out rooms and selling liquor to the gamblers. The stakes in those games were fairly high. They usually involved six to eight people, with a few bystanders. These onlookers often waited for someone who went broke to leave. At that point, one of them would take his place at the table. It was not uncommon for twelve to fifteen men to participate in these games in one night. After three or four hands had been played, the crooked gambler would say, "I don't like these cards. I have a feeling they may be marked." He would then glance around and spot one of the youngest onlookers, a boy of about eighteen years of age. He beckoned the boy to the table and said to him, "Here's five bucks. Get us two new decks of cards from the corner drug store."

Away went the lad. Meanwhile, the game was suspended while they were waiting for the new cards. Five or ten minutes later the boy appeared with the cards. They opened up the new deck and began to play. On the first hand, our gambler did not fare too well. He won a little in the second hand, nothing on the third. On the fourth hand he made a pretty good haul. Next hand, nothing. The whole scene was quite normal. As the evening progressed, he slowly but surely was winning. Many of the players ran out of money. By the designated quitting time, he had won most of the money. The other players did not become suspicious. They thought he was a good player with a little luck thrown in.

The truth was, these were all marked cards. He bought those cards earlier, opened them up and marked them. Then he sealed them again. The boy who went to pick those cards up was his accomplice. I am not sure where they stashed those cards. The young man probably had them in his pocket the whole time. His going to the store to buy them was just a pretence. What has always puzzled me is the average layman cannot detect marked cards. It is done in such a subtle way that only a card shark might notice it. All that illegal money did not do him any good. He died relatively young. I am sure he took none of that money with him.

When I was three months shy of being fifteen years old, I was involved in a maternity case which I will never forget. Here is what happened.

My brother, Jack, and his wife, Ann, lived in a small house located on my parent's yard. They were expecting their first baby. It was due in the beginning of May but, lo and behold, one stormy night in the middle of March Ann went into labor. My brother was beside himself with worry. He rushed over to our house to inform us what was happening. Ann would need to travel to the nearest hospital, but the roads were blocked with snow for at least the first five miles, and Swift Current was twenty-eight miles away. It was decided that we would hitch a team of horses to the car and pull it to where the road was open. Jack ran back to their house. I quickly dressed and rushed out to the barn and threw a set of harness on the horses.

We attached the team to the car with a logging chain. The horses were prancing around but I had good control of them. My brother

142

bundled his young wife into the car and he sat beside her and steered. Meanwhile, I was trying to figure out where I could sit. There really was not much choice. I simply climbed on the hood and away we went.

The thing that amazes me to this day is how I did not slip off that slippery cold metal hood. The horses were pretty frisky, we made good time. There were spots where the drifts were two to three feet deep. Every time we hit one of those drifts, the horses really dug in. They jerked that little car through them like a toy. There were stretches of open road but just when we thought we had reached open road another drift made its appearance. Finally after about five miles, we hit a better road that was open. We unhitched the horses, Jack started the car, and I watched the taillights disappear in the dark.

I climbed on one of the horses and headed for home. I was pretty chilly by the time I got to the barn. I unharnessed the horses, threw them a little feed and headed back to the house at approximately four in the morning.

There is one footnote to this story. Three or four days later when the roads had opened up, Jack and Ann came back home. No baby. It was a false alarm. The little girl (Gayle) was not born till May 11. I'm sure glad I did not fall off that hood. If the car had run over me and the horses had taken off on a dead run, it could have been a disaster. I still believe in guardian angels.

There are dozens of stories about bulls killing people. I know of at least seven such incidents myself. Often, it involves Holstein dairy bulls, but there are others as well. One incident I know of did not cost human life but it did cost a horse its life. My Uncle Abe was trying to sort off an ornery bull from some other cattle. Suddenly, the bull turned on the horse. Before my uncle could manoeuvre the horse out of the way, the bull took a mighty lunge and buried one of his horns deep in the horse's belly. He then ripped it sideways, there was an enormous gash, a whole bunch of the horse's insides fell out – but not on the ground because they were still attached inside the belly.

The bull kept on hooking at the horse which went down. At that point my uncle bailed off and headed for the buildings about a quarter of a mile away. A race horse or a greyhound could not have caught him.

The horse was not dead but he was beyond repair so they had to destroy him. I do not remember what they did with that bull. My guess would be he got a fast trip to the stockyards or packing plant where he would be turned into baloney. Years later, when my uncle recalled that incident, he still turned a little pale. It was his favorite horse.

Bert Hargrave was a rancher from Walsh, Alberta. He became a Conservative Member of Parliament in Ottawa. He used to also run the Walsh Community cattle sale. I had many good visits with Bert. He phoned me regularly from Ottawa to find out what was going on in the cattle industry, especially in the marketing end of things.

One day, he told me an interesting story. The home ranch where his parents lived was about forty miles from Medicine Hat. At election time that is where they had to go to vote. I was surprised there were no polling stations closer. Maybe there were, but his parents preferred to go into Medicine Hat to vote. Remember, this was eighty-five years ago, in 1916. At any rate, they drove a team and democrat to Medicine Hat for the vote. It took a long day to make that forty miles. They stayed the night and the next morning they went to vote. There were only two parties to vote for. He voted Conservative. She voted Liberal, or vice-versa. That meant they cancelled each other's vote. That caused no rift between them. That's what democracy is all about. The next day they loaded their democrat up with supplies and headed back to the ranch.

Grant McEwan tells the story about an interesting incident that happened shortly after the turn of the century. It concerned some homesteaders who had come from England. Many of those British folks were remittance men, but not all of them. However, some of them came from cities and life on a lonely homestead on the prairies was quite a culture shock. They learned by talking and watching what their neighbors did. They also were the life of social circles. Many of them could play instruments. Quite often they had house parties.

One English chap had imported a Shorthorn bull from England. He was very proud of this bull. One night there was a party at his house. They were dancing the night away, with a few drinks in between. About midnight they stopped dancing for a bit, for a bite to eat. During this intermission, the host was boasting about the good bull he had imported from England. Some of the guests said, "Why don't you show us the bull?"

He took up the challenge, went to the barn where the bull was tied, and brought him to an open window at the house. The bull was gentle and well halter broke. All the people, including the ladies, admired the beautiful beast. Some even patted him on the head. The owner of the bull handed the halter shank through the open window, where one of the men tied it to the leg of the organ. The host came back into the house and received compliments on his good bull.

After about half an hour or so, they decided to strike up the band (the organ and a few violins) and start dancing again. The sudden noise of the music spooked the bull. He whirled around and took off back to the barn. With his departure, the organ took off as well since it was attached to the halter shank. There was one small problem. The organ was slightly larger than the window opening. That changed in a hurry when a good section of the house was ripped off as the organ sailed through the window. End of party! No organ to provide music. By the time the bull arrived at the barn there was not much left of the organ. I hope the homesteader had enough money to import another organ from England, or maybe he ordered one from the T. Eaton Co. in Toronto or Winnipeg.

Earl Galvin told me about an interesting incident that happened years ago. In the area where he was raised near Moose Jaw, there was a small country store. When he was a boy, he often went there with his dad. Times were tough, this was in the Dirty 'Thirties. His dad often charged his groceries and when a little money would come in, he would pay the store bill. Sometimes it took awhile before he could pay. Toward the end of the Depression, his dad passed away and by this time, Earl had left home.

No matter how many years go by, childhood and youth memories linger. He often thought about the old storekeeper. Sometime in the 1960s, Earl was in Moose Jaw on business. While he was there, he decided to drive to where he grew up. Sure enough, the old store was still there. He walked in and, to his surprise, the old storekeeper was still there as well. He was old and frail looking. Earl introduced himself. The old gentleman was happy to see him.

In the conversation that followed, Earl asked him, "When my dad passed away, did he owe you any money?"

The old man rummaged through an old desk. He came up with a dog-eared ledger and thumbed through it. "Yes, he did owe me several hundred dollars." This debt had been incurred at least thirty-five years ago. Earl asked him the exact amount. At that point, he pulled out his cheque book and paid the debt. (I think he tacked on a little extra.) When Earl handed him the cheque the old man was overcome with emotion. Tears welled up in his eyes. It was not the money involved. It was the human kindness which touched him. To think that a long-departed son of the district would return and pay his father's debt.

A chap I used to work with told me an interesting story one day. One year, on Christmas Eve, the family was visiting in the front room laughing and joking. Around eleven at night, the wife went into the kitchen to check on a turkey she was defrosting on the kitchen table. Lo and behold, the turkey was gone. Upon investigation they discovered someone had slipped in the back door and hoisted the turkey. On Christmas Day all the stores were closed so they had no way to replace the stolen turkey. I do not remember what he said they had for Christmas dinner – probably hamburger. Meanwhile the thief had a feast. I hope he did not choke on a turkey bone.

Red Wheatcroft was one of the largest cattle dealers in Canada during the 1950s, '60s and '70s. He told me about an incident that happened to him in Mexico. Red had a villa or a houseboat, or maybe both in Mexico. Every winter and, sometimes in summer, he would fly to Mexico – often with his own small plane. One year, when he was returning to Canada, something befell him that could have cost him his life.

I am not sure whether it was an oversight or he underestimated how much gas he needed to get to the United States where he usually filled his plane with fuel. At any rate, he noticed that his fuel gauge was on empty. He was still over a hundred miles from the United

States border. He had no choice but to land. As he searched for a place to land he noticed a cluster of buildings with some flat ground nearby. He circled once then dropped down and landed safely. Before he even got out of the plane, he was surrounded by Mexican soldiers with machine guns levelled at him.

Red thought he was toast. He said they were young ragtag men, who probably had a scanty education and likely never wore shoes until they joined the army. They looked like they were anxious to become heroes by capturing a foreigner (a gringo) who had dropped out of the sky in a little plane.

He raised his arms, then tried to explain to them that he was out of gas. Of course, they could not understand anything he said. After a few minutes, they pointed him to a building a little distance away and marched him over to it. In the building were a few senior officers who could understand a little English. In spite of this, they acted like they might throw him in jail. After half an hour of babbled conversation, he got permission to phone his lawyer. The lawyer asked him if he had money with him. It so happened that he had a fair amount of American money on him. The lawyer advised him to give them a bribe of at least three thousand dollars. So, after a little more discussion with his captors, he gave them three thousand dollars on the condition that they would give him enough gas to get to the United States, which they did. Red said that was about the best money he ever spent in his life. For awhile, he thought he was either to be shot or thrown in jail.

If some of Red's family or friends happen to read this, forgive me if the details of this story are slightly different than I remember them. This happened about twenty-five years ago. The moral of the story is, never run out of gas in a private plane when flying over Mexico. Another thing to watch out for in Mexico is drinking the water and eating the salads. I know many folks who have come back from Mexico with a good dose of Montezuma's Revenge. It can hang around for months. I know one case that lasted for years.

CHAPTER TWENTY-FIVE

GEOGRAPHY AND HISTORY

By now, most of you know that I am a geography buff and a history buff to a lesser extent. For as long as I can remember, geography has held a fascination for me that I can really not explain. I have spent hours looking at world maps yet I feel that I have much more to learn about this old planet. I also have a lot of geography books. A number of them have been given to me by our children, for Christmas, my birthday, or Father's Day. I have received *National Geographic* magazine for the past thirty-eight years. My wife's parents gave me the first subscription and I have subscribed ever since. I had read a few issues of the magazine when I was about twelve years old. I am not sure where they came from. We did not receive it in our home.

It is absolutely incredible what a variance of topographical features we have on this planet. There are mountains, plains, forests, tundra, volcanoes, and all kinds of interesting geological formations. There is also a huge temperature, vegetation, animal and insect variation on this earth. Then there are the oceans, which cover over seventy percent of the earth's surface.

I do not believe in evolution, but I do believe that man and creatures do adapt to the environment they live in. Polar bears would not fare very well in the tropics, nor would penguins. Monkeys would have a tough time surviving in the Arctic or Antarctica, although there are snow monkeys in parts of Asia.

Insects thrive in most areas of the world, including mosquitoes and black flies in the north. In summer, they are so dense they are like a low cloud in motion. They make life miserable for man and beast. However, the largest variety of insects live in tropical and hot climates. Many of these insects are poisonous if they bite or sting you. Birds thrive on insects. That is why in the jungles of the world, bird life is abundant.

As I already said, over three-quarters of our planet is covered by water. Oceans cover seventy percent, with other waters like lakes, rivers, glaciers, creeks, ponds and dams, another five percent. It is the oceans that affect much of our climate. When the Pacific warms a few degrees, El Nino develops. This causes rain and flooding in some regions, drought in other areas.

Most major storms form on the ocean before they move onto land.

The Gulf Stream in the Atlantic Ocean greatly affects the weather in Northern Europe. In northern Norway, which is on the Arctic Circle, the weather is relatively mild, even in the winter because of the influence of the Gulf Stream. It does snow, but it melts when the temperature rises above the zero mark, which happens on a regular basis.

Most of the rain we receive is the result of evaporation from the oceans, even though it may be two thousand miles away. Some inland lakes and other small bodies of water also contribute to, or cause, rain.

How the ocean tides are connected to the moon is a mystery. I know it is the gravitational pull of the moon. If you can explain exactly how it works, you are wiser than I am. I am a person who observes things as they are, not what causes various phenomena we have. I leave that to astronomers and scientists to figure out – things such as ocean tides, sun spots, northern lights (aurora borealis), earthquakes, volcanic eruptions, meteorites. How about the earth making a complete revolution every twenty-four hours? Everything stays in place. It does not dump us out to float in outerspace.

The weather, soil and terrain dictate what people do in the various regions of the world. These things not only affect what people do for a living, they also shape our cultures. People who live in coastal areas are often fishermen or seafaring people. The British and many other European countries, large and small, explored much of the world in the four centuries before 1900. They not only explored, they conquered and colonized a number of countries and areas of the world. During the reign of Queen Victoria the sun never set in any part of the world that did not belong to the British Empire.

The countries and people that those Europeans annexed as their possessions had long-standing customs and cultures. They were subjugated by their new masters. Britain, France, Spain, Portugal and Holland were the most prolific colonizers. To a lesser degree were the Belgians, Germans, Scandinavians and Italians. In fact, the Italians were the latecomers in the practice, taking over Ethiopia in the 20th Century.

In the past two centuries nearly all these countries have gained independence, starting with the United States in 1776. It was not the Natives of North America who got their independence. It was the colonists who had immigrated from Great Britain and other European countries from 1492 to 1776.

Canada stayed loyal to its master, Great Britain. In fact, there are still vestiges of the past in our country such as the Queen's face on our stamps and currency. We also have a governor general in Ottawa and lieutenant governors in the provinces. They are the Queen's representatives.

Then there is the unelected Canadian senate, which is a copy of the British House of Lords. The only difference is the Lords are hereditary whereas the Canadian senate is appointed by the Prime Minister, who acts as a dictator, even though he is elected by the people.

It is time Canada becomes a republic and a real democracy. By now the folks who are staunch loyalists may be very angry with me. That is your privilege, as we live in a partial democracy, where we have freedom of speech and freedom of the press (at least most of the time).

All my life I have had a fascination about Oceana. It encompasses 3.3 million square miles. Two-thirds of it is in the South Pacific Ocean. It breaks down into four regions: Melanesia, Micronesia and Polynesia. The fourth region consists of Australia, New Zealand and Papua, New Guinea. There are thousands of islands, some fairly large, some medium size, others small. In fact so small they are called islets. Hundreds of these little islands are not inhabited. There are also many atolls and coral reefs. An atoll is a small island of coral, usually in a ring or horseshoe surrounding a lagoon.

When the European explorers reached this area of the world, after months of hardship, including sailing through the rough waters of Capehorn at the southern tip of South America, only six hundred miles north of Antarctica, they thought they had reached Paradise. And in a way they had. Palm trees swayed in the breeze, various fruits, beautiful weather, sandy beaches and the ocean which was teaming with fish. Maybe most interesting were the topless, dark haired lasses that seemed to be everywhere. Those sailors had not seen a woman, in some cases, from six months to a year. You do not have to have much of an imagination to know what happened. It was reported most of those women were quite willing to do a little cohabiting with those men. This resulted in offspring whose skin was a shade lighter but who retained dark hair and other features of those people.

Many of those men had wives at home so after a few months or sometimes a year, they sailed back to Europe. The South Pacific became a memory. Although some men made several voyages to the region, I am sure they never revealed to their children that they had half sisters and brothers in the South Pacific. I read of some men who remained on the islands all their life.

Unlike North America, most of those islands are still inhabited by a large majority of original natives. The two exceptions are Australia and New Zealand where Europeans outnumber the natives by a huge percentage.

We have been to Australia, New Zealand, Fiji, Tahiti, Bali and Hawaii. The weather in all these places is idyllic, except for an occasional tropical storm. The other islands and small nations I only know by what I have read about them. We also have two sons, Leland and Ward, who spent some time there. Ward is a geography professor in Auckland, New Zealand.

He wrote his thesis for his doctorate on the Solomon Islands. This entailed living with the people for periods of time. Today he is one of the world's leading experts concerning these islands.

Following are the nation's names and capitals of that vast region:

Australia	-	Canberra
New Zealand	-	Wellington

Fiji	-	Suva
Palau	-	Koror
Kiribati	-	Bairki
Marshall Islands	-	Dalap–Uliga-Darrit
Federated Micronesia	-	Palikin
Samoa	-	Apia
Soloman Islands	-	Horiara
Tongo	-	Nuku' Alofa
Tuvalu	-	Funafuti
Vanuatu	-	Port Vila

The colonizers were the British, French, Dutch, Portuguese, Spanish and Americans. Later Australia and New Zealand got involved as well. A few countries have their own currency, but a number of them use their former master's currency. All the above counties have gained their independence.

There are still a number of dependencies and territories that are funded by countries like Britain, France, the United States, Australia and New Zealand.

Here are some of them:

French Polynesia	-	Papeete
American Samoa	-	Paso
Cook Islands	-	Avarua
Quam	-	Agaha
New Caledonia	-	Noumea
Niue	-	Alofi
Norfolk Islands	-	Kingston

Following are some who do not have a capital – they are governed by their colonial masters:

Ashmore and Cartier Islands, Baker and Howland Islands, Christmas Island, Coco's Islands, Coral Sea Islands, Jarvis Island, Johnston Atoll, Kingman Reef and Midway Islands.

During the Second World War, the Japanese invaded large sections of this area. Some of the fiercest fighting in this region resulted in the deaths of thousands of American and Japanese soldiers, airmen and sailors. The most casualties took place at Quan Canal on the Solomans, Quam, Okinawa and Iwo Jima. Someone said when the war was raging that Paradise had turned into hell.

The Islanders have a long history and tradition of sailing on the huge open seas with their dugout canoes either to explore, fight or fish. There are thousands more islands, some without names.

I have often thought it would be nice to own one of those little islands. A few individuals have owned their own island. However the monotony of sailing or sitting under a palm tree everyday overwhelmed them and they returned to civilization.

So I guess I will let it remain a dream, not a reality.

From Biblical times to the present, we have had wars and revolutions where one country conquers another. The human spirit is very resilient. People who were under the rule of another nation, sometimes for a few hundred years, retained most of their customs, cultures and most of their religious beliefs. These things were usually practised underground and at secret meetings.

Religions, including Christianity, have survived for decades, even centuries, even though the masters forbade it. The government imposed severe restrictions and stiff penalties on people whom they suspected or caught in these activities. Some examples are the former communists in Russia and Eastern Europe. They were atheists, but the church did not die out. Although its activities were held in secret meetings, if discovered the practitioners were sent in exile to Siberia.

In the Eighteenth and Nineteenth Centuries, the British were the easiest masters of their colonies.

They established British parliamentary rules and the British judicial system, which had mellowed from the days when they exiled many minor and a few major criminals to Australia. In places like India, they allowed the people to continue practicing their religion. They also tolerated the caste system. I think it made it easier to control the people. Each caste, from highest to lowest, knows its place in society.

The British governors worked with the upper castes so, although ruled by the British, a small percentage of privileged Indians had a good lifestyle and some input in the government. Some of the other countries in Europe which claimed various countries and regions in Africa were often cruel masters. They exploited the people. Often the borders of the African colonies were drawn up with no regard for the tribal homelands. Under the European's iron rule, they forced the mix of tribes to work. When the truth really came out is when these countries gained their independence. In the past fifty years, Africa has been a bloodbath. One of the main reasons is long standing tribal hatreds. If the Europeans had paid some attention when they carved up Africa, much of today's conflict and bloodshed could have been avoided.

As already stated, the British possessions in Africa fared slightly better when they got their independence. Although in recent years even those countries are having internal tribal problems as well.

In Mexico, Central America and South America, the Spanish imposed their rule and religion on the people. They killed thousands of natives who resisted. Today, over ninety percent of these folks are Catholic. They have all gained independence, including Brazil which belonged to Portugal.

The problem with both Africa and Latin America is the governments have a tendency to be unstable. Since gaining their independence, nearly every country has either had a coup which ended with a dictator in control – often an army general who engineered the coup or a major civil war which claimed thousands of lives. Hopefully, in the next fifty years the people will see the futility of this constant conflict.

In my opinion the Muslims are the most successful in forcing their religion on the people and areas they conquered. Today there are millions of Muslims in a number of countries that they overran and conquered in the past five hundred years.

The Jewish people are scattered all over the world. They have retained their religion and beliefs. A few have departed from Judaism, but not many. Jewish folks do not have a tendency to convert other people to their religion. It does happen sometimes through marriage.

The Romans, who ruled the Middle East including Israel, were not a religious people. But to their credit they let the Jews practise and worship in their synagogues with a few restrictions. It was the Romans who crucified Jesus. It was not because of what Jesus stood for or preached. It was done to please the people, who thought Jesus was a blasphemer and an impostor. In reality, he was God's son.

Once again, I got carried away. When I started to write this book my intention was to stay away from politics and religion – especially politics. The truth is if a person wishes to write or discuss world history and geography, it is almost impossible to exclude those two subjects. They impact everyone.

I have hardly scratched the surface of the history and geography of the world. It is such a big topic that it overwhelms a person just thinking about it. All countries in the world have a unique history and culture. They produce different products and grow different crops that are suitable to their area. As the world shrinks and becomes what they call a global village, it behooves everyone of us to know as much as we can about other countries and their people.

In the past, many people in North America knew very little about other countries except for a winter holiday in some tropical resort. The United Nations is a little too pink to suit me, but they do help to link the world together. It would be nice if, in the foreseeable future, this world could become one happy family with only a few squabbles. Not the bloodshed we witness these days.

CHAPTER TWENTY-SIX

MOUNTAIN OR VALLEY?

Where would you sooner be, on a mountain top or in a valley?

Most people would say mountain top. In fact, great moments in our life are called, mountain top experiences. This expression comes from the idea we are all reaching for the top. On this earth, mountains are the greatest height we can reach using our two legs. It has always been a mystery to me why people risk life and limb to climb a mountain.

I am sure that once at the top it is an exhilarating experience although it is only a brief stay. Hopefully it is a clear day so you can see in all four directions. Basically what you see are more mountains. However, almost half the time at that altitude there are clouds which obscure your vision. If it is over fifteen thousand feet, you have trouble breathing on your own. You may set up a pup tent for a few hours but that is about the only residence you will ever have up there. Nothing grows. The only thing to eat is a few chocolate bars and some tidbits you packed up with you. Then it is down again.

The descent is just as dangerous if not more so than climbing up. There are numerous stories about mountain climbers losing their life on either the ascent or the descent. Mount Everest (over twenty-nine thousand feet) has claimed dozens of lives. What for? Just for the glory and recognition that many people crave. There certainly is no scientific reason for those climbs. Not like they have for those outerspace flights where all kinds of experiments take place.

How about valleys? When we are depressed the term often used is 'we are in a valley'. In other words, the valley is the opposite from a mountain top experience. To me, that is twisted logic. I like valleys better than mountains. Although mountains are nice to look at from a little distance, if I had a choice to sit on top of a mountain where the wind usually howls or in a calm valley, I would choose the valley.

Valleys are sheltered; the land is rich and fertile. Roads are easy to build and there are a few neighbors to visit. I can visualize no better way of life than a ranch in a wide valley where cattle and horses, even sheep, are peacefully grazing. Valleys usually are well watered by creeks and springs, thanks to the mountains. What this tells me is mountains and valleys complement each other.

We hear and read a lot about mountain ranches. They are very sought after and expensive. I think they should be called valley ranches, not mountain ranches. In Colorado, mountain ranches are two to three times as expensive as ranches on the high plains. Yet the average ranch on the plains will out-produce the mountain ranch per acre.

Ranches along the foothills west of Calgary, Alberta are so expensive that if you lived for two hundred years you would never recover your money. Very few of those ranches are ever for sale. Most of them have been in the family for three to five generations. Rich

Sketch by Christopher Bews at age twelve.

157

jaded oilmen and other professionals will pay almost any price to get hold of a piece of scenic grassland on the east slope of the Rockies.

We had a small ranch in that type of country once. But we had to sell it when cattle prices and a few other ventures did a number on me.

I got kind of sidetracked on mountains versus valleys. Mountain climbing is what I call an upscale sport. It costs a lot of money. When people achieve a difficult climb they become celebrities. Edmund Hillary was one such person. He was the first person, along with his Sherpa guide by the name of Tensing, to successfully climb the world's highest mountain, Mount Everest. For this feat he was knighted and forever after is called Sir Edmund Hillary. Without his Sherpa guide, he never would have made it.

Not many people get knighted who linger in the valley. Even though they may have contributed to society in worthy causes or helping their fellow men when those folks were in a deep valley literally as well. About the only Canadians who were ever knighted are a few newspaper tycoons who had connections in England.

The latest candidate to be offered that honour was Conrad Black. But our pork-barrelling prime minister, Jean Chretien, denied him that honor. Maybe Black would stand a better chance if he climbed a mountain. Instead, he stayed in the valley and became a billionaire by collecting ownership of newspapers like some people collect stamps.

Like I said, mountains are nice when you are in a beautiful valley surrounded by mountains a little distance away. I enjoy a brief vacation in the mountains, but when we leave and arrive on the open plains with a few hills and a few trees I always heave a sigh of relief. Being in the rugged mountains is like being in the jungle – they block your view. When I emerge from either one, I always feel like I was released from jail.

I consider myself a grassroots philosopher. Maybe that's why I like valleys and open plains better. Those areas grow a lot of grass.

CHAPTER TWENTY-SEVEN

SOME WISDOM FROM PROVERBS AND ECCLESIASTES

A wise man will hear and increase learning.

Fools despise wisdom and instruction.

Discretion shall preserve your understanding and will keep you.

The fool has said in his heart there is no God.

Let not mercy and truth forsake thee.

Trust in the Lord with all your heart and lean not on your own understanding.

Withhold not good from them to whom it is due.

Envy not the oppressor and choose none of his ways.

Wisdom is a principal thing, therefore get wisdom.

The lips of a strange woman drop as a honeycomb, and her mouth is smoother than oil, but her end is bitter as worm wood, her feet go down to death, her steps take hold on hell.

These six things doth the Lord hate yea, seven, are an abomination unto him, a proud look, a lying tongue and a hand that sheds innocent blood, a heart that deviseth wicked imaginations, feet that be swift running into mischief, a false witness that speaks lies, and he that sows discord among his fellow men.

A false balance is an abomination of the Lord! But a just weight is His delight.

A hypocrite with his mouth destroys his neighbor.

A virtuous woman is a crown to her husband.

Lying lips are abomination to the Lord, but they that deal truly are his delight.

He that is soon angry deals foolishly.

A soft answer turns away wrath, but grievous words stir up anger.

A fool despises his father's instruction.

How much better it is to get wisdom than gold, and to get understanding rather than silver.

Every word of God is pure, he is the shield unto them who put their trust in Him.

Who can find a virtuous woman? Her price is far above rubies. The heart of her husband doth safely trust in her so that he shall have no need of spoil. She would do him good and not evil all the days of her life. She opens her mouth with wisdom and in her tongue is the law of kindness.

The rod and reproof give wisdom, but a child left to himself brings his mother to shame.

Boast not thyself of tomorrow for thou knowest not what a day may bring forth.

A continual dropping on a very rainy day, and a contentious woman are alike.

A dog returns to his vomit so a fool returns to his folly.

A word fitly spoken is like apples of gold in pictures of silver.

It is better to dwell in the corner of the rooftop than with a brawling woman in a big house.

A good man is rather to be chosen than great riches, and loving favor rather than silver or gold.

Train up a child in the way he should go and when he is old he will not depart from it.

Make no friendship with an angry man.

A man that has friends must show himself friendly, and there is a friend that sticks closer than a brother.

All the rivers run into the sea yet the sea is not full unto the place from where they came then they return again.

He that loves silver shall not be satisfied with silver, nor he that loves abundance with increase.

As he came forth of his mother's womb, naked shall he return to go as he came and shall take nothing of his labour, which he may carry away in his hand.

It is better to hear the rebuke of the wise, than for a man to hear the song of fools.

He that observes the wind shall not sow, and he that regards the clouds shall not reap.

The words of the wise heard in quietness are better than the shouting of a ruler among fools.

No man has authority to restrain the wind with the wind or authority over the day of death.

Wisdom is better than strength. But the wisdom of a poor man is despised and his words are not heeded.

Remember also your creator in the days of your youth.

God will bring every act to judgement, everything which is hidden, whether it is good or evil.

All the above quotes are from the King James Version of the Bible.

CHAPTER TWENTY-EIGHT

EVOLUTION IN REVERSE

I believe in creation. It is clearly stated in Genesis that God created heaven and earth and all the creatures that inhabit it. I do not understand it, but I believe it. I have a friend who is an atheist or, if not an atheist, at least an agnostic. He believes in evolution. I find it hard to understand creation, let alone evolution.

There are more and more scientists that have abandoned the evolution theory. Theory is all it is, even though the schools teach it as fact. Do you believe that we washed up from the sea as a single cell from which all creatures like fish, birds and animals evolved? Then, finally, man arrived on this planet descended from apes or whatever.

Where is the missing link? It has never been found. There have been claims made that some skeletons, which were unearthed, were the missing link. But closer scrutiny reveals otherwise. This idea that man evolved from animals is silly. If we believe that then we may as well believe in reverse evolution. That is, that animals evolved from man. In many areas we are more primitive than animals.

Our bodies are not covered all over with hair like animals. We have not progressed that far yet. This thought struck me the other day as I gazed at my naked body in the mirror. (I don't do that very often. I don't like seeing my big tummy.) No hair to keep me warm in frigid weather. Not like the coyote which needs neither central heating nor clothes. Millions of years ago when men lived in caves they constantly shivered so slowly but surely some of his offspring started to grow more hair to keep warm. That was the beginning of animals. First monkeys, then others. Part of this evolution was body structure. Slowly these animals started to use their arms as legs. This gave them a lot more speed when they ran after their prey for supper. The animals had ample food while man was still struggling to provide for his family on two legs.

As for speech, the animals thought it caused too much trouble so they decided to use their senses of sight, smell and hearing to compensate for not talking, although they still communicate through wails, grunts and other noises only their own kind understand. A dog, coyote or any other member of the wolf family can hear ten times better than we can. As for smell, that is even more incredible. They can pick up a scent that we are another ten million years away from developing. That is why they use sniffer dogs at airports to sniff out drugs and the police use tracking dogs to catch criminals.

Most animals have better eyesight than we do. Many of them are nocturnal, which means they can see in the dark. That includes owls, members of the cat family, possums and others. We humans have not evolved to that level yet. Unless we have a flashlight, we stumble around in the dark.

The common housefly has about the most advanced eye of any creature. When their eye is put under a powerful microscope, it reveals an incredibly intricate eye that has capabilities we are not going to develop for another seven million years or more. When you are trying to have a nap and a fly keeps buzzing around your face, it can be quite annoying. Any attempts to swat it with your hands are fruitless. You have to get up, get a fly swatter, and even then, if you are not real fast, it will escape. The reason is it can sense and see in all directions at once.

As for parents, most animals are better parents than humans. If you do not believe me, try messing around with a baby grizzly bear if mother happens to be on the scene. Even a domestic cow with a new baby is protective.

Animals also have better teeth than we do. It may take another four million years to catch up to them in that department.

Animals never go to war with their own species like we humans do. Sure, coyotes catch rabbits for food, and lions kill wildebeest for the same reason. But they do not go to war against their own kind. If we had evolved a little faster so that we ceased to make war on our own kind, millions of lives would have been saved in the last five thousand years.

Lovemaking among animals varies a lot, but then so does it among humans. Wolves mate for life and a few others do as well. However, most practice polygamy and we are fast catching up to them in that area. We do not call it polygamy. Well, some do in Utah, but mostly we call it mate swapping or free love. There are more children needing homes and foster care than there are orphan animals. Animals seldom abandon their young. Sometimes an animal mother dies. When this happens, another nursing female will nurse the orphan as her own.

Our sex hormones have not quite evolved to where animals are at. They usually only mate during the rut season which lasts about two months. If we humans were that way, it would give women ten months of freedom from males. That way they could concentrate a little more on their careers. They might get pregnant, but that is no great hindrance for staying on the job these days.

Animals do not practice abortion. There are a few homosexuals among them, but not many.

Animals are on a great outdoor vacation most of the time. At least when food is plentiful. We humans are slowly catching up to them in that department. Many people also enjoy the great outdoors. Man has destroyed much of the various animal habitats in his search for food. We have caused our descendants big problems.

We humans have a pecking order. This is common in all segments of our society. It happens in homes, schools, sports, business or any other human endeavour. There are those at the top, those in the middle and all the way to the bottom. It is also evident in communities. We sometimes will not admit it exists. The order establishes itself by various means such as intelligence, good looks, strength and wealth.

Our descendants, the animals, birds and fish are more open about that pecking order. It exists big time. It is decided on strength and aggressiveness. If you have a pen of say one hundred hens, there is a complete pecking order from top to bottom. The top of the order gets to feed first and roost in their chosen spot. Woe betide the hen that tries to break that rule. She is put in her place in a hurry.

The same applies to most animals. We have had buffalo for quite a few years. Each buffalo knows exactly where he or she stands socially. Usually a big male is at the top.

The animals have modified the pecking order business of their human ancestors by eliminating such things as wealth and beauty. They use intelligence and strength. We are catching up to them. In some human societies strength too is the main criteria for holding power at the top.

Have you even thought how nice it would be if we had progressed as far as our animal descendants have when it comes to long dreary winter days and nights. Bears, ground squirrels (gophers) and a few other animals lead the way in that department. When cold weather arrives in the fall, they simply disappear underground for a winter's sleep. Their body functions slow down. In the summer, a gopher's heart beats approximately three hundred times per minutes. When it hibernates, it slows down to seven to ten beats a minute. A normal, healthy human heartbeat is from sixty-five to eighty beats a minute when sitting still. During the winter siesta, the hibernating animal does not eat or go to the bathroom. They are sound asleep when they give birth to their babies. No doctors or anaesthetic like we humans have. We are catching up in the birth process. Many women these days are having their babies the natural way.

What about birds, fish and insects? They are also descendants from homo sapiens. They too have evolved into intelligent creatures. Take birds, for instance. They till no soil, yet have lots to eat. A large majority depart for warmer climates for the winter. We finally caught on to that, since many humans now head south for the winter as well. The birds opted to go south rather than sleeping through the winter like some animals do. They have two legs like we do, but one day some of them decided they would rather have wings than arms. So from then on they practised flapping their arms. Eventually those arms became wings that carry them ten thousand miles to whatever destination they decided, all without radar or mechanical compasses. After a million years, we have finally mastered how to fly as well. The difference is, we have to use big cumbersome things called airplanes. We still cannot fly on our own.

No painful childbirth for birds. The female just lays a few round eggs, then sits on them two or three weeks, and bingo, there are the babies. The male often takes his turn on the nest as well. Some species, like the Canada goose, mate for life, although most birds practice free love like a large portion of the human race does.

Insects have really improved from the day they descended from us. The Bible mentions insects several times. Proverbs 6:6 *Go to the ant, though sluggard, observe her ways and be wise. Which having no chief officer or ruler, prepares her food in summer and gathers her provision in the harvest.* Proverbs 30:25 *The ants are not strong folk, but they prepare their food in summer.*

Bees have gone overboard. As they evolved, their motto was if you want to eat, you have to work. They carried the work ethic too far. Bees work hard all their life. No time for recreation. The exception is the Queen bee, which is the mother of the colony and the drones, which mate with her. Once a drone's duties are finished, the workers kill him. Not a bad system. It sure keeps welfare costs down.

The black widow spider has a unique system of reproducing her own kind. After the male and female mate, she eats him. This gives her enough protein to produce the eggs in her body. The male is only half as big as she is.

Not all evolution is good. Those spiders may have gone too far. Maybe that is just a male's view. Maybe our radical feminists think it is a great system. No men to put up with. Maybe in another million years we will have progressed to that process ourselves. There are several other insects with the same system.

Fish are also interesting. When that single cell washed up on the shore about a billion years ago, a few other cells must have remained in the ocean then evolved into fish – or maybe not. They probably also descended from humans. If they did, they sure have surpassed their ancestors in their ability to swim.

Some of the land animals saw the fish swimming in that warm, clear water so they took to the water as well. A few that come to mind are seals, otters, beavers, muskrats and whales. All these animals are having a whale of a time cavorting around in the water. Now, millions of years after, we've taken to the water as well. But we have a long way to catch up in our swimming ability to those fish and animals. Eventually, evolution will take care of that.

I foresee the time, a million years from now, when humans and dolphins will compete with each other in the Olympics.

Speaking about the Olympics, it is fortunate animals are not entered for competition (except in equestrian events). If animals

Of the five creatures pictured here, four can outrun humans, three can swim faster than we can. One can jump higher than we can. Two can smell better and one can hear better. Who said we are superior?
Courtesy Best Photo,
Airdrie, Alberta

along with humans participated in the track and field events, the animals would win most of the medals. Deer would win the high jumping with ease. I had one game fence builder tell me deer need a nine-foot fence to contain them. Elk need an eight-foot fence. There are several other animals that can high jump from five to seven feet.

In the running events, there are dozens of animals that can outrun humans in both short or long distances. A few of them are horses, dogs, antelope, impala, gazelles, cheetah, plus a number of other African species. Rabbits, coyotes, bears (for a short distance). Even a clumsy old cow can outrun a human.

We own a few buffalo. One day an old bull walked up to a Texas gate and paused at the edge of the gate. He haunched up and jumped across the gate. His back feet cleared the gate with ease. The gate is eight feet wide. If he had been running before he jumped, he probably could have jumped twelve feet. He weighs about seventeen hundred pounds.

So much for humans winning any gold medals in those events.

I suppose with time as we evolve we might give the animals some competition, but that won't happen for at least another three and a half million years.

I have never seen a mountain goat or sheep use ropes for climbing a mountain, have you? Who would you bet on climbing to the top of a mountain the fastest? A skilled human mountain climber with all the right equipment or a mountain goat or sheep?

Yes! Animals have it all over us when it comes to most athletic events, except for team sports. In team sports, some humans really get rough. I have never seen an animal hit someone on the head with a hockey stick or choke an opponent in a wrestling match. If we wish to teach our descendants some manners, we had better clean up our own act first.

I hope you did not get bored or disgusted with what I just wrote. My point is that reverse evolution is just as plausible as humans evolving from animals. Neither one of them is true. I challenge you to carefully read the Bible, then make your own decision. The whole evolutionary theory holds no water.

Chapter Twenty-Nine

FISH

The most universal food in the world is fish, as well as some other creatures of the sea such as lobster, crab, oysters, shrimp, eel and a few others.

Every country, tribe and culture eats fish. There are salt water and fresh water fish.

Over half the world's countries, including a number of island nations, have access to an ocean and the fish that it yields. These countries represent approximately eighty-five percent of the world's population. Those countries that are landlocked usually have lakes and rivers where various types of fresh water fish exist.

Fish come in all sizes, from large sturgeon and sharks to tiny goldfish and guppies. The most common sizes are one to three pounds for trout. Many of the other edible fish weigh from three to fifteen pounds.

Fish are fierce predators. The larger ones eat the smaller ones. One day an angler caught a large fish. When he opened it up he found a mid-sized fish inside. When he cut that fish open there was another fish inside of it. He opened that fish and it had a wee small fish in its belly. He had hooked four fish at once. Each fish had swallowed a smaller fish. Sound like a fish story? The man claimed it was true. That is the law of the jungle and the oceans. The strongest prevails. It is also referred to as the balance of nature or survival of the fittest.

Several bird species also prey on fish. They are their main source of food. A number of animals have an almost exclusive fish diet, such as seals, walruses, otters, polar bears, black and grizzly bears and a few others.

One of the most feared fish is the piranha. They are found in the Amazon River and a few other rivers in South America. They are from twelve to fifteen inches long. They travel in groups, usually called schools. They have teeth as sharp as razor blades. When they attack an animal in the water they reduce it to a skeleton in a matter of minutes. There are countless stories of people swimming or falling out of a boat and being devoured by these fierce predators in short order. When floating down the Amazon in a boat or canoe it is a good idea to keep your hands out of the water and do not dangle your legs in the water. If you do, you might be minus a few fingers or toes. Another feared fish is the barracuda. Often when a person is considered ruthless, who cares little for other people, they are compared to a barracuda. People who cheat other people on loan interest or other shady deals are called loan sharks. Every year a number of people are either killed or maimed by a shark.

The oceans hold hundreds of different species of fish and sea creatures. A large portion of them are dangerous if you come in direct contact with them. But we humans are the worst predators of all. There are several ways in which we catch fish. In oceans, the most common method is a long net stretched in a certain fashion. The net is hauled in with a catch of fish. These are commercial fishermen and they exist in every country of the world. Over the years there have been major disputes and skirmishes between nations about fishing rights off the coastal areas of countries. Canada has had disagreements about fishing off its coastal waters with the United States, France, Spain and Japan. In the end, those disputes were settled, not always to the fishermen's satisfaction. In international waters, it's a free-for-all. Another method of fishing in both oceans and lakes is trawling. Nets are also used on big lakes. Much of the fishing in lakes and rivers is the line and hook method. Sport fishermen like fly-fishing. This takes quite a bit of skill. Not everyone can cast those lines with enough expertise to catch a fish.

In the northern regions of the world a lot of ice fishing is done. They chop a hole in the ice, then lower in the line with bait on it. On some lakes a huge amount of fish are caught through the ice. The most common fish caught that way are whitefish and pike.

The image that sticks most in our mind is of a young boy sitting on a creek bank with a fishing rod and line dangling in the water hoping to make a catch. Often his dog is sitting nearby.

An avid fisherman means just that. For most of his (or her) life he remains an ardent fisherman. These people absolutely live for fishing trips, either to some northern lakes or mountain streams. A number of them take up deep sea fishing, usually for salmon or sturgeon.

One of the sticky issues these days is the fishing rights of Natives. They are allowed to fish anywhere at any time of the year. This is supposed to be for their own consumption. What is happening is quite a different story. They now often fish commercially. This is just not right. Other commercial fisherman have to obey all the rules, as to when and where they can fish.

A good example of this kind of activity took place at Burnt Church, New Brunswick. The MicMac Indians claimed they had a right to commercially catch lobster any time. The Federal Fisheries agents pulled several thousands of their lobster traps from the water. This caused a major confrontation. The other commercial fishermen in that area were really miffed and angry at the Natives for cleaning out a large percentage of the lobster before the season opened for them to catch lobster.

I know the answer to the problem. Throw the season open all year round for all fishermen, Native or otherwise. That would settle the dispute once and for all. Within two years there would be no lobster left. At that point we would have to import all our lobster from the United States and a few other countries where they catch commercial lobster. We import most of our fruit and vegetables now (at least in winter). We may as well add lobster to the list.

Back to fish. Today, there are a number of fish farms and hatcheries that help to replenish dwindling fish stocks. I think that fish will be available into the foreseeable future at a price. All through history fish has been part of the menu for rich and poor people. In the future it may be so expensive that only rich folks will be able to afford fish. Fish eggs or caviar has been a rich person's fare for centuries. Alaska King crab has also become pricey in the past few years. Hopefully normal fish won't follow suit.

A cattleman friend of mine, Jack Daines, said to me that the French actress Brigette Bardot is a real friend to cattle people. I said, "Oh, how is that?"

"Well," he said, "She spearheaded the drive against seal hunting in Newfoundland, which has been drastically curtailed. Since then the seal population has dramatically increased. Those seals have eaten most of the fish, so we can sell more beef." As some of you know, I like beef, but I also like fish. I do not want a steady diet of fish. It is nice to eat about once a week. There is a theory and maybe theory is all it is, that fish is brain food. If that is the case, then most of us should eat it at least three times a week.

People also keep fish as pets. Maybe the reason is a fish has very little emotion but lots of action. People admire this and get attached to them. But it's a cinch a fish doesn't get attached to a person.

Fish are kept in large and small aquariums where the fish cavort around. They often give them names, some examples may be: Charlie, Speedy, Tiny, Slowpoke, Spot, Tempest, Easy Bait, Pretty Boy, Lucky, Junior (my sister-in-law Leona's fish). You can't teach a fish any tricks. A dolphin is intelligent and does perform for people. However they are mammals, not fish. There is a smaller version of a dolphin that is a fish.

There are many fish stories which, of course, means the validity of the story is questionable. Often those stories are about the big one that got hooked and then got away. One of the biggest fish stories is in the Bible. This happened when Jonah disobeyed God. In Jonah, Chapter 1, verse 17, we read: *Now the Lord had prepared a great fish to swallow up Jonah. And Jonah was in the belly of the fish three days and three nights.*

While in the fish, Jonah repented his sins. It says in Chapter 2, verse 10: *And the Lord spake unto the fish and it vomited Jonah upon dry land."*

This is quite a story. When the Lord said He prepared a fish, He was not joking. He must have turned off its digestive juices or Jonah would have been turned into dung. The other amazing thing is how did Jonah breathe? God must have put Jonah's lungs on hold for three days. With God, all things are possible.

Ten countries in the world catch approximately seventy percent of all the fish that are caught each year. They are Japan, which has the biggest catch by far, China, the United States, Russia, Peru, Norway, Canada, Spain, the United Kingdom and India. This is according to figures released by the United Nations.

CHAPTER THIRTY

WISE QUOTES

Employ your time in improving yourself by other men's writings, so you shall come easily by what others have laboured hard for. -Socrates

Whenever I go into a large bookstore or library, I am always amazed by the number of books and articles that have been written. Some are pretty trashy. But the large majority of them are well written on thousands of different subjects. When Socrates was alive the amount of published material was small. Even in those days, what people read could change their lives. Many people could not read or write. It took until the 20th Century for reading to become almost universal – at least in the western world and in some eastern cultures as well. The explosion of knowledge in the past one hundred years can be attributed to people's ability to read what others have written. Much of that wisdom is written from a philosophical aspect and came from philosophers of the Middle Ages.

On the following pages a number of wise sayings and quotes will appear. There are some things we quote almost every day of our life yet we have no idea who said or wrote them - author unknown or anonymous (anon). Others were written hundreds of years ago, as well as in more recent times. The identity of who said or wrote them has been preserved. We see them in our newspapers, magazines, booklets and even advertisements. So I am taking the privilege of printing a few of them in this book giving credit to the writer. When I quote my family's favorite sayings, they may not have originated with them. The ones where I sign my name are the ones I have coined and, to my knowledge, I have never heard or read any of them before.

I selected the following sayings for the wisdom they contain. If we apply that wisdom to our daily life we can become better individuals.

Most people are waiting for something to happen – good or bad. It usually does. -Anon

Time is precious. It is the only non-renewable resource we have. Once gone, you cannot get it back. -Anon

A sharp tongue is like a sharp knife. Once the cut is made, it is hard to repair the damage. -Anon

It is a curious fact that of all the illusions that beset mankind, none is quite so curious as that tendency to suppose that we are mentally and morally superior to those who differ from us in opinion. -Anon

No opportunity is ever lost – someone else picks up the ones you miss. -Anon

Laugh and the world laughs with you. Cry and you cry alone. -Anon

Building boys is better than mending men. -Anon

The man who does not read good books has no advantage over the man who can't read them. -Mark Twain

Kindness is a language which the deaf man can hear and the blind man can read. -Mark Twain

Character is like a tree and reputation like its shadow. The shadow is what we think of. The tree is the real thing. -Abraham Lincoln

Success is to be measured not so much by the position one has reached in life, as by the obstacles which we have overcome while trying to succeed. -Booker T. Washington

Great minds have purposes. Others have wishes. Little minds are tamed and subdued by misfortune. But great minds rise above them. -Washington Irving

Real joy comes not from ease or riches or from the praise of men, but from doing something worthwhile. -Wilfred T. Grenfell

Adapt the pace of nature: her secret is patience. -Ralph Waldo Emerson

Patience is a virtue. -Anon

The poor have little: beggars none. The rich too much: Enough not one. -Benjamin Franklin

The great pleasure in life is doing what people say you cannot do. -Walter Bagenot

I have experienced that pleasure myself.

You will find as you look back upon your life, that moments that stand out are moments when you have done things for others. -Henry Drummond

The woman who helps her neighbor does herself a good turn. -Brendon Francis

Cheerfulness means a contented spirit! A pure heart, a kind and loving disposition. It means humility and charity. A generous appreciation for others, and a modest opinion of self. -William Makepeace Thackery

Every man must live with the man he makes of himself. -James M. Lawson

The first virtue of all great men is that they are sincere. -Anatole France

Everybody loves a fat man except when he sits in front of you in a theatre or church. -Anon

A cluttered desk, a cluttered mind. -A.J.E. Child

His desk was always in perfect order. I used to jokingly counter that with an empty desk, an empty mind. It didn't apply to him. He had a very good mind.

A stranger is a friend we have not met yet. -Will Rogers

Teenagers, if you are tired of being hassled by unreasonable parents, now is the time for action – leave home and pay your own way while you still know everything. -Anon

Actions, not words, are the true characteristic mark of the attachment of friends. -George Washington

A friend is a present you give yourself. -Robert Louis Stevenson

Lazy people often kill themselves working. They try to do everything at once to get it over with. -My mother

The morning hour has gold in its mouth. The evening has lead in the rear end. -My mother She believed in getting up early in the morning to get your work done. -L.F.

One day a guest, three days a pest. -My mother

Too soon old, too late smart. -My dad

Old age does not come with ease. -My dad

When my dad misplaced or lost his keys, glasses, or whatever, he would reach his hand to his bum and say, "I am sure glad it's fastened to my body or I might lose it too."

Another one of my mother's sayings was, *Never put off 'til tomorrow what you can do today.* Good advice.

Self praise stinks. -My mother Most people, including me, could benefit from that advice.

Empty vessels make the most noise. -My wife, Edna

It's a great life if you don't weaken. -Edna

Still waters run deep. -Edna

A stitch in time saves nine. -Edna

Cows may be dumb, but they are good company on a remote ranch. -Leonard Friesen

Parents must be good teachers. When their sons and daughters reach sixteen years they know much more than their parents do. -Anon

If you are stuck on yourself, no one sticks with you. -Anon

When the wisdom of old people is ignored, all of society loses precious knowledge. -Leonard Friesen

A woman's ways will forever be a mystery to man. -Leonard Friesen We have been married for fifty-four years and my wife is still a bit of a mystery to me.

Choices we make always have consequences, good or bad. -Leonard Friesen

Labour saving devices save a lot of time. The question is, why are we busier than before? -Leonard Friesen

Excess alcohol consumption by people is the same as gopher poison to gophers. The difference is a gopher dies a little faster. -Leonard Friesen

A picture is like a time capsule. When you look at a photograph fifty, sixty or one hundred years old, your mind goes back to that era. It is almost as though you are there at that moment. -Leonard Friesen

Three elements that man cannot live without are air, water and fire. But all three are deadly when out of control. -Leonard Friesen

When you have a job to be done, get a busy person to do it. -Anon

You never miss money until you have none. -Anon

Honesty never costs, it always pays. -Anon

Without ambitious, greedy, hard working people, the developed countries of the world would still be backwater, third world countries. -Leonard Friesen

When I was in either grade four or five, our teacher told the class to make up an original four-line poem. She gave us ten minutes to come up with our composition. I was sitting by a window where I could see the mid-morning sun. As I contemplated the wonders of nature, these words came to me:

The sun shines in the day time
The moon and stars at night
I shine all the time
But I don't produce a light

If memory serves me correctly, she gave me the best mark in the class for that little piece of prose. Unfortunately, I never followed up on writing poetry, although I enjoy good poetry. Over the years, I have composed little jingles for my wife, usually when I was going away some place. Here are a few examples:

When night falls and the sky is black
Just remember in a few days I will be back.
So cheer up; in the morning the sky will be blue
When I come home, we will kiss and I will say how much I love you.
A wife like you is worth more than silver or gold
These days, there are not many wives as faithful as you, or so I am told.
You are not only a wife but a mother to boot
This is worth more than all this world's loot.

The above poems are amateurish, but those little things, among others, have kept our marriage going for fifty-four years. Here is one that is not original with me but is a little ditty that I thought applied to my wife.

Roses are red, violets are blue
In this whole world there is no one quite like you.

When I was going to a small country school in the 1930s, every student had a personal autograph book. Just the other day I found one of these old books in a drawer with some other old papers. I thought it might be interesting to share a few of the autographs written by my friends who were between twelve to fourteen years of age. These were written in 1939.

Dear Leonard:

When you get married
And you get cross
Pick up a broom
And say you are the boss

Your friend, Archie

Dear Leonard:

Love is like an onion
You take it with delight
But after it is gone
You wonder whatever made you bite

Your friend, Effie

Dear Leonard:

Love many
Kiss few
If you will love girls
Girls will love you

Your friend, David

Dear Leonard:

When you stand beside a tub
Think of me before you rub

With love, Victor

Dear Leonard:

The higher the mountain
The lighter the breeze
The younger the couple
The tighter they squeeze

Your friend, Violet

Here are a few more, written by my sisters:

Dear brother Leonard:

Let your life be like a snowflake: leave a mark but not a stain.

Sister Cathryne (twenty-nine years of age)

Dear Leonard:

True worth is in being, not in seeming. In doing each day that goes by some little good, not in dreaming of great things to do by and by.

For whatever men say in their blindness and in spite of the fancies of youth, there is nothing so kingly as kindness and nothing so royal as truth.

Your sister Susie (17 years of age)

I have another sister, Helen, who also wrote in my autograph book. But it must have been in another book and I can't find it. Sorry, Helen.

Here are a few wise sayings by Adrian Rogers:

It is better to be divided in truth than united by error.

It is better to speak the truth that hurts, then heals, than falsehoods that comfort, then kills.

It is better to be hated for telling the truth than to be loved for telling a lie.

It is better to stand alone with the truth than to be wrong with the multitudes.

It is better ultimately to succeed with the truth, than to temporarily with a lie.

Never approach a bull from the front.

Never approach a mule from the rear.

Never approach a sidewinder from the side.

And never approach a fool from any direction. -Bryn Thiessen

To end this chapter I want to share something that Anne Van Wagner Young wrote many years ago.

180

Footprints in the Sand

One night a man had a dream. He dreamed he was walking along the beach with the Lord. Across the sky flashed scenes from his life. He noticed two sets of footprints in the sand. One belonging to him, the other to the Lord. When the last scene of his life flashed before him, he looked back at the footprints in the sand. He noticed that many times along the path there was only one set of prints.

He recalled that it happened at the very lowest and saddest times in his life. He questioned, "Lord, you said that once I decided to follow you, you'd walk with me all the way. Then why, during the most troublesome times when I needed you most, would you leave me?"

The Lord replied, "My precious, precious child. I love you and would never, never leave you. During your times of trials and suffering, when you see only one set of footprints, it was then that I carried you."

We all leave footprints for our children and grandchildren to follow. Maybe when there is only one set of footprints, He is carrying all of us!

CHAPTER THIRTY-ONE

THE GREEN-EYED MONSTER

Jealousy is alive and well; it manifests itself early in life. It is sometimes referred to as envy. Call it what you will, it is real.

The Bible has countless stories about jealous people. Cain was jealous of Abel so he killed him. Joseph's brothers were jealous of him. They sold him to the Egyptians where he became a slave. That little ploy backfired. Joseph started out as a slave. Years later he became the second most powerful person in Egypt next to Pharaoh.

Saul was jealous of David so he attempted to kill him. There are dozens more stories about jealous people in the scriptures.

People sometimes equate jealousy with greed. I disagree. Greedy people often create jobs for other people. They achieve wealth for themselves as well as for those who work for them. Most greedy people have a lot of self-confidence. They are aggressive in their business dealings and, believe it or not, are basically honest.

As for jealousy, I see absolutely no good ever come from jealous people. They have a tendency to slander those people they are jealous of. Jealousy often afflicts people with low self-esteem. They always think the next person got all the breaks.

Jealousy let run amok turns into hatred. It is very unhealthy physically, mentally, and spiritually. It eats away at the insides of a person. The old adage applies: It's not what you eat, but what's eating you.

There are several areas where the Green-eyed Monster manifests itself.

Let's look at a few.

As a child, jealousy usually comes from someone having a better toy or bicycle than one does. As teenagers, it often is clothes (especially girls). It is also common for plainer looking girls to be jealous of girls that are considered pretty. (Often the plainer looking girls become better wives than the pretty ones.)

In some high schools, it is considered cool to hang out with other students who have a somewhat lower IQ. They band together to put down the students that are good scholars. The less gifted hang titles like Nerds on them. What it amounts to is outright jealousy.

As we become adults, most of us deny that we are jealous of our fellow man. This is not the case. I pride myself that I am not jealous. Generally speaking, I am not a jealous person. However, every once in a while, I have a slight twinge of jealousy. Usually I get over it when I think of what I have often told people. What I said to them was, "There is not a jealous bone in my body." At that point, I decide to live up to that principle. I actually enjoy talking to successful people.

Many a jealous spouse has taken the life of their partner in a fit of jealous rage. The newspapers, radio, and TV report these kinds of murders on a daily basis somewhere in the world. The results are devastating. One partner dead (sometimes both when they turn the gun on themselves), the other partner in jail for a long stretch. For women it is usually not very long. I know of several cases where a woman who killed her husband or lover only got a few years. I also know of a few cases where a man only got a few years. Whether a long or short jail terms, their lives are wrecked.

Another group of people who are subject to a lot of jealousy are siblings. Often it is over an estate after the parents have passed away. We all know of families where this has happened. I personally am aware of at least twenty or thirty such situations in my lifetime. Often those brothers and sisters do not speak to each other for the rest of their lives. How sad.

Many of us know the story in the Bible about the prodigal son. He got his inheritance when the father was still alive. He left home to a far away land. There he spent all his money on fast living with the "wine, women, and song" routine. When he was flat broke, he returned to his father's house. His father welcomed him with open arms. He put on a feast to celebrate the son's homecoming. There was one person there who did not appreciate all that activity one bit. That was the prodigal son's older brother. He had stayed home and worked all those years with his father. The father reassured his oldest son that "what I have is also yours. We thought your brother was dead, but he is alive, so we are celebrating his return." For the complete story read the gospel of Luke, chapter 15.

The world is full of prodigal sons and daughters. In nearly every case, when they return home their parents welcome them. Sometimes the parents are not as fair as the father was in the Biblical story about the prodigal son.

I know of one case where a son, who was "the apple of his mother's eye", left home for a number of years. He kept in touch. When he finally returned home, he inherited the ranch while his siblings got very little (the father had passed away).

Another area where jealousy flourishes is in the business community. When someone in a certain line of business becomes very successful, his competitors often make snide remarks such as, he cuts corners. In other words, he or she is dishonest, which usually is not true. Or, they may say, he or she charges a lot of money for inferior goods or services. No wonder they make a lot of money. In some cases the competitors say their competition works the system. In other words, they have connections to government funds, or some other cheap source of funds. Whatever they say, it all boils down to jealousy.

Often people with lesser ability become very jealous of people who have ability. Be it in sport, academics, business, or any other area of life. It is almost as though they think that putting their fellow men down will build them up. The fact is the opposite is true. Praising other people for a job well done can be far more rewarding than being jealous of them and trying to put them down.

I said earlier that I am not the jealous type. I must confess, in one instance in my life, I had a certain amount of jealousy and dislike for a certain individual. I thought he was very stuck on himself, and had made most of his money from his father's wealth. It so happened that he and I ended up on the same board of directors. After I got to know him better, I discovered that I had completely misjudged him. His aloofness was actually shyness. He was an OK guy. What that taught me was, never be jealous or prejudge someone that you really do not know. For that matter, do not judge anybody. Just keep your own affairs in order.

There is a lot of jealousy in our political system. Often when people wish to be elected to office, they resent their opponents to the point where they "bad-mouth" them beyond reason. Often, the person they are "bad-mouthing" has a lot more ability than they do. Jealousy clouds their thinking. If the more intelligent opponents have one weak spot or fault, the opposition hammers away at it. This ploy is often successful. This can result in the jealous, slightly less intelligent individual being elected as a Member of Parliament in Canada or to the United States Congress in the United States. It puzzles me how the public can be hoodwinked into voting for people like that.

Winston Churchill once said that democracy is a very poor form of government, but is still the best we have discovered this far.

If you happen to be a person who has a problem with the Green-Eyed Monster, get rid of him. He is like a monkey on your back. I guarantee, if you manage to eliminate him from your life, you will be a much happier person.

CHAPTER THIRTY-TWO

OUR FIVE SENSES

We all know what our five senses are. Let us take a close look at how they impact each one of our lives. I will list them, not in order of importance but alphabetically: Hearing, sight, smell, taste, touch.

Animals have those exact same five senses. So what sets us apart from animals? Humans have another five senses - at least that is my view. Here they are:

- **Awareness** of a higher power (God)
- **Awareness** of our mortality (we are all destined to die)
- **Conscience** is the biggest difference between animals and us.

One day when we were gone, the door to the canary cage came open. Our canary, Fred, flew out. Guess what? Our pet cat, Petey, had himself a canary lunch. When we came home all that was left of the canary were a few feathers. The cat had eaten the whole bird, including the beak and feet. This cat is well looked after. My wife makes sure Petey has lots of cat food and water available at all times. I suppose he wanted a change of diet. A cat is a cat. Their instinct is to hunt. What we found interesting is that Petey did not appear to have one ounce of remorse for what he had done. His conscience did not bother him. He walked around as nonchalantly as though nothing had happened.

- **Love**
- **Emotion**

Some of you folks will not agree with those last two senses, love and emotion. Some people say animals do possess them. They do to some extent, but in a different way. In animals, love is actually instinct to protect their young and to get along with their fellow species. Animals do have memory, but not in the comprehensive way we humans do. Elephants have a long memory, so do many others. That is why we can train dogs, horses and other animals to do certain things. However, there are other areas where their memory is short. For instance, when you wean a calf from its mother, both mother and calf will bawl for four or five days. But within ten days they have forgotten about each other. After two months that bond is completely wiped out. How about when a bull, a stallion, a dog or most other animals mate with the female. They forget all about it. When the babies are born the male could not care less, except in a few animals that mate for life. That's enough about human/animal comparisons.

Back to our five basic senses. Hearing has a major impact on our life. It helps us communicate with other people. It helps us enjoy music and the sounds of nature such as birds singing, coyotes howling, the lonesome hoot of an owl, the rush of a waterfall, even the thunder in a lightning storm, and hundreds of other sounds. Our hearing can also warn us of impending danger.

A large portion of people are hearing impaired. I know quite a few of them. I admire them for the way they cope with their handicap. Hearing aids are of great help, although in some severe cases they do not help. There are thousands of people who have lived useful, fulfilled lives with no hearing whatsoever. They communicate through sign language. As we get older hearing often diminishes. Mine is still good and my wife's is even better. She can literally hear a pin drop ten feet away. Well that may be a little exaggeration.

In my opinion, sight is the most treasured of the five senses. Shortly after birth, our eyes open to a wonderful magic world. As young people and adults, we begin to appreciate what a large world we live in. Beauty is in the eye of the beholder. When we fall in love, there is nobody as wonderful or beautiful in our eyes than our beloved one. Besides all the beauty of nature, eyesight has some practical everyday uses such as reading, writing, driving a vehicle, walking and a hundred other daily rituals.

It is a fact in our society that we have a number of people with poor eyesight. These days it can be corrected with the right kind of glasses, and also with laser and other surgical procedures. In spite of this, there are some people who are blind. Some are born that way. Others lose their sight through a disease or an accident. Sometimes that disease is diabetes. I thank God for my good eyesight.

Smell, in my opinion, is not quite as important as hearing and sight. Nevertheless, it is nice to have a keen sense of smell. I read not too long ago that our mind can recall a smell as well, if not better, than what we hear or see.

I can remember many types of smells from my childhood. I can vividly recall what our kitchen smelled like when my mother was cooking some of my favorite foods, such as fresh baked bread and buns, or roast beef, or the turkey at Christmas. I can also recall what our garden smelled like, especially the flowers. Roses were my favorite. I also remember what new mown hay smelled like.

There are hundreds of other smells, some good, some bad. Now that I am older every one of those smells are still with me. The sense of smell is also a safety feature, such as smelling deadly gas leaks before it does you in. Even with food it is wise to smell it if it is spoiled or rancid.

We spend a fortune on lotions, perfumes and other cosmetics to ensure that we smell nice, and what about bad breath? In my lifetime, I have met several people who almost knock you over with their bad breath. In most cases I don't think the person realizes how offensive their breath is. We always keep a bottle or two of mouthwash around.

I remember the exact smell of the perfume my wife used on our very first date fifty-five years ago. I thought it was the most heavenly smell that I had ever experienced. It was the smell of excitement.

My mother's smell when I sat on her knee as a child was a smell of fragrance, security and safety.

One of the most revolting smells is that of dead animals in the heat of summer after they have been dead for several days. I am told an even worse odour is that of a dead person, when found in a car after a week or so. I have never experienced that smell. I often marvel how doctors and other officials can perform an autopsy on a body like that. That is not a good note on which to leave the topic of smell. My parting suggestion is, do not forget to smell the roses, our time is short.

What can I say about taste? We all enjoy the sense of taste. Without taste it would be a pretty bland world. Our taste buds develop early. As infants we enjoy milk. As a young child we soon let mother know what we do not like by spitting out food that does not appeal to us. Eating, like I mention in the chapter about food and restaurants, is one of the great social pleasures of life. We need a balanced diet every day of our life, so we may as well enjoy it. A large part of our working life is spent working to provide food for ourselves and our family. In third world countries it can account for as much as eighty percent of their income. In North America it is fifteen to twenty percent, depending on whose statistics you believe. Next time you dine savour your food. Millions of people have little food to savour.

The last sense I will write about is touch. The sense of touch can bring more pleasure or pain than any other sense. Just what is touch? It is the nerves in your body that can feel the lightest contact with another body or object. Some people are very sensitive to touch. Others seem to have very little sense of touch.

Some people resent being touched by another person. Others enjoy the physical contact. These likes and dislikes are often the result of a person's childhood. One experience of bad touching can affect a person for life.

By nature I am a toucher, but I have trained myself not to touch people, especially females. These days that can be a dangerous game. Even the most innocent touch could lead to a sexual harassment suit. Most societies in the world express their like for a person by giving them a hug, usually as a greeting or a farewell. I think it is also a good idea to give your kids a hug every day.

Then we have male/female touching. As teenagers there is nothing like touching the person you love, or think you love. Even holding hands can send shivers up your spine. Kissing can actually make you dizzy. The grand finale of touching, of course, is the foreplay before intercourse. This is a very sacred act and should only take place after marriage. However, these days and even in the past, people broke God's rule and had sex before marriage. I am not sitting in judgment on your social actions. Many people have broken that rule, then later married and raised good families.

Touching can also mean pain. If we get a sliver it hurts us so we take action to remove it. The fear of pain by forceful touching such as a kick by a horse helps us to avoid dangerous situations. Spanking, which is outdated by now, warns us to behave ourselves or suffer the consequences of a forceful touch by a stick, a belt or a hand on our posterior.

I probably did not write anything about the five senses that you did not know. Every once in a while it is good to stop and reflect on how fortunate we are to have all five senses and the part they play in our daily lives.

CHAPTER THIRTY-THREE

RAILROADS AND TRAINS

There are many things and practices that we take for granted today. Trains fall into that category. They have been around for about one hundred and seventy years. For almost two centuries before that they used small rail cars in mines pulled by horses (ponies would be more correct). James Watt, a Scotsman living in England, invented the steam engine in 1769. He patented a better version in 1781. It only stood to reason that steam locomotion could be used to pull railroad cars on steel tracks above ground.

Railroad construction was very slow. In fact, it remained in an experimental stage for about forty years. The first public rail line was built in England in 1825. The first rail line in the United States was in New York State in 1830. There was a steady increase in rail transportation after that, with a number of railway companies formed. By the time the civil war took place, the United States had over thirty thousand miles of rail and track.

After the civil war, things really took off. One of the regions where thousands of miles of track were built was in the American West. Several lines were built through the mountains to the West Coast.

This replaced stagecoaches for long distance travel. The stagecoach survived another twenty or thirty years for shorter trips where there were no railroads.

In Canada we followed a similar pattern. There were some railroads in eastern Canada in the 1840s, 1850s, and 1860s. It wasn't until the late 1870s and early 1880s that the westward expansion began. The CPR rail line reached Calgary, Alberta, in 1881- the year my father was born. Building a railroad through the Rocky Mountains to the West Coast was a monumental task. There are a number of tunnels between Banff, Alberta, and the Fraser Valley of the West Coast. The Spiral Tunnel at Field is incredible. It spirals through several mountains. If you are riding on a car at the back of the train you can actually see the locomotives (there are usually three) going the other direction, since each car is linked to the one ahead of it. It is like a snake.

I have been on that train several times, including when my wife and I went to the West Coast on our honeymoon in 1946. Our honeymoon lasted four months. By today's standards a strange thing happened on that trip - my wife became pregnant. Nine months later our first son Leland was born. These days when people marry, the first baby is often on the way or already born. On the other hand, many couples do not have their first child until five or ten years later. In the old days, nine months to a year was the rule.

Back to the railroad and trains. A number of folks were and still are railroad buffs.

The old steam engine whistle was something that most people enjoyed. I sure did. The engineer pulled the whistle cord at every crossing, usually several times. In spite of this, several thousand people worldwide have been killed at railroad crossings.

In 1941, my Uncle Nick Friesen was killed at a level crossing a few miles east of Walbeck, Saskatchewan. Some years later my cousin Mary and her husband Jake Rempel were killed at a crossing about two miles west of where my uncle was killed. Several other people I knew were also killed at railroad crossings.

Both my son Leland and I have had close calls at railroad crossings in the United States. His happened in Montana. Leland and my nephew Neil Friesen went to Montana to pick up a horse. On their way back they approached a railroad track lying in a valley. The road was quite icy. It was at dusk. Suddenly they noticed a train coming full speed. Leland slammed on the brakes, the truck and trailer slid. When they finally came to a stop the front of the truck was only a few feet from the tracks at the precise moment the train thundered by. They were pretty shaken up, but alive. They got the horse home safe and sound.

My little brush with a train took place in Kansas. I was on my way home from our ranch in Colorado. About two miles south of

Whithams feedlot there is a level crossing. I was driving along in deep thought when suddenly I heard the train whistle. I glanced to my left and there was this train coming full throttle. I had no time to stop because I was only about one hundred feet from the crossing. The train appeared to be about the same distance away. I was driving fairly fast. I had no choice but to beat the train so I tramped on the gas. That old Ford truck shot over those tracks with only a few feet to spare. I thought for sure the train would clip the rear end of the truck. It was a close call but, like Leland and Neil, I survived.

I know you folks reading this can tell similar stories about close calls by either yourselves or people you know.

Every year, somewhere in the world, major train wrecks take place. India is notorious for train wrecks. They average three hundred wrecks a year. Some are minor wrecks. Their trains are usually crowded.

People ride on the roof of railway cars. When a wreck occurs, it often kills and maims hundreds of people. India also has one of the largest networks of railroads in the world. This is a legacy the British left. It allows millions of people to have relatively cheap transportation.

Another interesting railway is in Russia. Every day the Trans Siberia Express train leaves for Vladivastok - fifty-seven hundred and eighty-seven miles away from Moscow. It takes nine days to make that journey. I have often thought I would like to take that rain ride, but I guess I never will. I have read several stories about that trip. The train passes through some of the most hostile environment in the world. There are some stretches of decent farmland, also some heavy forests. Six thousand miles covers a lot of terrain. That is a quarter of the way around the world. It passes through seven time zones.

In 1925, the first diesel locomotive made its appearance. This was about one hundred years after the first steam locomotive came on the scene. It was slow to catch on. By 1945 there were quite a few diesels but it was not until 1953 that about half of the locomotives were powered by diesel. By 1965, the changeover was almost complete except for a few remote areas of the world. There were also some steam locomotives for tourists, which there still are today.

Today, there are highspeed trains in several parts of the world, including Japan and Western Europe. Some trains can reach speeds up to two hundred miles per hour.

When we were in Japan we took a ride on one of the bullet trains. We rode from Tokyo to Osaka. On this train they said we were travelling one hundred and fifty miles per hour. The landscape as we gazed out the window was just a blur.

The train was completely computerized. The control panel was in Tokyo. They had an engineer sitting in the driver's seat. Someone told us he had absolutely no control - he was only there to make the passengers feel more at ease.

An interesting aspect of that ride was how the people were boarded. There was a huge mob getting on. Believe it or not, the fact was they had "people pushers". Their job was to get everyone on board in a specific time frame. This sometimes meant they had to push the last passengers on before the doors closed. Otherwise, someone may have been caught in the door. The people pushers had to make sure the door closed within seconds of the allotted time.

For a hundred years railroads moved freight and people. There were freight trains and passenger trains. The passenger trains travelled at higher speeds. Freight trains may pull up to one hundred and twenty cars which slows them down.

These days in North America the percentage of people travelling by train is small. In the United States, they have a passenger service, usually only a few cars, called Amtrak. In Canada, the passenger train service is called Via Rail. In other parts of the world, there are still a lot of passenger trains. Many of these countries do not have the highway networks like we do in North America. Air travel is much too expensive for the people in less developed countries.

A large part of the romance of the cattle industry in the early west involved railroads. In those days, there were only a few rail lines. After a while, a number of branch lines were built. This meant that nearly every small town had train service. The railroad station was usually in the center of town. People congregated there to meet people who came off those trains. Or they themselves boarded the train for a trip somewhere. The station agent also was the telegraph person. Many telegrams were dispatched from there on a daily basis. Not quite as handy as fax machines today.

Usually the stockyards for shipping livestock (mostly cattle) was located a short distance from town.

Before Texas had railroads that connected them to larger Midwest and eastern United States urban areas, the cattle were trailed to Kansas where they had large stockyards in towns like Abilene, Hays, Dodge City, Newton, and other locations. Here the cattle were loaded into stock cars.

The word cowpuncher (cowboy) had its origin from cowboys with sticks poking the cattle to make them walk up the chute into the boxcar. Those cattle cars had slats, which circulated the air, especially on hot days.

From 1870 (in Canada, 1881) to about 1980, millions of cattle, sheep and hogs were shipped by rail. Our outfit shipped several hundred thousand cattle by rail in a fifteen-year period. The packing plants and people like Red Wheatcroft shipped even more. After 1980, cattle trucks pretty well took over the transport of all livestock.

The railway certainly did a good job moving stock for over one hundred years. I have great nostalgia for those days. Sometimes between the packing plants and people at the stockyards, whole trainloads of cattle were loaded out in one day. Occasionally, two train loads.

The steam locomotives had cow catchers in the front of the engine. They were designed to scoop up any stray cow, horse, buffalo, or other animal that happened to stand on the tracks or cross them. The cowcatcher consisted of a curved round of sturdy tines about two feet above the tracks. Their purpose was twofold. Number one, they prevented a lot of damage to the engine, and secondly and more important, they kept whatever it was the train hit from going underneath the train, which could cause a derailment. It was not only animals that got caught up in it from time to time. It was also vehicles, cars, trucks, and horse drawn wagons and sleighs. I remember once in the small town of Herbert, Saskatchewan, where a drayman got hit by a train. He was driving with a sleigh. Sometimes when there was a heavy load on the sleigh, the sleigh got stuck on the tracks. The steel runners on the sleigh grinding on the steel railroad tracks caused this. He got stuck just at the moment a train came barrelling down on him. The horses were already over the tracks, but the back runners were still on the track. At the very last second the driver leapt from the sleigh in the direction that the train was coming from, just missing the engine as he rolled into the ditch beside the tracks. On impact, the cowcatcher gathered up the sleigh, dragging the horses to their death. They were still firmly attached with the heavy harness. The man was not hurt, only in shock and badly shaken up. No deliveries that day.

Our neighbor, Chris Olsen, told me what he saw one day on the CPR mainline between Waldeck and Swift Current. There was a severe blizzard in progress that caused about thirty horses to huddle on the tracks. They were trying to find shelter in a cut where the railroad passed through a hill with high banks on either side of the tracks. Suddenly, a fast passenger train bore down on that herd of horses. It was what they called a fast express. Believe it or not, that old steam engine had a full head of steam and was travelling at ninety miles an hour, When it hit the horses, it literally made mincemeat out of them. According to Chris, there were pieces of horse meat and legs scattered for a quarter of a mile. Some parts of horses were hanging on barbwire fences. He said it was the most gruesome sight he had ever seen. Approximately half the horses were killed. A number of them were badly injured and had to be put down. Only a few escaped injury. I have read where this sort of accident happened many times in the early days in the west. Those trains would not have travelled that fast, but fast enough to kill quite a few buffalo, and some cattle and horses. Surprisingly, very few trains got derailed from those collisions thanks to the cowcatcher.

During the depression of the 1930s, thousands of men rode the freight trains free. Jobs were few and far between. This caused the men, mostly young, to hop on the freight train and head to a different part of the country looking for work. As the depression deepened, the number of those men increased until the freight trains looked like cows covered with lice. Each train had dozens of men crowded on them. I remember as a child seeing those men, standing in the doorway of empty cars, huddled on flat deck cars, even on the roofs of rail cars. Their food consisted of handouts, hence the nickname, hobos. Sometimes they would take little part time jobs for very little pay - often only a meal or two.

The railroad police made an effort to rid the trains of these men, but it was a lost cause. For every one that they chased off the train, a dozen more took their place. It was something like swatting mosquitoes in a swamp. There was an endless supply.

The police could do little but chase them off the train. There was no use arresting them. The courts and the judges would simply dismiss the charges of trespassing. There was no way the jails could have accommodated all those men. A few committed small felonies, which landed them in jail for short periods. That was not all bad. It meant free room and board.

My wife's parents lived close to the railroad tracks. She told me it was not uncommon for some of these men to come to their door looking for a bit of work and food. The majority of these tramps, hobos, bums or whatever name people hung on them were average young Canadian and American boys caught in the worst depression ever experienced in the western world. A few became professional hobos who liked that lifestyle better than working. When the Second World War came along in 1939 these young men evaporated like a morning mist. They went into the armed services and served their country well.

There is a lot more that could be written about railroads. One thing I will mention is we are moving more goods by rail today than ever before. A big part of that freight is loaded on semi-trailers minus the truck. It is called piggy backing. Sometimes, long trains only consist of flat cars loaded with trailers.

Material like grain, oil, and coal are more suited to ship by train than truck. Especially coal and grain. In Wyoming and other places those long coal trains can be seen every day. Much of that coal is hauled to West Coast seaports where it is dumped in ocean freighters for a trip to Japan.

Another thing railroads specialize in is container shipments of goods. They are unloaded with cranes into ocean liners that deliver the goods around the world.

In spite of other forms of transportation like trucks and airplanes, trains are here to stay. Their operations in the switchyards are completely computerized.

Were you aware of the fact that railroads spawned a lot of bigamy? On a train, there may be engineers, stokers, brakemen and conductors. I knew quite a few of them. Some had two abodes - one in Calgary and one at the other end of their run, usually somewhere in the interior of British Columbia. They would leave Calgary in the morning and get to their destination in late afternoon or early evening, when another person would replace them for the rest of the trip to the coast. The next day they would return to Calgary. This went on for years. It worked out to about four nights in Calgary and three nights in Revelstoke, Kamloops, or somewhere else.

Here's where the bigamy came in. A man alone in a town gets pretty lonely. They naturally meet women in restaurants, bars or other public places. Before long, they had a regular girlfriend. After several years they often married them and had children, although some just lived common-law. They told these women they were single or separated from their wife.

Meanwhile, wife number one was holding the fort in Calgary, busy raising their children. She was completely unaware of wife number two. I am sure both wives must have wondered why their husband was so tired. I guess they put it down to the CPR working him too hard. They would both have a ton of compassion for the poor fellow.

I know of several cases where this arrangement went on for over twenty years. When the case finally comes to light is when the man retires. Which wife does he choose to retire with?

Another problem arises when one wife dies, and the children from both wives are more or less grown up. The third problem arises if he happens to die. At this point, the two families meet for the first time - both mourning their wonderful husband and father. I know of one funeral where three women showed up. He was a real Romeo. He had three on a string at once.

Not all men are cheaters. A friend of ours by the name of Norman Johnstone was on a run like that. He was away about three nights a week. He was completely faithful to his wife. He was as straight as a string. He was a good Christian man. Do not get me wrong. I know of several Christian men who kicked over the traces. Norman was not one of them. He lived by the teachings of the new testament: One wife until death do us part.

Over the years railroad companies have been one of the largest employers of people. In many towns where they had switching stations, marshalling yards, or divisional points they were the community's largest employers.

CHAPTER THIRTY-FOUR

LAWS, RULES AND REGULATIONS

Without laws and rules, we would have anarchy. These days we have far too many rules. When God gave Moses the Ten Commandments, He knew that people would not obey all of them. They were given as a guide on how to live. All through history men have been obsessed with rules. Some kings ruled with an iron fist. For the least little infraction a person could be executed. Thousands of British subjects were exiled to Australia, sometimes for only small thefts or because they broke some minor law.

Thousands of people from Europe immigrated to North America to escape the rules imposed on them. Men long to be free. For many years, The New World - Canada and the United States - had relatively few laws and rules, but in the last fifty years we have almost as many rules and regulations as they do in Europe. Someone told me just recently the problem with our country is we elect politicians that make promises of enacting legislation to appease small pressure groups so Parliament or Congresses pass more laws and regulations. It would be refreshing to hear some candidate for office say, if elected, they would work hard to rescind a bunch of laws and regulations instead of enacting more. I would agree with him a hundred percent.

I mentioned the Ten Commandments in the Old Testament. In the New Testament, Jesus was outspoken against the Pharisees who totally lived by rules. They themselves had a lot of shortcomings, but on the outside, they put on quite a front about how they obeyed all the laws. Anybody that did not live up to the rules was looked down on as a second class citizen. They called them publicans and sinners. Jesus, more or less, said let's use some common sense. His stand was, we need to obey God, not man. The Pharisees refused to do any work on the Sabbath. Jesus said, if your ox falls in the well on the Sabbath, go ahead and pull him out. He also said that He came into the world to set men free, not to bind them. Since that time, two thousand years ago, many Christian churches are so full of rules that they can hardly function. We humans need some guidelines, but when traditions become laws, we are in trouble.

One reason laws are so popular with leaders, church or secular, is it gives them control. This is how the Communists managed to stay in power. They had absolute control. Dictators operate the same way, they make their own rules and you better obey them or else.

We are regulated by all kinds of goofy little laws. Fortunately, many of them do not get enforced. There just are not enough police officers to do that. We have strict building code laws, water use laws, weed control laws, hunting and fishing laws, seat belt laws, load limit laws, speed limit laws and tax laws. The above-mentioned laws have some merit, providing they are carried out with common sense. Take speed limits, for instance. On our road, there is a high school with a high fence around the playground and no development across the road from it. No students ever cross that road. Despite this, the speed limit past that school is 18.6 miles an hour, or thirty kilometres an hour. That is the standard speed limit past elementary schools in densely populated areas, which is OK. The problem? No common sense is used. The high school with no one crossing the road has the same speed limit because that is the law.

I do not smoke, nor do I think smoking is good. But, some of the laws now are kind of ridiculous. I personally think alcohol consumption does ten times more damage to society than smoking, yet very little is said about that except the, "If you drink, don't drive" slogan. I agree with that, however, beyond that, drinking is still promoted as the 'in' social thing to do.

We have seat belt laws to protect ourselves from ourselves. Sky diving, heli-skiing, mountain climbing, auto racing and bull riding are all dangerous sports. Yet, there are no laws prohibiting or restricting such activities. Besides, thousands of dollars are spent each year rescuing these kinds of people, plus the medical bills they incur. This activity, versus seat belt laws, seems a little inconsistent.

Believe it or not, I always buckle up.

Lawyers also thrive on laws. That is their business. I am always astounded to read how many people have broken serious laws, and got off because of some technicality, even it was quite evident they were criminals, all because a lawyer found a loophole in the law.

In the 1930s in the United States, there was a lot of criminal gang activity, yet often these gangsters never got prosecuted. Al Capone is a good example. He committed a multitude of crimes, including murder. Strange as it may seem, none of those charges stuck to him. What they finally nailed him with was tax evasion. I guess taxes are more important than human life.

There is no doubt in my mind that we are over regulated. The sad part is, it will get worse. It is very simple to enforce all those regulations with computers. Once you are put on a computer for breaking some small rule, it stays there indefinitely. I am not sure how long the statute of limitations apply.

I know of several instances were people were denied entrance into the United States for an infraction they committed years ago. About three years ago, there was a couple and their two children who had tickets to go to Hawaii for a two-week vacation during the Christmas holidays. When they got to the United States Customs office at the airport, the parents were cleared because they had proper identification papers. However, their two children who were a little under ten years old, did not have their birth certificates with them. Immediately the customs official became suspicious that maybe the children were being kidnapped in a custody dispute. I am sure in his heart he knew this was not the case, but like all officials, he wanted to show his authority. At that point he began to check out the parent's background. Suddenly, he came up with a gem. Seventeen years before, when the husband was fifteen years old, he had a brush with the law. He was not jailed for his offence. He was fined five hundred dollars and put on probation for a little while. That was the only time he ever ran afoul of the law. He had a good job with a perfect track record, got married, and had two children. Would you believe that the customs officer refused the family entrance into the United States. The rules say that if you have any criminal record whatsoever, you may not enter the

United States, even for a two-week holiday. Without computers, this mistake from seventeen years before would never have been discovered. Don't get me wrong, I am not in favor of mollycoddling criminals. But in this case, there was ample evidence that the young man was on the level. He was a young person when this offence took place. Meanwhile, all kinds of crooks and criminals slip into the United States every day. They know how to work the system.

Incidentally, that family did not go to Hawaii that year. Rules are rules and must be enforced whether they make sense or not.

The army is all rules. The reason is quite obvious. Without rules there is no control. In the military, that is of utmost importance. If a soldier is ordered to the front lines, even if he knows it means certain death, he obeys and may die in combat. War is a horrible thing, but because of leaders and nations lusting for power and control, other countries are forced to fight for the freedom of their own country. I am a pacifist at heart, but I know there are times when we need to stand up and fight for what is right.

In raising a family, rules come into play big time. In some homes, the rules are so stringent that when the children reach adolescence, they rebel. Every year, millions of children run away from home. On the other hand, if a home has no rules, the results are not much different.

The key is to have some flexibility in the rules. They should be set up as guidelines and administered with lots of love.

I am aware of different families where all three methods have been used. The results are quite predictable. The rigid rule and the no rule families nearly always end up a mess. Whereas, the more reasonable, loving family usually turns out good. I am sure you have all heard about the person who said one day, "Before we had children, I knew six ways how to raise children. Now that we have six children, I seem to have no definite way on how to raise them."

It doesn't look like we will have less laws anytime soon. Recently, I read where on average in the United States, 150,000 new laws and about two million new regulations from various local state and federal governments are put into place every year. In my opinion, this is a tragic situation.

Laws, rules and regulations are necessary in governments, armies, churches, schools, homes and society in general. The important part is how they are administered. It would be nice if all segments of our society were blessed with a big dose of common sense. The possibility of this taking place on this old planet is remote. Meanwhile, let us make the best of our own situations. We in the western world are blessed in spite of all the rules, regulations, and problems we face every day. Maybe it is not the rules that are out of order; maybe it is me, and millions of others like me. I am not fond of Big Brother standing over me with a big stick. Are you?

Chapter Thirty-Five

SHEEP DOGS AND COMPUTERS

Sheep have been a part of the culture of the human race for thousands of years. Sheep are mentioned hundreds of times in the Bible. It tells about the great flocks, owned by many characters in the Old Testament.

It was shepherds who heralded the birth of Jesus Christ. He was born in a stable, with animals around him. I am sure it included sheep. Later on when Jesus was ministering to the people he told the parable about the ninety-nine sheep which should be one hundred. One had gone astray. The shepherd searched diligently until he found the lost sheep. Jesus is often referred to as the Lamb of God. He went as an innocent Lamb to the slaughter (the cross).

For several years when I was a young man, I was a sheep and lamb buyer for Burns Foods. I got to know sheep real well. Sheep have a gentle nature; they are not the least bit dangerous. The only exception is mature males (rams). They may butt you if they consider you a threat, especially during the breeding season. As for ewes and lambs, like I said, they are completely harmless.

Sheep are followers, just like ninety-seven percent of humans. If the leader goes over a cliff, the rest will blindly follow. The problem is that there are very few good leaders in sheep or humans. In the Middle East, the sheep always followed the Shepherd. Occasionally an old ewe or goat will take on that role.

I have loaded thousands of sheep into railway cars (sometimes alone and sometimes with help). What we did was get hold of a front leg of a lamb or sheep, then drag it up the loading chute. It would unwillingly hop along behind you on three legs. The other sheep followed on behind, right into the boxcar. They did not stop to consider that the sheep you were pulling was unwilling to go. They blindly followed it.

The same method was used to move sheep up a long ramp to the fourth floor of the plant where the killing floor was located. During all this activity, the sheep never made a noise, only an odd little bleep.

In sheep ranching areas of the western United States and Canada, ranchers employ sheepherders with good sheep dogs. Sheep are vulnerable to predators such as coyotes, wolves, bears, and even untrained domestic dogs. When I was a boy, we had a small flock of sheep. One Sunday afternoon, our neighbor's dogs destroyed that little band of sheep. Several were killed, and a number of them maimed.

A shepherd must constantly be on guard to protect the flock. These days, some people use goats or donkeys to scare away predators. There are also big white dogs (Great Pyrenees) that are trained to live with the sheep, day and night.

Shepherd, the sheepdog, does a good job of holding the flock in a tight bunch on the Bar S Ranch, west of Nanton, Alberta. Clay Chataway is on the left, and Rick Neville is at right.
Courtesy Lee Gunderson

Now, let's look at the human equation. People are much like sheep in a number of ways. We are more violent and only slightly more intelligent, but most of us are followers. I could cite hundreds of examples, but I will confine myself to a few.

It starts at an early age. At the toddler stage, we follow mother and dad around. If we have older siblings, we copy everything they do. Once school starts, we almost become clones of our fellow students. Our fear is that, if we dare to be different, we will be ridiculed and become outcasts. By junior high school, the peer pressure becomes intense to dress alike, to eat the same food (with the girls, it often excludes meat), to listen to the same music, and have the same hairstyle. Following high school graduation, we finally feel a little more individualistic: the peer pressure in colleges and university is not as great. One reason is that students have selected different career choices. Courses vary greatly from high school, where everybody, more or less, studied the same subjects. So, for the next five to ten years, we become more independent thinkers.

Once we have settled into chosen careers, get married (many live common-law), and have children, we may fall back into the flock or herd mentality, doing exactly what friends and neighbors do. The style of clothes (especially women), the same cars (it's not our fault that cars these days are also clones), and the same political views. Actually, there is a split here: some are right-wing, others left-wing. Whichever political group we believe in, we will blindly follow, even if the leaders of those parties turn out to be scoundrels (Chretien is a good example).

The big multinational corporations and other large companies and advertising agencies have a heyday taking advantage of this follow-the-leader mentality. If all the people are buying a certain product, we better get in on the act, lest we get left out (keeping up with the Joneses).

The stock market is a prime example. Just recently, there was a big rush to buy stocks in a gold mine in Indonesia. It was called BreX. People who had never before purchased stocks suddenly became experts on how to get rich via the stock market. This attitude also included many who bought stocks regularly. They all caught the gold fever. Everyone was buying - it must be a winner. Well, it did not turn out that way.

It was a giant hoax - a fraud. Actually, it was both. The shareholders who got caught still holding the shares howled like a hyena caught in a trap. They launched major lawsuits in both Canada and the United States in an effort to claim back their losses. I was completely puzzled by that action. Where did they expect to get that money? The shareholders who bailed out early and made a fortune certainly were not going to give up that windfall money. The brokers who traded the stock said they did not know it was a hoax. They said people called them and said just buy the stock.

I may be an oddball, but I was not once tempted to buy that stock even before the price got ridiculous. If it's too good to be true, it's usually not true. My theory was that, even if there was gold in the Indonesian mine, the dictator Suharto would find a way to stop the gold from leaving Indonesia. Apparently, this thought never occurred to those greedy investors. This whole scam ballooned up to six billion dollars.

Back to computers. Multinational corporations, as well as other large companies, are enslaving millions of employees. The tools to help create this situation are computers.

Control is the name of the game. With these advanced computers, the rules of the company can be rigidly enforced. You either shape up or ship out. This total work-to-rule takes away an individual's ability to think for themselves.

I realize that, on assembly lines, everyone has to work by the rules, or it could create all kinds of problems, even endangering people's lives. However, most jobs have room for flexibility and innovation, but the rules prohibit that. I dare say that eighty-five percent of today's employees do not like their jobs. They are stuck in a rut. Their only relief is weekends and holidays. The only light at the end of the tunnel is retirement, and that may be another ten, fifteen or twenty years away.

Now, let me explain how sheep dogs and computers are the same. They both are tools of their masters. The sheep dog's master is the shepherd. The computer's master is the boss of a large corporation. A good sheep dog will hold the flock together in a small area. If one sheep happens to depart from the flock, the dog immediately brings it back in a great hurry. If an employee strays away from the team rule program, the computer quickly whips them back into line. The people in control of the computers feel a huge surge of self-importance and power.

Humans have always enjoyed power. That is what spawns dictators and corrupt political leaders that lust for power over other people. If I had a choice to be a sheep dog or a computer operator creating misery for other people, I would choose to be a sheep dog. I could save some sheep from being torn to pieces by a predator. I could also enjoy the great outdoors, not stuck in an office on the forty-ninth floor of a skyscraper located in a congested, polluted big city, punching a computer along with the rest of the company clones. Sorry folks, if I hurt your feelings or stepped on your toes. I know computers are here to stay, and in many ways, they are a wonderful tool, which has been great for business. But I foresee major problems in the future. Our privacy will be a faint memory, and so will I.

I must sheepishly admit that the computer was a great help in making this book a reality.

Chapter Thirty-Six

RENTING OR LEASING

These days, renting or leasing is big business. I stand in amazement when I hear and see what people rent or lease. I know I am in the minority but I am from the old school. To me, renting certain things is like buying a dead horse.

Of course, there is a big difference in what you rent, or for how long. I have rented dozens of cars from rental agencies at airports. I have also rented hundreds of hotel and motel rooms, even golf clubs or skis, when it is not practical to pack our own along.

There are other machines or tools that make sense to rent. They are things that you only need occasionally, so it is not wise to buy them. When I said I was amazed at what people rent, I am talking about long-term rentals and leases. One example is cars and trucks. Today, about half the vehicles are leased - usually on a three-year lease. At the end of that period, you have the option of purchasing it.

Even large corporations do this. I realize many people cannot afford to purchase vehicles for cash. However, they can purchase them using a payment plan. I would much sooner do that. I like the feeling of ownership. I have been fortunate in my lifetime. I have bought sixteen brand new cars and trucks and about a dozen used ones. I paid cash for every one of them, with the exception of a 1947 Studebaker (it was a bit of a lemon). For one year, I drove a lease car. The company I worked for leased it. My theory is do not buy a vehicle until you can afford it. I dislike making payments on something that wears out and depreciates fast. Even when I drive a rental car from an airport, I have an uneasy feeling when driving it.

The picture changes when it comes to renting or leasing business premises or houses. If young people waited until they could afford to pay for a house, or even make a down payment, they might never get a house of their own. Their best option is to rent as reasonably as possible, save their money and, when they have saved enough money to make a down payment, take the plunge and buy a house. Realtors call them starter houses. Eventually, when the babies come or their financial lot improves, they can buy a bigger house. If everything goes well, they will own a good house free and clear in about twenty-five or thirty years. That is a long time, but it is a lot better than renting a house all those years. I know of a number of people who rented a house all their lives. In the end, what did they have? A dead horse, or should I say a dead house (no house).

I read not too long ago that a house is the most valuable monetary possession that at least eighty percent of Canadians and Americans will ever own. Worldwide, ownership of houses or apartments is very small, something like around twenty percent. Millions of people in large cities live in rented houses or apartments.

In slum areas of the third world countries, people may have their own little hovel constructed of materials dragged home from the dump. The land the little shelter sits on is not theirs. They are squatters. One notch up from that are slightly better houses owned by slum landlords. They rent these ramshackle houses out to folks who have some sort of job.

Large property corporations own most of the world's high rise office buildings. There is not much choice for most corporations or private individuals but to lease their business spaces from the property corporations. There are some folks who even rebel at that. One example is my wife's nephew, James (Jim) Regier. He owns a small engineering firm with about a dozen or so employees. What he did was buy an old church. He remodelled and refurbished it to suit his needs. He owns it. No more high rent or lease payments. No hassles with increased rents by a landlord two thousand miles away.

The most common thing people rent or lease is land. Like housing, most of the world's farmers rent or lease the land they farm. In feudal England, ninety percent of people were serfs. However, in reality, things did not change all that much. Even today, over half of Britain's farmers are tenants.

I read a book several years ago called *Britain's Four Hundred Richest People*. It surprised me that a least half these people were large estate owners. This included Prince Charles and Queen Elizabeth, along with a number of Lords, Counts, Viceroys, or some other titled sorts. Collectively, those two hundred people own millions of acres of land. The land is rented out to farmers, although usually a fairly large portion is reserved for fox hunting or other equestrian activities.

In Russia, private ownership of land is still almost nil. Even before the communists took over in 1917, few people owned their own land under the czars. Today, it is a hotly debated issue. There are still enough communists in government to block privatization of land.

In Mexico, Central America, and large portions of South America, land reform is a big issue. Up to this point, not much reform has taken place. I had first hand experience when I was in Colombia. In that country, a few people own the bulk of the land (at least the good land). The rest of the people are more or less peons. Much of that land had been granted to rich families by the King of Spain several hundred years ago.

Africa is such a mess that I am not even going to give my opinion about land on that continent. A few of those countries have some semblance of order, but the majority are in chaos. In Zimbabwe, masses of hoodlums are invading and taking over farms from white people. The government sanctions this action.

In Continental Europe, land is so high in price that there is no hope of young people ever owning any, except by inheritance.

Asia, including India and China, is a mixed bag. There are a number of small landowners, but the bulk of the farmers are tenants.

When all is said and done, we, in Canada and the United States, are a pretty lucky group. We still have a majority of farmers who own their own land. I am not sure for how long, though. Farms are getting bigger and bigger.

The ranching end of things is slightly different. In both Canada and United States, millions of acres of grasslands and forests are owned by the people through the government, not much different than in Russia. Most of those ranches hold long term leases on that land. For how long? More and more pressure is being exerted by special interest groups like radical environmentalists, animal rights people, endangered species types, water rights people, fishermen, hunters and other recreational users. The problem is, this land is not for sale. In time, these radicals will have all the politicians in their pockets. They already do. No more grazing livestock on land that is only suited for that purpose. I will not live long enough to see it happen, but I believe that, one hundred years from now, North Americans will be in the same mess land-wise as most of the world is today. Or is that too pessimistic?

Several years ago, an enterprising person in the United States started a Rent-a-Husband business. He set some ground rules. A woman could call the agency and ask for a rented husband for a day. She was told that the man they would send over would do all the things a husband is supposed to do, but never does. He would vacuum and dust the whole house. He would bring her breakfast in bed, if he arrived early enough. However, he was not allowed into bed with her, just as her rules for her husband were, if he brought breakfast to bed for her, which he seldom did. Another job the rented husband had was to pick up the real husband's clothes and hang them up.

After cleaning up the house, his next chore was to clean up the real husband's mess in the garage, and then wash the car. After all those mundane chores were finished, she asked him to fix the latch on the bathroom door so she would be assured privacy for her two-hour bath. While she was having a bath, he went to do a little shopping. This included dropping off the tomcat at the vet to get him neutered. The shopping list was simple - distilled water, diet coke, chicken breasts, skim milk, yokeless eggs, stone ground whole wheat bread, diet Jell-O, the *Enquirer* magazine, and a small bottle of Viagra for her real husband.

When he got back, she had him fix several other things that her husband had neglected to do for months. She paid him, and he was on his way home.

After he left, she reflected on how the day had gone. It was perfect. The thought occurred to her that, at last, humans had caught up to bees. The queen rules supreme. The worker bees do all the work, just as the rented husband had done. All she had to do now was wait for her drone husband to come home. We all know what the drone's job is. What that rented husband did was strictly a figment of my imagination, although I remember that one of the rules was no physical contact or hanky panky with the rented husband.

We used to rent out houses and several small apartment blocks. These ventures were kind to us, even though our rents were cheap. I found an old receipt book the other day, and I was shocked at how cheap the rents were in 1973. Here are a few examples:

- a two-storey house on Twenty-Ninth Avenue SW in Calgary - one hundred and twenty dollars per month
- a small bungalow on Fourteenth Street West in Calgary - eighty dollars per month
- a large apartment - one hundred and fifteen dollars per month, including stove, fridge, washer and dryer
- a two-bedroom house with a third bedroom downstairs - one hundred and forty dollars per month
- another bungalow in Altadore - one hundred and ten dollars per month

We had six small apartments with two rooms in Ogden for thirty dollars per month, each. We had twenty-three houses and suites all rented at similar prices when the government, in their wisdom, put on rent controls, because rents were too high in some bureaucrat's opinion. I decided to bail out of the rental business. We sold all those properties and bought land.

Today, those properties would rent for seven to ten times as much. I have no regrets. The land did well for us.

Renting and leasing is here to stay. In my opinion, the renter or leaseholder gets the short end of the stick, unless the rentals are short term. In that case, it is wise to rent and not buy. About the only things that cannot be rented are toilet paper and toothbrushes.

CHAPTER THIRTY-SEVEN

UNDERDOGS

The Funk & Wagnall dictionary describes an underdog as one who is at a disadvantage in a struggle; a probable loser; one who is victimized or downtrodden by society.

In my opinion, there are two types of underdogs - the real ones, and the ones who perceive themselves as such.

Some people like to be underdogs. They seem to think that somehow it will give them an advantage in society or, at least, elicit some sympathy from others. Underdogs and unsung heroes are distant cousins. The difference is that most unsung heroes do not feel sorry for themselves, whereas underdogs thrive on pity from others. Both are sort of at the bottom of the ladder, while the higher-up people got the best breaks in life's game – or so it seems to the underdog.

In politics and sport, people often claim the underdog position. They think that they will catch their opponents off guard and win an election or a sporting event. In politics, there have been hundreds of situations where the underdog became the winner. One such situation comes to mind. In 1948, Harry S. Truman ran for president of the United States. The polls indicated that he would lose, but Harry kept on plugging away. Lo and behold, he beat his opponent by a comfortable margin.

People like underdogs because most of us identify with them to some degree. I think that is because we ourselves often have the underdog complex – real or imagined.

Another underdog who turned that situation into triumph was Ralph Klein, when he became the mayor of the city of Calgary. People thought that this TV reporter had little chance of winning, but he did. Today, he is the premier of the province of Alberta.

In sport, it is even more common to seek the underdog status. The upsets by underdog teams are legion. The coaches think, and rightly so, that if the opposing team underrates them, they will have a much better chance of winning.

The other advantage of being the underdog is that when they lose, it's no big deal. However, if you win, it's a real feather in your cap. The favored team wins? So what. They were expected to win. When they lose to the underdog, they take a lot of flak from sports fans.

In individual sports like golf, tennis and boxing, underdogs often come up the winner – especially in boxing. Rodeo is not different. The real good hands usually win. However, every once in a while, an unknown competitor will win big. One year at the Calgary Stampede, a nineteen-year-old rookie by the name of Jerry Sinclair won the Saddle Bronc championship. He beat all the top hands. Later, he went on to win three Canadian Saddle Bronc championships.

One year, a ranch hand from Montana won the steer-wrestling event at Calgary. He only went to a few rodeos during the season. Yes, underdogs do win quite often.

In business, many upstarts pass those who have been at the top for some time. In the United States, ten cattle buyers decided to start a packing plant venture. They called their outfit Iowa Beef Packers. A few packers such as Swift, Armour, Cudahay, Hormel, and a few others had dominated the packing industry. In a short period – say ten years – those old time packers were gone. Iowa Beef Packers became the largest beef packer in North America. If those early packers had modernized and changed their methods, this would never have happened. The reality is that when an underdog rises to become the top dog, he remains there until another underdog replaces him.

Once a top dog is toppled, he seldom becomes an underdog. He simply disappears from the scene.

Then there's pecking order – especially in families. It results in some family members becoming underdogs – or sometimes called, a black sheep. I have observed that a family underdog rarely succeeds in losing that image. As an adult, he or she often feels like a victim, trodden down by society. In politics, sports, or business, being an underdog can be advantageous. But, with a family member, that seldom is the case. Once an underdog, always an underdog.

These individuals often feel hard-done-by. They whine and complain that no one gives them a chance to improve their lot in life. Once that mode of life has been entrenched in a person's mind, it is hard to shake it off. Education and a geographical change can sometimes help to get rid of the underdog inferiority complex.

In this world we have people who are wise and dumb, rich and poor, good and bad, happy and sad, gifted and ungifted, positive and negative, winners and losers, talkative and silent. And we have top dogs and underdogs, plus all levels in between. Most of us fall into the in-between category. Whatever our lot in life, let's make the best of it.

CHAPTER THIRTY-EIGHT

UNSUNG HEROES

This world is full of heroes that most people have never heard of. Every so often we hear or read about an exception, when someone saves another person or persons from a house fire. Usually they receive an award from the police, fire department, the local community, or even a national honour.

My mother was an unsung hero. She was the wife of a homesteader who, in 1906, moved onto a homestead site that had no buildings. They arrived there on July 6, 1906. She had a one-year-old baby and was expecting another one that was born on February 12, 1907. By October, dad had erected a house (a shelter would be a better description), plus a little shelter for a team of horses, and a few cows and pigs. Those of you who are history buffs have read about the terrible winter on the prairies of 1906 and 1907. There was three feet of snow piled into huge drifts. The temperature hovered between ten degrees below and forty degrees below Fahrenheit for almost five months. Twice a week, dad had to hitch up the team and head for the river brakes, about two miles away, to bring in a load of wood to heat that leaky shack. Guess how they watered their stock and how they procured their drinking water? They melted snow on a wood stove. They did not have a well.

What did they eat? Home-baked bread, home-made butter, salt pork, biscuits and milk, and the odd rabbit that dad shot. Not a well balanced diet, but it kept them alive.

The next winter, they fared a little better. They had planted a garden, including potatoes. With the home-canned vegetables and potatoes added to their larder, their diet was a little healthier. Imagine what it must have been like for a young mother with a couple of babies waiting for her husband to come home with a load of wood that he had to chop into stove-length pieces?

The closest town and post office was twenty-eight miles away. Needless to say, they never went there during that winter. There were a few neighbors in the area who braved the elements and made that two day return trip a few times in that five month period, and brought back everyone's mail and a few supplies that were essential. Those pioneers helped each other whenever possible. That is the only way they could survive.

There are thousands of stories about homesteaders and the women of that era. They faced untold hardships. The end result was that they paved the way for generations to follow. Many of the sons, daughters, grandchildren and great-grandchildren became outstanding citizens of this country. They served their country in the armed forces and in other civic positions. Not only did many become outstanding farmers and ranchers, many got educated and became professionals in a number of different fields. Yes, those women and mothers were real people and unsung heroes. Of course, their husbands shared that honor as well.

Some other unsung heroes are people who work for large or small companies behind the scenes. The credit for a company's success is usually given to the CEOs, presidents, vice-presidents and department managers. Without the support staff at the lower levels, those people at the top could not have succeeded. Sure, the employees get paid for what they do. However, many of them do a lot of extra work that often goes unnoticed. The real loyal employees always strive to make their boss and people in management positions look good, even when some of those people at the top have flaws in their performance and character.

In politics, there are people who are called, king makers. These are people who work hard and intelligently to promote someone running for political office. These kingmakers make all the right moves and have the right contacts for the client. Often they are also fund-raisers. When that candidate attains office, they will sometimes give their promoters a job in their office. Sometimes, those folks who got their man or woman elected are forgotten. Those people are unsung heroes.

I know a lady who is constantly looking where she may help someone in need. This includes a variety of areas such as physical, mental, spiritual, or any other thing that besets the human race. She spends hours with a mentally challenged young woman. She and her husband invite less fortunate people to their house for a meal. She finds fault with very few people. She has a ton of compassion. And I know a number of other things she has done to help people. The beauty is that she expects no monetary return or recognition for her activities. That's what I call an unsung hero. Their names are Harold and Grace Preet.

People who have the gift of visiting people who are in hospitals and sick at home do a ministry that has helped people overcome great odds in their struggles to become well again. Pastor Tony Hanson and his wife Esther are good friends of ours.

He goes the extra mile to visit and counsel sick people. In fifty years, he has visited thousands of people in hospitals. He has a way of talking to people that touches their lives. A number of people have given their heart and what's left of their life to the Lord through his wise counsel from God's Word. When those people pass away, they will definitely go to Heaven. He takes no credit for himself. He gives it all to God.

Only one life 'twill soon be past.
Only what is done for Christ will last.

Some of you reading this may not believe in prayer. I do. I am not talking about public prayer, although that is good. What I am saying is that, as the Bible says, "The prayer of a righteous man availeth much."

The silent prayers of millions of people, including parents, have changed the lives and events of countless people. The Bible says, "Before you ask, I will answer."

Some may say, if that is the case, why bother to pray? Let me put it this way. If you know your child wants a certain thing, rather than just give it to them, you want them to ask for it. In most instances, you will give it to them when they ask. However, once in a while, you may decide it would be better if you did not give it to them. That is like God. He does not always grant us our request. We cannot understand why. In the end, it usually turns out to be okay. All things work out for the best to those who love God.

Once, in a United Church, I saw a plaque that said, "Prayer may not change things, but it changes you."

Prayers by parents and other people are truly unsung heroes in this world.

Abraham Lincoln once said, "God must have loved the common man, because he made so many of them." I would add that a large percentage of those so-called common men are unsung heroes.

I think a large number of teachers are unsung heroes. I still remember many things and principles I learned from my teachers. It stays with a person for life. Those teachers worked for very little pay. They truly liked children and young people, and did their best to instruct those kids.

A few years ago, my wife and I met a man who had been a grade six student at the school where my wife taught. He said to her, "I have always remembered the manners you taught me fifty years ago."

Other professions where unsung heroes abound are in the health field, such as nurses, doctors and other medical staff. Even some lawyers have helped people through difficult problems, for little remuneration. Our lawyer, Don Kelly, did it for us. I think most of us have considered ourselves unsung heroes at one time or another. It sort of makes a person feel good about themselves. Agreed?

CHAPTER THIRTY-NINE

YEARNING FOR THE PAST

One cliché that I often quote is, nostalgia is a great liar. That is not altogether true, since many things from the old days were very good. This is often proved when old ideas or customs are revived in our present day society.

Has it ever occurred to you that yachting is a direct descendant of the old sailing ships? Those old sailing ships were a lot of work to operate, especially in a major storm. When that happened, all hands had to be called on deck to lower sails and bail out water to keep the ship from swamping and then sinking. The ocean floor is littered with vessels that sank in the past five hundred years. Compare that to today's luxury passenger ships and huge freighters and tankers that ply the oceans these days. Few sink.

It is the nostalgia of the past that causes people to enjoy yachts and other smaller sailboats. There are all kinds of motor boats and modern ships, but somehow they do not present the same challenge as do boats with sails.

Or, how about the revival of the old steam locomotive and the early versions of the diesel engine. Now there are areas in North America where these trains with their old coaches are making a comeback. Not to haul freight, but rather, tourists who yearn for the good old days when traveling by train was the main means of transporting people long and short distances. Those of us old enough to remember have a great nostalgia for the sound of the old steam engine whistle.

In the high country of Colorado, they still have an old fashioned train on a narrow gauge track, hauling tourists for a bit of a sight seeing trip. The railroad goes over an enormously deep gorge. People line up to get on this train.

In Canada, the CPR announced in early 2000 that a train would leave Calgary and go through the eastern Rockies, circle back in southern Alberta, and arrive back in Calgary three days later. The train consists of refurbished passenger cars and coaches. The price tag for this little trip is only about seven thousand dollars per person.

My wife and I, along with three other couples, had a nice trip from Calgary to Vancouver and back in two of the last private railroad cars in existence. The trip was courtesy of the Calgary Exhibition and Stampede. When we got to Vancouver we were guests at the annual fair at the Pacific National Exhibition.

It was an enjoyable and relaxing trip. We had our every whim catered to by two good chefs. There were two cars, so we had a lot of room. From the 1880s until the great depression of the 1930s, private cars were owned extensively by wealthy people. Every industrialist worth his salt had one. It was a status symbol.

The ones we were on were hooked behind a freight train. We were held up for a few hours by some railroad workers on strike. This was in a scenic area in the Rockies, so we suffered no hardship. We had lots of good food and good company. Eventually, we were allowed to continue our journey.

That trip was a glimpse of the past. It was fantastic. As far as I am concerned, it sure beats today's frenzied rush to get from point A to point B by jet plane or high-powered car. In this case, nostalgia was not a liar.

How about horses?

In the old days, horses were the mode of transportation – whether ridden or driven. When the railroads made their appearance, the horses were pretty well eliminated for long distance travel. No more stagecoaches or pony express mail delivery. When the automobile was invented, huge numbers of horse drawn vehicles became redundant. Can you imagine New York City full of horse drawn carriages? There must have been a lot of manure to clean up.

Then, somewhat later, farm tractors began to proliferate, until all farming was done with tractors. With the advent of trains, cars, trucks, and tractors, horses should have been eliminated. However, this was not the case. There are more horses in North America now than there was one hundred years ago. Why? Because people long for the good old days when a horse was king.

The way horses are used today is vastly different from the old days. They are used almost exclusively for pleasure, although there are still some ranches that use horses to feed their cattle. Horses are much better in deep snow than trucks or tractors. I better lay off on the horse subject, since there is a whole chapter on horses in this book.

You do not have to be old to yearn for the good old days. It afflicts all ages. I have heard several of our grandchildren talk about the good old days. They were referring back about ten to twelve years.

The most any person can recall eyewitness events is ninety-five years – that is if they happen to live to one hundred and their mind is still sound. That is why it is so important to record our history for future generations. There are many history buffs that know exactly what went on one hundred, two hundred or even one thousand years ago. This is because someone recorded it.

There is also oral history. It sometimes is not too accurate. Every time a story is handed down from one generation to the next, some details are lost. Often the incident is embellished, so in five hundred years it can become more fiction than fact. That is why it is so important that our present history be written down so our descendants will have an accurate account of what our society was all about. Today, this history may be recorded on computers. I would feel much safer if it is written or printed on paper. Who knows when a computer virus or a Y2K-like bug might wipe everything out.

Once again, I quote Sir Winston Churchill, who said: "When people disregard history, they may not have much of a future."

Often when I autograph a book for someone I write: History is a great teacher. It helps us avoid mistakes in the future.

CHAPTER FORTY

RED TAPE

Red tape is something most of us encounter on a daily basis. I abhor red tape. Whenever I have looked into red tape that involved anything I was doing or working on, I discovered that ninety percent of the red tape could have been eliminated, and the transaction or whatever the issue, could have been resolved in a relatively short period. Instead, unnecessary red tape dragged it on.

Funk & Wagnall's dictionary defines red tape as rigid official procedure involving delay or inaction, from the tying of public documents with red tape.

Red tape and bureaucrats are bedfellows. Bureaucrats thrive on red tape. So do some businesses. The legal system loves it as well. To top it off, red tape is a lawyer's delight.

Years ago, I made an application to move a house onto a lot. I thought this would be a simple operation, but I found out that this was no simple matter. The trips to city hall to get permits almost wore me out. I could not believe all the paper shufflers I encountered in my visits. Finally, when I was almost ready to give up, all the papers were in place, including permission from the police department to move the building during non-rush hour traffic.

A close friend of mine who developed small acreages around the perimeter of Calgary said the hassle was unreal. Sometimes, a certain document or papers lay on the desk of a minor municipal civil servant for weeks. All that was needed was for that person to sign it. Those "little Caesars" really feel their power by interpreting everything to the letter-of-the-law. They are in no hurry to issue any permits or sign documents. Often this costs the person trying to conduct business thousands of dollars in lost time and other expenses incurred because of this delay. All because of bureaucratic red tape.

Have you ever considered how many skyscrapers we have in our large cities? Every one of them is full of people shuffling papers. They go from the lowest file clerk to CEOs of major corporations, and all the folk in between. This is private industry. At least twenty-five percent of that daily activity could be eliminated if the governments and the corporations themselves got rid of a bunch of red tape that is totally unnecessary. There is an upside to it. It employs people. However, these people could be gainfully employed in some other sectors of our economy producing goods and services that stimulates our economy and improves everyone's lifestyle.

In government and corporations, business forms should be simplified so they can be filled out in a few minutes, instead of an hour or two. Nine times out of ten, the main reason for the red tape is the tax department. Thousands of accountants work for people and companies to try and find all the loopholes they can. Hence, all the 'T's must be crossed and the 'I's dotted. Luckily, there are a few loopholes that the bureaucrats have not plugged. If it were not for those loopholes, many businesses would go down the tube.

The red tape in the tax department is threefold. First, there are bureaucrats writing down rules. Next, are the accountants and lawyers trying to work within those rules, while at the same time, trying to save their client some money. When the return is finally filed a second set of civil servants takes over. Their job is to ensure the taxpayer is giving them every cent they think they are entitled to under the tax laws.

Another tangle of red tape is our court system. Every day in our newspapers, radio and TV, we hear or read about court cases and inquiries that go on for months. Inquiries often go on for years. There are thousands of pages of legal jargon and opinions written during some of these inquiries, and almost as many in some court cases. Lawyers get rich from these cases. Often the government (us) gets stuck with the bill from both the prosecutor and the lawyers for those on trial.

Maybe the justice of the old west was a better system. Give them a fair trial of five minutes to maybe one day. If found guilty, justice was swift and sure. Either hang them or put them in jail and throw away the key. In reality, our justice system should be somewhere in between.

These days, in some states, prisoners are on death row up to fifteen years. Finally, they meet their maker after a dozen appeals. Meanwhile, thousands of dollars have been spent, even though everyone knew what the outcome would be for the last ten years. It would be refreshing if common sense would prevail in all the red tape in our society.

Sex, poverty, hot tempers and a host of other things cause marriages to break up. One cause that we seldom hear about is when one partner is full of red tape, whereas the other partner likes to do things simply and in a common-sense manner. This problem, among others, is called incompatibility.

I know of cases where the husband is such a fussbutton that a simple job is made into a big production. In other situations, it is the wife who demands that her husband be more articulate.

This can cause major friction. Red tape people see those who are not full of red tape as careless individuals who like to cut corners. In fact, the end result of the so-called corner cutter is that they perform better than the ponderous red tape person's final result.

Hot beds for red tape are the United Nations, all federal, state, provincial, county and municipal governments, police departments, the whole judicial system, large multinational corporations, private businesses, the army (everything in triplicate, sometimes as many as five copies), the medical and education systems, plus a large percentage of private individuals.

In other words, every one of us is touched by it, either by our own actions, or that of others who impose red tape upon us.

Right now, I am going to my accountant who is working on my tax return. I am unable to untangle the red tape involved in that exercise.

CHAPTER FORTY-ONE

MISTAKEN IDENTITY

One of the first stories about mistaken identity is recorded in the Bible. In that ancient culture, the oldest son always received the birthright. In other words, he inherited his father's estate. In Genesis, Chapter 27, the Bible tells the story about Isaac and Rebecca, and their two sons, Easu, the eldest and Jacob, the youngest. Jacob was Rebecca's pet. She and Jacob schemed as to how he could receive the blessing from Isaac. Isaac was old and his eyesight was dim.

Jacob with smooth skinned. Esau was hairy. Rebecca put some kid (goatskin) on his neck and arms. When Jacob came to receive the blessing, his father felt the goat hair and thought it was Esau, so he blessed him. That, in essence, was willing his whole estate to the youngest son instead of the oldest, as was the custom in that culture. Jacob remained a schemer for the rest of his life.

One day at the Calgary Stockyards, a farmer spoke to one of the commission men about selling his cattle. The commission man happened to know that the farmer had him mixed up with a packer buyer, so he strung the farmer along for a while. Then suddenly, he said, "You can keep your lousy cattle. They are just a bunch of scruffs anyway."

The farmer's mouth dropped open. He was totally surprised. He had sold cattle to that packing plant before, and had always received good treatment. The commission man walked away, leaving the farmer muttering to himself. A bad case of mistaken identity.

A number of years ago, my sister Tina and her daughter Pat were going to set up a daycare center in their home. In other words, a baby-sitting service. They went down to city hall to apply for a permit. When they arrived, they went into what looked like the right office. After waiting for a little while, they were ushered into a back room. Here they had to strip down for a thorough physical examination, including x-rays. They thought that all of this activity was kind of strange. When it was over, they discovered that they had come to the wrong place. What had just taken place was an examination for TB.

The permit they required needed no such examination. They had a good laugh over the whole misunderstanding. Incidentally, they were both given a clean bill of health.

One area where mistaken identity often occurs is on the telephone. Some pranksters can really imitate other people's voices. This can lead to some embarrassing conversations. This has happened to me several times. My nephew, Loran, is very good at that game. He does not fool me too often, anymore.

I have heard of others where serious consequences took place from what someone told them on the phone. At that point, it is not funny anymore.

An old rancher in southern Alberta decided he and his wife should retire, so they bought a house in their local town. His wife enjoyed living in town. As for himself, he still preferred the country. Nearly every day, he drove to the ranch, where his son lived. Once in a while, his wife would go with him.

On day, when they returned from the ranch, they walked into the house. Nature was calling, so the rancher quickly walked to the bathroom. When he opened the bathroom door, he was shocked by what he saw. Strewn all over the place was ladies' undies. Peeking from the shower curtain was a pretty young lady's face (the shower was going full blast). At that point, it was a toss-up as to who was embarrassed more, the rancher or the young lady. He beat a hasty retreat. He told his wife what had just happened. They were both puzzled by the unusual situation. In a few minutes, a hastily dressed and very embarrassed young lady emerged from the bathroom. An explanation was in order.

Here is what happened. The young lady was a nineteen-year-old girl. Her neighbors in the country were very close friends of their family. Two weeks previously, they had moved into town. The girl was away at school in the city when they moved, she had never seen the house. The second day, after she had come home from school, she decided to go to town and visit her friends. When she rang the doorbell, there was no answer, so she opened the door and walked in (those days, thirty years ago, few people locked their doors in the country or in small towns). After waiting ten minutes or so, she decided to have a shower. What better way was there than to spend half an hour, while waiting for her hosts to arrive? The problem was that she was in the wrong house. The folks she wanted to visit lived next door. After, that explanation, they all had a good laugh. Then the rancher quickly headed off to the bathroom to do what he set out to do when he entered the house. They became good friends.

I knew of a set of twin girls, my Dad's cousins, who were identical. When they were nineteen years old, they each had a boyfriend. One day, they decided to play a little trick on them. It so happened that they both had a date to go to a party.

When the first boy showed up at the door, the twin he was not going with came to the door and went with him in his car. Half an hour later, the other boy showed up. The other twin, who was not his girlfriend, went with him. Neither one of the young men caught on that they were with the wrong girl. This was a number of years ago. In those days, most men were real gentlemen when it came to courting a girl. All during the evening, the boys were totally unaware of the situation. They talked and held hands, but that was it. However, things took a funny turn when they took the girls home.

Like I have already mentioned, they were gentlemen. But, even in those days, it had a limit. Necking and kissing has always been a part of courtship. So, when they parked their respective cars, the natural thing to do was to put their arm around their girl. At this point, the girls could hardly keep their secret. The next step was kissing. At this point, the girls did not cooperate. The boys were both puzzled. After a few more attempts to kiss, the boys gave up in disgust. At this point, the girls revealed their true identities. Needles to say the boys were shocked. They quickly changed partners and the good night kisses were the most passionate ever (they married the girls).

The story is told about a Texas oilman who heard about a brilliant university professor, who was an expert on geology. The oilman approached the professor with a proposal. He told the professor that he would pay him good money if he would go to various universities and other functions, and deliver a dissertation on the subject of geology. He would supply him with a limousine and a uniformed chauffeur.

The professor accepted his offer. Away he went with the chauffeur, and things went well. He received great receptions everywhere he went to give his lectures. The chauffeur always sat in the back of the auditorium. After about ten speeches at different locations, the chauffeur said to the professor, "I have listened closely to what you say, and nearly every speech is the same. I bet I can give that talk just as good as you do."

The professor said, "Okay, we will switch tomorrow night." Before they arrived at the place, they exchanged clothes, the professor put on the chauffeur's uniform and the chauffeur put on the professor's suit.

The chauffeur was introduced as the professor who would deliver the speech, while the professor sat at the back of the room. The chauffeur spoke eloquently for three-quarters of an hour. The professor was shocked at how good he was.

After he had given his talk, the meeting was opened up to questions from the audience. He answered all the questions, until one student asked a technical question that was difficult to answer. The chauffeur-turned–professor looked the student right in the eye and said, "The answer to your question is easy. In fact, it is so simple that I am going to ask my chauffeur to come up and give you the answer."

Wilbur and Orville were two brothers who liked hunting ducks. One fall, they had driven around the country for hours with no luck. Suddenly, they say some ducks on a pond close to some farm buildings. Being law-abiding citizens and good sports, they decided to ask the farmer for permission to hunt on his land.

When they stopped in the yard, Orville went to the house to ask permission. Wilbur was on the slow side, although not retarded. He stayed in the pick-up. When Orville knocked on the door, a gruff old farmer came and asked what he wanted. Orville politely asked if they could hunt on his land.

The farmer said, "No way. I don't like hunters."

Orville was about to leave when the farmer said, "Just a minute. I will let you hunt, on one condition."

"What is it?" asked Orville.

"Well, we have a thirty-year-old horse behind the barn that is not well. Nobody in our family wants to shoot him," said the farmer. "If you will shoot him for us, I will let you hunt here."

As Orville walked back to the truck, a thought struck him, why not play a little trick on Wilbur? When he got there, Wilbur asked, "What did the farmer say?"

Orville told him the farmer was a cranky old coot, and would not let them hunt on his land. With that, he took his shotgun and said, "We will get even with him." He walked toward the barn. Wilbur was about ten paces behind him. When Orville got behind the barn he saw the horse, along with a few good cows. He walked up to the horse, levelled his gun, and shot it at point blank range.

Just then, he heard two loud gunshots behind him. He quickly turned around and saw Wilbur with a smoking gun in his hand. "I don't like that old farmer either, so I shot two of his cows," he replied.

Needless to say, no roast duck that night, only a lawsuit to pay for the cows and for trespassing on private property. Orville had permission to go behind the barn, but Wilbur did not. After an incident like that, the farmer's hatred for hunters became greater than ever.

One of the embarrassing things in life that often happens is when you meet someone whom you have not seen for awhile. You start talking to them about things from the past, about which they know nothing, because they are not the person that you think you are talking to. It has happened to me several times.

One evening at a social function, I met a lady I knew. I visited with her for at least fifteen minutes. I did not know that she was not the person I thought I was talking to. In fact, she did not say that I must be mixed up, because she did not know what I was talking about.

About a month later, I met this woman and mentioned our conversation at the party. She looked at me kind of blank, and said she wasn't there. Then it dawned on me who I had actually been talking to. I knew both of those women. They are totally unrelated and have different interests in life. But they look identical. I must have looked silly to both of them.

Some mistaken identity stories end up with positive results. James Dobson tells the story about such an incident.

In a certain school, there were two boys named Billy. One was an excellent student, well behaved and with good manners. The other Billy was always in trouble. He caused lots of problems for the teacher. His marks told the story. He was not concentrating on his studies.

One day at a PTA session, a parent asked the teacher how her Billy was doing at school. "Oh," said the teacher. "I really like him. I think he has a great future. In fact, he is my favorite student."

The next morning, the bad Billy came up to the teacher and said, "My mother told me what you said about me. Thank you for talking so nice about me."

Suddenly, it dawned on the teacher that she had thought the parent was the good Billy's mother. She did not tell the bad Billy that she had made a mistake about who she was talking about.

A strange thing happened. In the next few weeks she noticed a big change in bad Billy. He caused no more problems, did his assignments, and in general was a good student. This is one case where mistaken identity worked a miracle.

Chapter Forty-Two

IS THIS THEFT?

We all know what theft is. However, there is one type of theft that often goes undetected, and that is the stealing of ideas and sometimes, patents.

Patent thefts are often detected and end up in court. When it comes to ideas, they can be difficult to prove.

Over the years, millions of ideas and inventions have been stolen. Sometimes, the thief gets rich from some idea that originated with someone else. There are countless ways in which it can happen. Sometimes it comes from a casual conversation. Sometimes an idea is shared with a friend, someone you trust. The next thing you know, the person you trusted has stolen your idea. He uses it as though it was his idea to begin with.

My uncle, Peter Friesen, was quite an inventor. He was also open about his inventions. Needless to say, other people stole many of his inventions. There was one invention that caught the attention of a large machinery company. They paid him a small fee for the patent then proceeded to make a ton of money from it. My uncle was a good-natured Christian man, and took it all in stride. Some people would have sued the company for more money, but he just let it pass. Maybe better luck next time. He passed away a number of years ago.

I have been involved in the cattle business all my life. It is a very honest business. In spite of that, I can recall numerous times when ideas and what to do were copied by others.

One example is that of castrating bulls weighing from eight hundred to eleven hundred pounds. They make good steers when they finish out at thirteen hundred to fourteen hundred pounds. Thirty-five years ago, I was one of the few people doing that. Today, there are a lot of people in that game. It was not original with me. A few people had done it for the past seventy-five years. The reason I mention the bull story is to illustrate why some people copy ideas. They hope it will make money for them. It usually does. The whole cattle industry has evolved from somebody's ideas. If an idea turned out well, everyone copied it. It included such things as grain feeding cattle, artificial insemination, rotational grazing, breed and genetic selection.

This copying of ideas is not only done in the cattle industry, but also in all other businesses. Like I said earlier, many of the folks with the original ideas or inventions are often left in the dust.

Let me ask you who invented the wheel? Glass? Paper? Or thousands of other things we take for granted. If you look in an encyclopedia, you might get those answers. But, in our busy daily lives, we pay scant attention to the originators of the products and things we use. In a sense, it was a good thing that people stole other people's ideas, and began mass producing the various equipment and products we have today. In some cases, the inventor did cash in big from his own idea.

The most accomplished copiers are the Japanese. Wherever they go, they carry cameras with them. The pictures that they take are not always of scenery and family. Often, they take pictures of equipment or methods used in other countries. Those pictures, along with a few questions, give them enough information so that, when they get home, they begin to make the same products, maybe with some slight alterations or improvements.

Of course, the Japanese have plenty of their own ideas, especially in the field of electronics. One Japanese prisoner of war told his American captors, "We have lost the war, but we will win the next commercial war."

This was when the war was over and he was being released. What he said surely came to pass. In the next fifty years, the world was flooded with Japanese goods from small appliances to cars and trucks. This resulted in a high standard of living in Japan. They also have the longest life span of any country in the world. In the old days, Japanese goods were considered inferior. Not any more. They produce and manufacture high quality goods.

Stories abound about large oil companies buying or suppressing people that have come up with inventions to drastically reduce the fuel consumption of the internal combustion engine that all cars, trucks, tractors and other motors use. Most of these stories are hearsay, and cannot be substantiated.

One day a person that I knew well phoned me. He was looking for an investor in a patent that he was working on, which would cut fuel consumption in half. He said he had tested it and it worked. He said he needed money so that, after he registered the patent, he could start producing his invention.

He also told me that he was taking a big risk by phoning me. His fear was that some big oil company might tap into the phone line. If that happened, he though he would be in danger of getting snuffed out (killed).

I wished him well, but did not invest in his venture. He died from natural causes not too long after. I guess his invention died with him.

To plagiarize is to write something that someone else has written, and then claim the story as your own. As a writer, it is sometimes difficult to know where to draw the line as to exactly when it is plagiarizing.

In our lifetime, we read thousands of newspapers and magazine articles, as well as books. All this knowledge and information gets mixed in with our own life's experiences. Whenever someone writes a book, the copyright is mentioned. It usually states that no part of that book may be used by anyone, unless they have written permission form the author or publisher.

I have read hundreds of books, where I know for a fact that the author did not have permission to write certain excerpts that were in the book. I have written a column for twenty-five years, plus four books and some things I have written have been copied by someone, with some slight changes. It does not really upset me, although it would be nice if a writer gives credit as to where he got his information.

There is one book that we can freely quote without permission, and that is the Bible. Some folks might not even agree with that. These days, there are so many new versions, that even the Bible should not be misquoted, in the opinion of some people. I still like the King James Version, quaint language and all.

One day, some folks decided to have a banquet to honor a famous author. It was a good evening, with several speakers heaping praise on the accomplishments of the writer. One of the speakers posed the question, "Sir, to what do you credit your great success as a writer?"

Without hesitation, the author replied, "Plagiarism."

This was an answer that no one expected. Of course, much of that plagiarism would have been disguised with a few key changes.

If we could not quote or write anything that someone else has said or written without their written permission, it would be a dull world. Most writers, speechmakers, and newspapers would cease to exist. Maybe a little theft of ideas is all right if carried out with discretion.

Art is another area where copying other people's work is routinely done. Few artists will own up to that. I have seen dozens of pictures that were copies. In most instances, they were copies of lesser-known artists. It would be pretty risky to copy Charlie Russell or Frederick Remington, or any of the famous European masters. I have never seen a fake copy of the Mona Lisa, although I have seen many prints of the original.

Artists often paint a picture from a photograph. We own a number of original oil paintings and, to my knowledge, the bulk of them are originals. The last painting that I asked a well-known artist to paint for us was from a photograph. I told him to make a few small changes, because the photo was a little blurred. He did an excellent job. It was a photo of our son (now deceased) riding a saddle bronc at a college rodeo.

CHAPTER FORTY-THREE

HOUSEWORK

For centuries, the words housework and housewife were synonymous. Women got married, had babies, and did housework. Even today, women do more housework than men do, although there has been a change in the last twenty to thirty years. These days, many husbands share in the housework. In a few cases where the wife is the main breadwinner, the husband does all the housework.

When someone has a tidy, well-run house, no one notices. It is a thankless job. Accolades are far and few between. Even though men do some housework, in this chapter I will assume that women do the bulk of it. Consequently, I will use the words, she, her or women rather than person.

There are three main types of housekeepers. One is the tidy, clean freak – a very fussy woman who always keeps things immaculate. Another description is prissy. They will work day and night if need be to keep everything shiny and sparkling clean, including the inside of every cupboard and closet. There is not a speck of dust anywhere. Dust or a mess simply freaks them out.

This kind of housekeeper will often excuse herself for a bit of a mess when someone drops in unexpectedly. When you look around, you cannot help but notice that there is no mess nor clutter in sight. Everything is clean and in perfect order. At that point, you cannot help but stare at the lady, and wonder if she has all her marbles. Somewhere in her childhood she, along with many others, picked up this paranoia about housework. Maybe her mother was like that. Or maybe just the opposite - her mother may have been messy, so when she grew up, she was determined to keep her own house spotless.

Sometimes traits like this afflict men and women when they lack confidence in themselves. They are always out to prove they can do the job, so they overcompensate.

At the other end of the spectrum is the woman whose house is always in shambles. Often, a woman like that is a happy-go-lucky individual who has little concern for a little mess here and there. There is always tomorrow for cleaning it up. In my lifetime, I have been in a number of houses like that. Some were extremely filthy and so full and messy you could hardly find a chair to sit on. There was dirty laundry, empty boxes, dirty dishes and cigarette butts on the table, along with a bunch of old newspapers. In the midst of this mess, there was a carefree, cheerful woman asking if she could serve me a cup of coffee. Seldom does a sloppy housekeeper like that make any excuses for the mess.

I once knew a lady who was raised in a tidy, orderly home. When she got married and set up her own household, it was a different kettle of fish. Her house always looked like a tornado had gone through it. She and her husband seemed very happy. In fact, she was much happier than her "prissy" mother was.

You may think I prefer a messy house, rather than a tidy one. That is not the case. What I am saying is, either messy or tidy, women can have a good personality. Only in a different way.

My guess is that only about ten percent of all housekeepers fall into either the clean freak or the outrageously messy categories. Ninety percent are between those two categories. I call them the common sense ones. The common sense, or average housekeeper, likes to keep things clean and tidy, but will tolerate a certain amount of mess, especially when there are young children or teenagers in the home. A person feels comfortable with people like that. These women, quite often, are very intelligent, and realize that there is more to life than striving to have either the cleanest or dirtiest house around. My wife falls into the common sense category.

If you read this and happen to fall into the ten percent category, I am sure that you are not very happy with my assessment. If you are honest with yourself, you know what I wrote is the absolute truth. That does not mean that you will change, or even want to change. Old habits and character traits are hard to break.

There are a huge variety of tasks that a housekeeper has to do every day, such as tending to the children, washing floors and walls, dusting furniture, washing clothes, washings dishes and vacuuming. One of the biggest chores is cooking and baking.

There are good cooks and poor cooks in all categories of housekeepers. Some messy women are good cooks and some tidy housekeepers are poor cooks. In the common sense category, there are both good cooks and poor cooks, just like in the other two categories.

In many households, cooking is a joint effort by husband and wife. One of our sons-in-law is an excellent cook. Our daughter is quite happy to let him do it.

Now that I am semi-retired, I help with the housework, including cooking.

Two or three generations ago, it was common for people to have a hired girl for doing housework. They were just ordinary folks and those girls received very little pay. Some families had four, five or more daughters. I knew one couple that had eleven daughters. In those days, most young people quit school at fifteen years of age. The girls usually got married from eighteen to twenty years of age. It was in that timespan, from fifteen until they got married, that they worked for other people as domestics.

I am talking about an era from the turn of the 20th Century until after the Second World War. Since then, young people got more education and there are many more job opportunities. The hired girl practise is pretty much a thing of the past. These days many households hire a cleaning lady who comes in about once a week. There are also nannies to look after children while the wife works. Most of these nannies come from overseas, many from the Philippines, also Mexico and Central America.

I know of a strange case about sixty years ago, where the wife and the hired girl both had a baby one day apart. Both were sired by the husband. I do not remember if he hired another girl to look after the extra workload. If he did there probably were three babies born at the same time a year or two later. These folks lived approximately nine miles from our place. I did not really know them, I did see the husband a time or two. They were not Mormons.

Forty years later, we had a regular cleaning lady who came once a week. We had a big house, almost eight thousand square feet on one floor. The night before the cleaning lady was to come, my wife was as busy as the cleaning lady. She cleaned up, put stuff away and, in general, tidied things up. I used to "kid" her by saying you have all the work done. Why bother having a cleaning lady? My wife would reply, "I just don't want our house to look like a total mess when she arrives in the morning. Furthermore," she said," there is a lot of dusting to do."

Some areas of the house such as the formal dining and living room often did not get used for weeks on end. Most of the activity took place in the family room, the games room and the swimming pool area. There also were six bedrooms, five bathrooms and thirteen sinks. Needless to say, the cleaning lady never ran out of work!

In England, in the Fifteenth and Sixteenth, Seventeenth, Eighteenth, Nineteenth and Twentieth Centuries, titled families had a lot of help, both men and women. There were housekeepers, cooks, nannies, butlers, gardeners, stable hands, chauffeurs and footmen. I do not think all that help made the people particularly happy. Their whole life was centered on keeping up with the Joneses. They were and still are, in a constant battle with the British tabloids to keep them from reporting all the extra marital affairs that are ongoing things in those circles. If you do not believe me, take a look at Kitty Kelly's book, *The Royals*. It was well researched.

In the Bible, we read about a household of two women, Mary and Martha. Mary liked to visit, while Martha was committed to work and providing food. Jesus said to her, "Martha, Martha, thou art careful and troubled about many things; but one thing is needful, and Mary has chosen that good part."

Maybe there is a lesson in that for all of us. It is better to relax and visit than to fuss around to ensure that everything is perfect.

CHAPTER FORTY-FOUR

NEVER SAY CAN'T

When I was in school, we had one teacher who absolutely forbid us to say "can't". She was so adamant about it that you risked getting the strap if you used the word. I think that was a good lesson for me. In my lifetime, I have not used that word for any task facing me, no matter how difficult. I am not that pure that I have never used it. These days, I say it quite often, in the phrase, "I can't remember the date," or your name, or a number of other things. I use it very seldom when it comes to challenges that most of us face on a daily basis, thanks to my former teacher, whose name I can't remember.

All through history, men and women have achieved great feats. They often stood alone. Everyone else said it couldn't be done. I am sure the average person today or in ancient times would have said it was impossible to build the Pyramids of Egypt. It just can't be done. They did it, even though it cost the lives of thousands of slaves. Some of those pyramids are over four hundred and fifty feet tall. It is impossible to imagine how they managed to pull those huge slabs up and place them into perfect positions with only ropes and human strength. Some of them are over four thousand years old and still in good condition. The Pharaoh's overseers never entertained the idea that it couldn't be done.

It was another one of those atrocities against the human race that one can hardly comprehend. Those slaves worked hard in the scorching sun. If they slacked off, an overseer's whip would be applied to their backs. So the project progressed with blood, sweat and tears. Those pyramids were constructed as tombs for Egyptian kings.

This is quite different today, when a large number of people are cremated. There is no monument of their past existence except for a small urn of ashes and the ashes are often scattered on the ocean, plains or mountains. I am not criticizing that, although I still prefer burial with a gravemarker.

I always tell my wife that, if I happen to die before she does, I have no request as to what she does with my body. It is our souls that need to concern us. If we have accepted Jesus Christ as our Saviour, then when we die, our souls shall soar to much greater heights than an earthly pyramid.

We must never say it can't be done. God made provision for us so it can be done. It is a risky business to turn our backs on God when we are still alive.

How about the world's other projects that have been built? The naysayers of all generations have said it can't be done. Yet, in every generation, there are people who are risk takers, and never say it can't be done. Some of those challenging man-made projects are railroads through the mountains, numerous canals and tunnels, subways, super highways, the great wall of China, huge churches and cathedrals (St. Peter's in Rome took nine hundred years to build), plus many more. If the builders of those projects had listened to the "it can't be done" crowd, none of these things would have been built.

The Wright brothers never said can't. They had absolute faith that man could fly through the air in a contraption called an aeroplane. That's a far cry from today's supersonic military and commercial jet planes. All through the evolution to today's planes, people said it couldn't be done.

There are a number of things that we take for granted today that people with a positive attitude have discovered, invented and manufactured such as glass, the wheel, steam and fuel engines, electricity (which spawned the electric light bulb), radio, TV, computers, and other gadgets of every description that make life easier.

How about the little challenges we all face on a daily basis? Often, we as parents, hear our children say, "I can't do it." Of course, that applies to adults as well.

I am not mechanical, so whenever something happens to our cars, trucks, or equipment like household gadgets, I avoid saying, "I can't fix it." Rather, I say, "It is just not my line," and let someone repair it who knows what they are doing. I avoid saying, I can't do it.

Several years ago after a knee replacement operation, I was taken to physiotherapy. As I was lying on my back, my physiotherapist told me to slowly lift my leg off the bed. I tried, but I just couldn't lift it, even an inch. I told the lady I just couldn't do it. She gave me a severe look and told me in no uncertain terms that there is no such thing as "can't". Immediately, images of my teacher from half a century ago flooded in and I summoned all the courage that I could muster. Sure enough, I was able to raise my leg about two inches. Each session after that I raised it a little more. In two weeks, I had no problem raising it all the way up. If I had stayed with my I-can't-do-it attitude, I would probably have a stiff leg to this day. I thanked her for being tough with me.

I do not know how many young people will read this. If you do, I hope you will resolve in your minds not to take the I-can't-do-it attitude towards life. The world would be a better place for people if we have a positive outlook rather than an I-can't mentality.

When a baby takes its first steps, it thinks that it is hard to do, but the baby is anxious to walk like its parents. After a few faltering steps, the baby suddenly realizes it can keep its balance and begins to walk. This is an early lesson on the I-can't mentality.

Whether as children we are aware of this I-can outlook, I am not sure. I am sure that any challenge faced and overcome as a young child, has a great influence on our attitudes when we become adults. I know of one child that overcame a stutter in his speech. He became a good preacher as an adult.

CHAPTER FORTY-FIVE

EVERYBODY SHOOTS FROM THEIR OWN CORNER

All through history, people have looked out for "number one", themselves. Many people do not really care how their actions or activities impact on other people's lives. There are countless situations where someone gets hurt by the selfishness of someone else. I will mention a few cases that I am aware of. It can be financial, moral, spiritual, or any number of things.

Several years ago, an old gentleman that I knew well, told me how delighted he was that interest rates were sky high. He said that he had a whole bunch of money in five-year term certificates that paid nineteen percent interest. He was not hard up. He received several good pension cheques. I said to John (not his real name), "How about your children and grandchildren? They are having a tough time paying high mortgage rates, in some cases losing their jobs because businesses were going broke, due to high interest rates." This was in the early- to mid-'80s. I got clipped pretty well myself. I was paying twenty-two percent interest on a four million dollar loan. I could tell he knew that what I was saying was true. In spite of that, he shrugged it off. He seemed to have very little concern about what was happening to a large segment of the population. Of course, it was not his fault that interest rates were so high. He was shooting from his own corner.

In large corporations, or even small companies, the pecking order is ruthless as to who gets a promotion. I once worked for a large company. What I observed there was that the middle managers were the worst. They were a little way up the ladder and their goal was to get to the top at whatever cost. They got to where they were by more or less cutting their fellow employees' throats. Once they got to that middle management position, they carried on the same kind of tactics, although maybe a little more refined.

I experienced it myself with one of my fellow workers. This chap would do anything to make me look bad, while trying to enhance his position. When a promotion came along, he got it. After that, he was quite nice to me, because he needed me. In the end he lost his job and, eventually, I got the job. In a few years, I got another promotion to the head office as the general manager of our department. During my tenure in that position, I always used the pat on the back, instead of the stab in the back approach. I am not gloating about what happened years ago. I only wish to point out that we can be decent and civil to our fellow employees, and still get ahead.

Another thing that happens quite frequently in large corporations is that incompetent people get promoted to middle management because they are easier to control. It is surprising how many companies want "yes men" that strictly adhere to company policy. They have very few ideas of their own.

A number of years ago, a man drove by our place with about a thousand pound round bale on the back of his pick-up truck. Somehow, the bale fell off on a high-grade road that goes by our place. The bale hit a wooden plank fence. The planks and several posts sheared off and splintered. The bale rolled about a hundred feet onto our property. He just drove off. A few days later, when there was no one around, he came back and got the bale. He never said a word about the fence, nor did he come to repair it. He did not care that it cost about seventy-five dollars to repair the fence. The least he could have done is given us that bale of hay. He was strictly shooting from his own corner.

Have you ever sat on a board with a dozen other people? I have, on a number of occasions. Sometimes the board functions very well. However, on some boards there is a lot of friction. Everyone has a different idea as to what should be done, so a consensus is hard to achieve.

One good example was the City of Calgary Board of Education (1999). This board consisted of seven members, all women. Everyone on that board seemed to have a different view and opinion on how things should be done. This resulted in a lot of bickering and mud slinging. They became totally dysfunctional. Finally, the Minister of

Learning (education) fired the whole board. This was an extreme case of everyone shooting from their own corner.

In sports, such as hockey, baseball, football, rodeo and others, they have referees or judges. Generally, these officials are competent and fair, but, being human, they are sometimes biased for or against a team or individual, and make bad calls in favor of friends or teams that they like. This is very evident in Olympic sports, especially figure skating. Members on the judging panel will almost always score the skater from their own country higher than the rest of the skaters.

I am a rodeo fan. Having watched for sixty years gives me a pretty good idea of what to look for in a good bronc ride. Most rodeo judges are fair, but every once in a while they are way off base. They either mark the contestant too high or too low. It is sometimes obvious that a judge favors certain individuals. A contestant that questions a judge about his low mark soon gets the reputation of being a complainer. Once that happens, his markings may even get lower.

I once saw a world champion bareback rider marked eighty-eight points. At the same rodeo, lesser-known riders were marked in the mid-seventies for rides that were every bit as good, including the spurring action. In rodeo, fifty percent is marked for the horse or bull and fifty percent on the performance of the contestant. One day, I saw a man on the ground when the whistle went (the ride lasts eight seconds), yet the judges marked him. Why? I guess they liked him better than his closest competitor who was known as a bit of a "complainer". The cowboy who bucked off before the eight-second whistle went home with a bunch of money. His competitor, who rode the whole eight seconds, went home with a much lesser amount of money.

One day, I heard a rodeo judge's remark about a contestant that he did not like: "I'll get even with him."

Tough penalty calls can kill any team on a given day, especially in hockey. It allows the other team to score a power play goal.

One sport that is honest, at least at the pro level, is golf. However, at the duffer level, cheating is rampant. I have seldom played a game of golf where my fellow golfers were honest in their scoring. Their excuse is, "Oh, well, it is only a game for fun, so why worry about a little cheating." The problem is that when the game is over, they boast about the low score they had.

I was golfing with a chap one day. I noticed on the first three or four holes, his score was considerably lower than mine was. So I made it my business to discreetly keep track of his shots as well as my own. What I discovered was that he marked his score one to three strokes less than he actually had. When we finished the eighteen holes, his score was much lower than mine was. In the clubhouse, he boasted about his good game. I never told him that I had kept track of his last fourteen holes. I let him revel in his good game of golf. He was not only shooting golf; he was also shooting from his own corner.

Big, multinational companies are notorious for shooting from their own corner. They have absolutely no regard as to how many small businesses they put out of business. A classic example of this is a relatively small mall close to where we live. There are about twenty-five small shops with a larger anchor store at each end. One of the anchor stores is a huge grocery chain with headquarters in San Francisco, United States. This store decided to enlarge its floor space. They built a large addition. There was nothing wrong with that, except that they made their own large entrance from the outside, at the opposite end away from the mall.

They left a tiny opening onto the mall with no check-out counter. Further more, the mall has a florist and a pharmacy, which sell greeting cards and other stationery. In spite of these outlets, the multinational grocery chain specializes in all three of these non-grocery items. In fact, they enlarged their card inventory on the card racks. There are no prices displayed, for a good reason. Their cards are two to three times as expensive as those in the mall. In at least three of those stores, one of these card stores is also a United States multinational. Its cards are also expensive. They trade on their so-called superior quality, which is a bunch of hooey.

Back to the grocery store. The reason that they can sell cards is simple. When people are grocery shopping, they suddenly remember Aunt Sadie's birthday, so for convenience sake, they toss a birthday card into their shopping cart, even though they are getting ripped off. I talked to some of the mall merchants after the grocery store had basically shut the mall off (before they remodelled and enlarged the store, their main entrance was in the mall). They told me that business in the mall had dropped off anywhere from twenty-five to thirty percent, because of so much less pedestrian traffic. This was rather a long-winded story, but this scenario is replayed throughout all urban areas in North America. The large get larger and the small independents get smaller and disappear altogether. That may be progress. The end result is that everyone becomes an employee of these large corporations. In most cases, there is little room for promotion. A large number of those employees are part time. That way the company escapes paying benefits.

The story I am about to relate does not completely fit, Shooting from your own Corner, and yet it does, to some degree.

The one-room country school that I attended often had discipline problems that were difficult to solve for some of the young women teachers who taught there.

One day Jake (not his real name) committed a misdemeanour that the teacher thought needed some corporal punishment. The strap was missing. Probably, one of the boys had stolen it and threw it in the pond. At this point, the young teacher became creative. She told Jake to go outside and find a branch or stick, with which she would administer the punishment. Jake left the classroom. In a few minutes he returned with a little twig, so small it would not hurt a mouse. The teacher was furious. She immediately ordered him to get a bigger stick. Out he went again. This time he stayed out quite a while.

When he finally made his appearance, he was dragging a big fence post, large enough to kill an elephant. The whole classroom dissolved in laughter. Even though the teacher tried to keep a straight face, she had to smile. She could see the humour in the situation. Jake went unpunished. That was one time that shooting from your own corner paid off. It also provided a little entertainment. Jake passed away several years ago.

Human nature is strange. We sometimes criticize other people, but we sure don't like it when someone criticizes us. Every person has some faults. We seem to have a great capacity to overlook our own faults. I believe that fault finding and criticism are the greatest destroyers of marriages. Maybe even more so than jealousy and that ranks pretty high.

When one or both spouses find constant fault with their partner, it leads to fighting and bitterness. Often, the criticism or fault is over a trivial matter. By the time it is over, it has blown into a major confrontation.

Often when a couple is going together before they marry, they are much more tolerant about each other's shortcomings. Once married, either one or both of them embark on a program of reforming their partner into what they consider the right type of person and spouse. The result of such action strains the marriage relationship until it finally erupts into a situation from which neither spouse can extract himself or herself. The story to the divorce court is that we are simply incompatible. That is the grounds for divorce, which is the most common.

If the couple had more tolerance for each other's little faults and accepted one another for what they are, pimples and all, much heartache could be avoided. Then, all our children could grow up with both parents in the same house.

Yes, shooting from our own corner in marriage is a dangerous game.

I have written several books in which I mention a lot of names of people and something about them (character sketches). I have had little criticism from them or their families. However, there have been a few. Every one of those criticisms was based on the fact that I had not written enough good things about their spouse or relative. People do not mind reading something negative about someone else. Just do not write anything negative about their family or themselves. I have had a number of people tell me that I was much too kind in my comments about someone they did not like or considered a rascal. My answer to them is, "How would you like it if I told the public all about your shortcomings?" That usually silences them.

Every morning when we get up, we should look in the mirror and say to ourselves: "Today I am going to consider my fellow man and avoid shooting from my own corner." We can overcome, if we try.

The young man that sweet talks a girl into having premarital sex is shooting from his own corner, or, should I say, lusts from his own corner. He often does not really care if she becomes pregnant. To me, that is utterly disgusting.

Shooting from your own corner can involve any or all of the following: dishonesty, greediness, ignorance, low moral character, laziness, self-importance, anger and revenge.

Most of us are guilty of shooting from our own corner at least once in a while. A good idea is to say to ourselves, "How would we like it if somebody else did to us what we do to them?" Or, as the Bible puts it, "Do unto others as you would have them do unto you."

Always strive to help rather than to hurt someone. Try a little love instead. This world has many good people who try to live by the Golden Rule. Are you one of them?

CHAPTER FORTY-SIX

THINGS THAT ANNOY

Have you ever stood in line at a bank? I am sure you have. What annoys me is that, after standing in line for ten minutes, you are finally at the front of the line. At the counter in front of you is a bank customer dealing with a teller. After all the transactions have been completed, the customer - often an older lady - continues to visit with the teller. When the teller more or less terminates the conversation, the lady starts fiddling around in her purse or handbag rearranging things. She puts her latest bank papers in a certain compartment, slowly zips the purse shut, and then slowly moves away. Now it's my turn. In a small bank with only four tellers, people like that waste at least an hour of other people's time each day. Are you one of those time-wasters who does not consider other people waiting in line?

How do you enjoy conversing with someone who talks steadily? When you say something, he or she has a glazed look on their face, not hearing a thing you say. When you finish your few comments, away they go again, filling you in on every small detail in their little world. This can happen on the phone or in person. One day a man said what a wonderful conversationalist a certain man was, when in fact; the man hardly said a word. Only an odd, "Yes, I agree," or shaking his head in the affirmative. It never occurred to the man that he had done all the talking, while the so-called good conversationalist had only been listening.

As we get older this can become a habit. I try to police myself in this respect. I am quite a talker myself, but I always try to listen to what the other person has to say. Next time one of you meet me, give me a test to see if I pass or fail.

How about public rest rooms? Nothing is as revolting to me as someone who is too lazy to flush the toilet after a bowel movement. Those are the kinds of people who seldom wash their hands after using the toilet. A man once spied on people's hand washing habits in three or four big cities. Of special interest to him were restaurant personnel such as waiters and cooks. What he discovered was that over half of the restaurant help did not wash their hands in the washroom. I guess it is a good thing our immune systems can handle a lot of germs. I often think of that survey when I eat in a restaurant. Service station operators have told me that the ladies rest rooms are much dirtier and messier than the men's rest rooms. Is this true, ladies? I would not know since I have only set foot in a ladies rest room twice. Both times by mistake. They looked all right to me, but then I did not stay long.

Smorgs or help-yourself restaurants and banquets can also test a person's patience. Some people take oodles of time deciding what they take. Sometimes you wonder if they are ever going to move. Often there are a half a dozen people ahead of you, each one a slow poke. This can be really annoying if there is a long line-up. The same thing happens at post offices, or any other place of business.

While we are no the subject, how about parking your car? When a parking lot is full, it is difficult to find a parking spot. Suddenly, you notice someone walking to his or her car. Here is your chance to park. You move the car into position ready to take their spot when they vacate it. Many is the time that a person will start the car and sit there doing who knows what for three or four minutes. It seems like half an hour. Slowly they secure the seat belt and move out. You have your parking space, provided someone who has just arrived doesn't slip in ahead of you. This has happened to me more than once. If it is an older lady, I just sort of grin and bear it. But, if it is some young buck, I have to bite my lip to keep from exploding.

Clichés can also get to a person. Often, when you go to pay your bill at a restaurant, the person at the till will ask, "How is everything?" I usually say, okay, even if it was not. I have found that to complain to that person is a dead end street, so why bother.

When someone says, "How are you today?" my wife answers, "How much time have you got?" End of conversation.

When I think of all the things that annoy me, condescension tops the list. This happens more as we get older. Most people do not do it on purpose. It happens when they assume they have to explain things to you because you may not understand what the topic of discussion is all about.

Nine times out of ten, I know the topic better than they do. An example might be, "Have you ever heard of the Catacombs?" My reply, "Yes, I have even taken a tour through those underground tunnels." One day, a younger woman (thirtyish) explained for two minutes to my wife how to use the phone. Or, how about, "Have you ever eaten in a Chinese restaurant?" Yes, hundreds of times.

"Do you know that every country in South America speaks Spanish except for Brazil?" Yes, I have known that since I was in grade three.

They mean well when they say to me, "Let me lift that for you." It may weigh twenty-five pounds. I can still lift two hundred pounds.

One that really blew me away was when a young medical person was surprised I could still trim my own toenails. Maybe the day will come when I do not know what the Catacombs are, or where South America is, or I am unable to lift twenty-five pounds. But until such a time, please do not rush me into becoming a helpless senior with not many mental facilities left.

Young people, please do not spoil our golden years by talking to us as though we have lost it. It can be annoying.

A few more things that annoy me, or should I say, I don't like or appreciate:

- Cranky postal employees (There are exceptions. The ones at our post office are good).
- Illegal strikes.
- All the plastic surrounding new cars, including those totally useless flimsy bumpers.
- Violence on TV and at the movies.
- Lumpy motel and hotel beds.
- Foam rubber pillows.
- Soya bean hamburgers.

- County and municipal politicians and bureaucrats who often act like little Caesars (there are a few good ones)
- Loud music in a restaurant, when you are trying to have a relaxing dinner.
- Parks overrun with gophers.
- A salad with all kinds of strange leaves, but not much lettuce.
- Cracked sidewalks and potholes in the road.

There is more that I do not like and that annoys me, but I think this is enough negativity for now. Let's move onto something more positive.

CHAPTER FORTY-SEVEN

ONE-LINER TIDBITS AND WISDOM

Pause to reflect on what you read after every line. In other words, take time for what the message or meaning of each saying is, and let it sink in.

- A man has no worse enemy than himself.
- Vanity is the quicksand of reason.
- The reward of suffering is experience.
- Talent without tact is only half talent.
- Mistakes are lessons of wisdom.
- No legacy is as rich as honesty.
- Originality is simply a pair of fresh eyes.
- Patience is bitter, but its fruit is sweet.
- The whole life is made up of unfinished business.
- Humility is to make light of oneself.
- Intuition is reason in a hurry.
- Doubt whom you will, but never yourself.
- Today is the day you worried about yesterday.
- Where we all think alike, no one thinks very much.
- Gratitude is the most exquisite form of courtesy.
- Leave hate to those who are too weak to love.
- Win or lose, never regret.
- The person who has everything should be quarantined.
- Kind words do not cost much.
- Children have more need for models than critics do.
- A contented man can't be sold a thing.
- Morning comes long before you are ready for it.
- Most of us can't stand people who are intolerant.
- Every change of scenery is a delight.

- Move slowly; never negotiate in a hurry.
- Action makes more fortunes than caution.
- A good idea shared with others will live forever.
- The wise man can learn by listening to the ignorant man.
- Few men have repented of silence.
- Architecture is frozen music.
- Chance usually favors the prudent.
- What is now proved was once only imagined.
- Moderation is the key to lasting enjoyment.
- Law can not persuade where it can not punish.
- Knowledge comes, but wisdom lingers.
- Praise makes good men better and bad men worse.
- When you are through leaving, you are through.
- Examine what is said, not who speaks.
- What we do not understand, we do not possess.
- Good fortune is not known until it is lost.
- Laziness is often mistaken for patience.
- Good humor makes all things tolerable.
- Weakness is the only incurable fault.
- There was a patient who received so many shots, he had to drink water to see if he leaked.
- Don't worry about your wrinkles. They only indicate where your smiles have been.
- Don't envy anybody. Every person has something no other person has. Develop that one thing in your life and make it outstanding.
- Every accomplishment, great or small, starts with the right decision – I'll try.
- Hope sees the invisible, fells the intangible, and achieves the impossible.
- You can't get anywhere unless you start.
- Kind words never die but without kind actions they can sound mighty sick.

- When all the affairs of life are said and done, more has been said than done.
- The world we live in hasn't changed on some things. People are still judged by their actions.
- By the time we find greener pastures, we are too old to climb the fence.
- The art of conversation consists of building on another person's observation, not overturning it.
- Most of us would be glad to accept good advice if it did not interfere so much with our plans.
- The problem with telling a good story is that it usually reminds another person of a better one.
- The advice that is most valuable comes from the one who is most reluctant to give it.
- Appreciation makes people feel more important than almost anything you can give them.
- Antiques – what your grandparents bought, gave to your parents, they sold as junk, and you bought as treasure.
- Some people will pat you on the back to make sure you've swallowed what they've just told you.
- May today be a beautiful day filled with joy and happiness – enough to share with those you meet.
- Folks in the medical industry are the only ones who benefit from poor health.
- Sound advice is just that – ninety-five percent sounds and five percent advice.
- Teamwork really works. Look at the Mississippi River – it's nothing but drops of water working together to move in the same direction.
- If you can laugh at it, you can live with it.
- Some people can adapt to any situation. If they fall in a lake they check their pockets for fish.
- No matter what your lot in life, build something.

- When things don't go right, at least we have the opportunity to try again with more wisdom.
- The happiest of people can enjoy the scenery when they have been taken on a detour.
- It isn't what you know that counts; it's what you think of at the moment.
- Just because today didn't go as planned doesn't mean something wonderful isn't headed your way.
- Those who just want to kill time need to learn the value of life.
- We all know people who have a lot of good in them. They must – it never comes out.
- Some folks are hard of hearing, others are hard of listening.
- If adversity builds character, then that explains why there are so many characters in this world.
- The best cures for despair are doing a good deed or soaking in a hot bath.
- The people we admire for wisdom are the ones who come to us for advice.
- If you can determine what is good advice and bad advice you don't need any advice.
- Hope is the anchor of the soul, the stimulus to action, and the incentive to achievement.
- Do something. Either lead, follow, or get out of the way.
- We increase our ability, stability and responsibility when we increase our sense of accountability to a higher power.
- He who hesitates is lost.
- Look before you leap.
- Many people buy on time but few pay that way.
- I only borrow money from pessimists. They never expect it back.
- Wisdom comes from good judgment, which comes from experience, which often comes from bad judgment.
- The harder I work, the luckier I get.
- When in doubt, don't.

- Always buy a good bed and a good pair of shoes. If you're not in one, you're in the other.

Desiderata

Go placidly amid the noise and haste, and remember what peace there may be in silence. As far as possible without surrender be on good terms with all persons.

Speak your truth quietly and clearly; listen to others, even the dull and ignorant; they too have their story.

Avoid loud and aggressive persons, they are vexations to the spirit. If you compare yourself with others, you may become vain and bitter; for always there will be greater and lesser persons than yourself. Enjoy your achievements as well as your plans.

Keep interested in your own career, however humble; it is a real possession in the changing fortunes of time. Exercise caution in your business affairs; for the world is full of trickery. But let this not blind you to what virtue there is: many persons strive for high ideals; and everywhere life is full of heroism.

Be yourself. Especially, do not feign affection. Neither be cynical about love; for in the face of all aridity and disenchantment it is perennial as the grass.

Take kindly the counsel of the years, gracefully surrendering the things of youth. Nurture strength of spirit to shield you in sudden misfortune. But do not distress yourself with imaginings. Many fears are born of fatigue and loneliness. Beyond a wholesome discipline, be gentle with yourself.

You are a child of the universe, no less than the trees and the stars; you have a right to be here. And whether or not it is clear to you, no doubt the universe is unfolding as it should.

Therefore, be at peace with God, whatever you conceive Him to be, and whatever your labors and aspirations, in the noisy confusion of life keep peace with your soul. With all its sham, drudgery and broken dreams, it is still a beautiful world.

Be cheerful. Strive to be happy.

Max Ehrmann - 1927

Chapter Forty-Eight

A FEW WAR STORIES

War always produces a lot of sad stories and the Second World War was no exception. Millions of people died, including thousands of Canadians. Each life was precious to surviving family members and friends.

In the area where we lived, many boys were in the armed forces serving at home and overseas. One such person was a young man who enlisted in the navy. His parents lived approximately five miles from our place. He was three or four years older than I was.

After some basic training, he was consigned to a battleship in the North Atlantic. One night a German torpedo hit their ship. Within minutes, the ship began to sink. The sailors all scrambled overboard into lifeboats. The problem was that there were almost twice as many sailors as there was room in the life rafts. As they floundered around in the water, those who could not get into a life raft clung to the sides of them, their bodies dangling in that cold water. Some of the men in the rafts took turns hanging onto the sides, while their fellow sailors climbed onto the rafts for short periods. As the hours ticked by, more and more of the men were overcome by hypothermia and dropped off into those frigid waters, never to be seen again. The boy from our neighborhood hung on for a long time. Finally, he too succumbed and disappeared into the icy waters of the North Atlantic. This story was told by the handful of men who survived. They were picked up by a rescue boat a day or so later. What a tragedy that whole affair was. The Navy was partly to blame. They should have had enough life rafts for every man on board that ship. There are hundreds of similar stories that have all but been forgotten, except by family and a few friends. This happened about fifty-eight years ago. Much of his family has passed away. How sad those young men gave their lives in war, all because of a madman called Hitler.

Some war stories had a different ending. I knew a man that was in the Infantry in the Canadian Army. His unit was in the midst of fierce fighting, almost hand to hand combat. Suddenly, he felt a searing pain in his lower abdomen and back. He buckled up and fell to the ground. His comrades dragged him behind an old barn. Fortunately, there was a medic present in their unit. When the doctor pulled off the man's uniform, he was amazed by what he saw. There were seven bullet holes in the front of him and seven holes in his back where they had exited. Apparently, he was the recipient of those wounds from a German machine gun. They were in a straight line from one side of his body to the other side. They must have been steel tipped not the mushroom type. The doctor gave him the best medical attention possible under those circumstances. They transported him to a field hospital, then later to a hospital in England. He credits the army doctor for saving his life.

The amazing thing is that those bullets missed most of his vital organs such as lungs, liver and heart. They also missed his spine or he would have been paralyzed. He eventually recovered. When the war was over, he came back to Canada. He got married and raised a family. He lived quite close to our family. I never actually saw the scars that the bullets left. He did show them to a close friend of mine. The chance of a man surviving seven machine gun bullets through his body must be about a million to one.

Human nature is interesting and has put a strong self-preservation into each one of us. None of us are in a hurry to die, even if we say we are ready to die.

A man that I knew well who was in the Second World War told me about being under enemy fire at close range. He was driving a jeep (I think in France) when suddenly there was a burst of gunfire. He stopped the jeep and dove under it. While he was lying flat on the ground, the bullets literally riddled the jeep. While lying there, he prayed to God for safety. He said, "Lord, if you spare me I will serve you or do anything you want me to be involved in." His life was spared. However, when the war was finally over, he forgot all about his promise to God. He was not a bad person, but there was not much evidence of his promise to serve God.

Situations like this have happened to a lot of people, maybe not as dramatic as bullets flying a foot or two above your head. But we humans have a tendency to resolve to do better to our fellow man and God when we find ourselves in a tight corner. Once the danger or problem is over, we forget what we resolved to do.

A paratrooper in the Korean War told me a story of an experience where he, along with others, parachuted behind enemy lines. The problem was that they misjudged where the enemy was. As they descended, the enemy opened fire on them. A number were killed in the air. They were dead when they hit the ground. My friend was hit as well. He passed out and does not remember hitting the ground.

In a fairly short time, he regained consciousness. He heard the enemy walking around among the dead and dying paratroopers. He lay stock still as though he was dead. Just then, a soldier walked by him and gave him a couple of hard kicks in the groin with his big army boot. When a man's life is at stake, he can do super human things. This was a case like that. The pain from the kicks, along with his gunshot wound, was excruciating. He continued to play dead. Finally, the army moved on. At this point, he mustered all the courage he could and started to crawl in the opposite direction from which the enemy army had gone. A day or so later, a United States army patrol picked him up and took him to an army hospital. Fifty years later, he still bears the scars of that horrible encounter. War affects people adversely. It is kill or be killed. After a while, you become callous.

Another man that I know well, is a gentle soul, and he told me what a terrible thing war is. As an American, he was involved in some of the fighting in the South Pacific during the Second World War. One day, they encountered a large group of Japanese soldiers who were dug into a hillside. The exchange of gunfire was awesome. He reckoned that he killed twelve or thirteen enemy soldiers. Many Americans died as well. He was seriously wounded. In civilian life he would never think of killing a man, but in war, when it is kill or be killed, you go kind of numb and keep on firing at the enemy until one side gives up.

I must tell you another story about a friend of mine – Winston Churchill Parker. He experienced an unbelievable march during the Second World War. This story illustrates how terrible war is.

Winston was raised just south of Calgary in the Midnapore area. His parents immigrated to Canada from England, his mother in 1912 and his father in 1913. They met in Canada and were married in 1915. Mrs. Parker was a Churchill, a third cousin of Sir Winston Churchill. The Parker's had three children, sons Winston and Geoff and a daughter Jessie. Winston and Geoff were good horsemen. They rode with either western or English saddles. Both of them were good polo players.

When World War Two broke out they both enlisted and joined the air force. After some basic training, they were sent to England, where they ended up in different squadrons. One day the plane Geoff was flying in was shot down in the North Atlantic. They managed to splash down on the water and miraculously survived. The sailors from the destroyer they were protecting plucked them from the water. Geoff became a friend of mine after the war.

Winston's squadron was always flying at night on bombing sorties over Germany. On one such mission, as they were flying close to Hamburg, German anti-aircraft fire hit the plane that Winston and five other crew members were in. Winston was a wireless operator and air gunner. The plane still flew, but it was in bad shape. They almost made it to the Dutch border when it conked out. They had no choice but to bail out. One member of the crew was killed.

As soon as they had landed with their parachutes, the remaining crew members were taken prisoner. They were not beaten, but they were treated pretty rough. After some intensive interrogation, they were shipped to prisoner-of-war camps. They did not all go to the same location. Winston was shipped by train to a prison at Lansdorf called Stalag VIII B. It was close to the notorious Auchwitz extermination death camp. That was in April of 1942. For the first few weeks they tied his hands together with cords. Then a shipment of handcuffs arrived that, strange as it may seem, had been manufactured in England. Maybe the Germans had them in storage for a few years.

He spent ten or eleven months in handcuffs. Then they eased up and took them off. On the whole, his treatment was tolerable, especially when certain guards were on duty. As one can well imagine, it was a dreary experience.

News from the outside world was scarce. But word got around, maybe from the guards, that the Russian army was rapidly advancing towards their location.

Suddenly on January 22, 1945, they were ordered to get ready for a march. There were twenty-seven thousand men in that camp. They broke them into groups or columns of three thousand men, along with a number of guards who accompanied them. Conditions were appalling, as it was winter. Their clothes were not warm and their shoe situation was terrible. Winston told me he had a sturdy pair of shoes to start with. By the end of the march, he and most of the others were walking barefoot as their shoes were completely worn out.

They marched anywhere from four to fifteen miles a day, depending on the terrain and the weather. On most nights they found some shelter, either in an old barn or other old buildings, even in a rock quarry. A few times they slept outdoors. One night there was a fierce blizzard. They huddled together in the snow. They each had a blanket. In spite of this, on real cold nights, they shivered like wet pups.

As the weeks went by, a number of men died from either exposure or dysentery. Winston said, only the hope of freedom some day and a dogged determination kept him and the others going.

After three months, they arrived at Hanover, close to the Dutch border. At that point, for some reason or another, they were ordered to march back in the direction they had come from. Suddenly General Patton and the United States Army arrived on the scene. Apparently, the German guards knew that he was coming, as they all disappeared into the countryside. The men were a sight to behold, ragged and most of them barefoot with huge calluses in their feet, unshaven and some were sick.

They were transported to England. That was in April 1945. Winston weighed approximately one hundred and eighty pounds when the death march started. When he arrived in England, he weighed ninety-eight pounds. He was in the hospital for six weeks recuperating. After he was released from the hospital, he went to visit some of his relatives. His dad's cousin, Reg Parker, had been the chauffeur for five British Prime Ministers, including the Prime Minister at the time, Sir Winston Churchill. His uncle introduced him to Churchill. When Churchill found out he was related to him, he was quite delighted. He told his chauffeur to take him to the Parliament Buildings, then to take the rest of the day off.

He drove Winston Parker around London for the day. Winston told me it was an interesting time. Not only were the sights of London interesting, but also how the police cleared the traffic and the intersections when they saw the Prime Minister's limousine. Other folks on the sidewalks also recognized the car as well.

When Winston got back to Canada, he bought a place at Millarville and raised Hereford cattle. I bought a lot of his cattle when he brought them to the Calgary Stockyards. They were top quality calves and performed well in the feedlot. He also raised registered oats and barley seed. In 1989, Winston and his wife Phyllis retired to Okotoks were they are still involved and active in community affairs. Winston went on the "Hooves of History Cattle Drive" at Cochrane at eighty years of age.

I salute Winston and the thousands of other veterans who served their country well in both war and peace.

On the lighter side, an American told me about a conversation he had in Australia during the Second World War. The Aussie said to him, "We like you Yanks but there are four things wrong with you." "Oh," said my American friend, "And what are they." The Aussie replied, "One, you are over paid. Two, you are overfed. Three, you are over sexed. And four, you are over here." Of course it was said in jest so there were no hard feelings. This sailor came home after the war, got married and raised a good family.

There were millions just like him.

CHAPTER FORTY-NINE

WHO IS IN THE MINORITY?

In these days of political correctness we hear much about minorities. The term is sometimes used and abused in order to gain better jobs or higher social standing in the community.

Ever since creation, minorities have existed. The Bible is full of people who were in a minority situation.

In any country or area in the world where people live, there are bound to be minorities. In other words, because of national background or religion, small groups of people who have the least number of people are minorities.

In the United States, Afro-Americans and Hispanics are minorities. In Mexico, Central America, and South America, Protestants are in the minority because those countries have ten times as many Catholics as Protestants. In the Middle East, parts of Europe and most of Asia and Africa, Christians (Catholics and Protestants) are in the minority because there are so many Muslims. Nearly every country in the world has minorities, either by language, national background or religion.

In a democracy, or any other form of government, the majority rules. The people in the minority feel like their voices are not heard. This leads to unrest, which often leads to rebellion and civil war.

In many countries where there are minorities, governments attempt, and often do, introduce legislation, which they hope will prevent the situation from escalating into a full-blown rebellion.

In North America (Canada and the United States), we have an uneasy peace at the moment. The reason I say uneasy is that, in the United States, the black and Hispanic people still feel they are not fully integrated. In Canada, the French in Quebec are constantly trying to secede from the rest of Canada. In both countries, the Native people (First Nations) are on the verge of going on the warpath in order to gain huge land claims – vast areas they consider their land.

The history of Europe, Asia and Africa is littered with terrible atrocities inflicted on minorities. Even these days the strife continues. Newspapers are saturated with stories of severe persecution and even genocide. Some countries that come to mind are Iraq, (where the Kurds live in fear for their lives), Sudan (where over two million people have been killed in the last twenty years), Rwanda, South Africa, Spain, Sri Lanka, Pakistan, India (where the three religions - Hindi, Muslim and Sikh - live together) are hot spots. There are more countries that do not mix very well: Northern Ireland, Indonesia, Israel, Kosovo, and also several republics in Russia and dozens more around the world.

The minorities in these countries often become terrorists who kill thousands of innocent people. Their goal is to destabilize their government, which can be either a democracy or a dictatorship. They hope to overthrow the government or secede from the country.

In nearly every case, the root problem is religion. In Ireland, it is Catholic versus Protestant. In most other countries it is Muslims versus Christians. In the Middle East, it's Muslims versus Jews. It varies from country to country. In some places Christians are in the minority. In others, Muslims are in the minority.

In Africa, it is usually tribal tension. This is a recipe for rebellion and civil war. Rwanda, Sudan and Eritrea are some examples. In Zimbabwe and South Africa it is blacks against whites.

In North American society, the word minorities is bandied about freely. These people consist of visible minorities. What a pity that the color of a person's skin is such an important issue. It is the person's character that counts. Skin color and other distinguishing features should play no part as to how we perceive people.

The radical feminists always seek to join forces with minorities. They think that if all women endorsed that policy, they would have greater clout. This is somewhat of a contradiction, as slightly over half the world's population is women. How can all these women, plus the other groups, be called a minority when, in fact, they are the majority?

This begs the question, which is the minority?

From my vantage point, in Canada and the United States, it is the Caucasian male. If you doubt this, try and join a police force or any other government funded job. You will soon discover that, if you are a white male, your chances of getting a job are pretty slim. Women and minorities are usually the first choice. This stems from years of white male dominance. However, in my humble opinion, the pendulum has swung too far the other way.

As an older white male, I often get the minority feeling. This is not all bad since minorities often get sympathy from those in the majority. I do not feel persecuted by women. They treat me well.

For that matter, I also get along with the visible minorities that I know. I am always thankful that, in Canada and the United States, there is no religious persecution. I am Protestant and some of my good friends are Catholic and Jewish. I know very few Muslims or people of other faiths. But I am sure if I did, we would get along just fine. Like I said in one other chapter, when it comes to people, God is colorblind. We should be the same.

CHAPTER FIFTY

ADVERTISING

In North America and the rest of the developed world, advertising is the largest business that exists. In dollar volume, it exceeds the auto business, the computer business and the commodities people produce. It exceeds the movie business, professional sport, the pet food sector and even the welfare system.

The reason why advertising has such a stranglehold on dollar volume is because it gets a good piece of the pie in all the above-mentioned businesses and organizations, plus many more such as banks, real estate, politics and hundreds of other human endeavours.

I have no documented dollar figures to prove advertising is the biggest business of all. You do not have to be a genius to arrive at that conclusion. The only thing that might exceed advertising in volume is governments and their accumulated debt. It is in the hundreds of billions in Canada and stands at over five trillion dollars in the United States and it is climbing.

The methods of advertising are newspapers, TV, radio, flyers, signs of every description, huge billboards, hot air balloons, the sides of buses, trucks, business cards, brochures, sidewalk signs, the sides of buildings and, oh yes, the Internet. It is "big time" these days. Another method of advertising is word of mouth, which is the only free method there is.

The advertising executives and ad writers come up with some very creative ideas. Cows that can talk, people falling off buildings (I saw an ad like that yesterday), a man or a woman being jilted because of bad breath, scantily clad women almost half naked selling cars and a number of other products. Sleek cats and dogs (the result of a certain brand of pet food), old men and ladies (because of constipation), who have the cure. People calling home because the phone call is practically free if you are hooked up with the right phone company (this claim is usually grossly exaggerated, at least that is what our monthly phone bill indicates).

New houses, always referred to as homes, in exotic sounding neighborhoods like Poplar Grove, Ranchlands, Deer Run, Pine Ridge, Rocky View, Bayview, Lakeview, Mountain View, and a number of other views. The truth is, the only view ninety-five percent of these houses have is the neighbor across the street, or the neighbor across the back alley. On either side of the house is the blank wall of another house, unless you are located on a corner. There are exceptions to the rule. Our daughter Dee and son-in-law Roger have a house with a wonderful view of a valley below them and an unobstructed view of the Rocky Mountains. This is in Calgary, Alberta.

Without advertising, our western society and economy would shrink down to nothing (like many third world countries). However, I think it is grossly overdone. It can be outright annoying. Our mailbox is so full of flyers and advertisements of every description, there is hardly any room for legitimate mail. Every year, millions of trees are cut down to supply the paper for those daily advertisements.

Our daily newspapers have more than fifty percent advertising content. Have you ever read the weekend edition of the *New York Times*, the *Denver Post*, or any others big city newspaper? They are so huge you can hardly lift them, let alone read twenty-five percent of their content. A large portion of the paper is advertising (around sixty-five percent). These ads range from condoms to sanitary napkins to luxury homes and all things in between. There are thousands of classified ads in such small print that, if you are fifty years old or older, you can barely read them. I guess that saves on paper. If those ads were in larger print, the paper would be so heavy a large percentage of people couldn't lift the paper.

The three most prolific advertisers in the average newspaper are real estate, vehicles, and women's lingerie, especially bras. The bra-less era of the 1960s is a thing of the past, or is it? You be the judge.

One thing that bothers me about nearly all ads is the gross exaggeration of how good the products and services are, and how they will change your lifestyle and improve your quality of life.

In big cities there are dozens of agencies, especially in New York City, where the large majority of national ads are created. Ad agency services are not cheap. They rake in megabucks from corporations. Those ads are all tax deductible. Successful agency salesmen get filthy rich. I have to hand it to them; they use a lot of imagination and ingenuity. Sometimes a TV ad is more interesting than the program you are watching. But some ads are disgusting, others absolutely boring.

Once in a while, I watch an interesting television special that lasts one or two hours. The constant interruptions with ads diminish my interest in the program. I watched the show, *Who Wants To Be A Millionaire*, and I counted forty-one ads during the one hour show. The total time those ads consumed was fifteen minutes, ten seconds.

I guess somebody has to pay the bills for the cost of that show. Ads are a little like what Hitler once said, "If you repeat a lie often enough, people will begin to believe it."

When a highway billboard displays the name of a certain hotel or restaurant, your mind stores that name. When you arrive in a strange town, you have a tendency to look for that hotel or restaurant. It is the only name that registers in your mind.

Advertising breaks down into several areas. There are commercial ads, classified ads, personal ads, coming events ads. One type of ad, among others, where there is quite a bit of deceit is in the personal ads. The person, male or female, who places an ad for a mate, always portrays himself or herself as a great catch. For example: Middle aged lady looking for man from age thirty-five to fifty, must be of good character, with some means. He should be kind, loving, romantic, caring and intelligent.

She describes herself as soft-hearted, loving. She is of medium build who likes the arts and opera, reading, hiking in the mountains and fine dining.

If the ad brings a response, and after several phone conversations they decide to meet, the story may be quite different than what is said in the ad or in their phone conversations.

First of all, the man responding may be sixty-five years old, not fifty. Often he's a ne'er-do-well who is anything but intelligent. He may also have neglected to tell her that in his lifetime he has lived with a dozen or more women. He married about half of them. Those women kicked him out once they found out what he was all about. He never held down a steady job and, by the time he departed, a good chunk of the women's money had found its way into his pockets.

As for the lady who placed the ad, she too greatly overstated her attributes. For starters, she is well past middle age. As for weight, she is way past pleasantly plump. She may have been to one or two operas in her life. Her reading consists of a gossip column and a few cheap romance novels.

Maybe everything will work out since they both misrepresented themselves. The above scenario is a bit exaggerated. There actually are some mailorder marriages that do work out okay.

Advertising and sales are bedfellows. Advertising results in sales being made. I could write a chapter on salesmen separately, but I will incorporate sales and salesmen in this chapter. Salesmen are like ads. Some are totally above board. Others flirt with the truth. Some ads are very insistent. So are some salesmen. With the advent of modern shopping malls and now the Internet, door-to-door salesmen have almost become extinct.

For years, Watkins and Raleigh salesmen (peddlers) were a common sight in this country. There are also people selling life insurance (very persistent) and beauty products such as Mary Kay. There are encyclopedia salesmen. Some of the worst ones are vacuum cleaner salesmen. The man who came to our house was a salesman posing as a repairman. After briefly looking things over, he recommended we buy a new hose and a more modern head. Once again, we fell for his line.

Guess what? After using it about fifty times that outfit also quit working properly. I was too disgusted to bother calling him again. Now we are using a smaller, normal vacuum cleaner. It does not do a great job either. When will they ever invent a trouble-free vacuum that does a good job? Maybe never. In our fifty-four years of marriage, we must have owned at least a dozen vacuums with not good results. That proves the advertising and high-pressure sales tactics sell products, even though the consumer takes a hosing (no pun intended).

A whole chapter or book could be written on the consumerism mentality. I will touch on it only briefly, because it is a direct result of repetitive advertising. The constant bombardment by ads of what we need and are entitled to has dramatically affected the past two generations. They are what I call 'consumer junkies', people who have an emotional need to shop. It is this affliction that keeps many low and middle income people broke. Many people with large incomes, such as actors and sports personalities often die broke because they just kept on buying big ticket items. When their income declined, they found themselves in a tight financial corner.

Meanwhile, the large corporations, often multinational firms, take in millions of dollars in profits at the expense of the folks with consumerism mentality. These people often end up exactly the opposite as to what the ads said as to how their lives would improve by buying all those consumer goods.

In most homes, there is ample evidence of the buying frenzy. Closets, basements, and garages are full of consumer goods that are not needed and seldom used. Our house is no exception. We, as well as many other folks, have garage sales to try and get rid of some of this stuff.

I personally am quite ticked off when we have a garage sale. Shoppers try to steal the good items and, as for the more junky items, nobody wants them (can't say I blame them).

The result is that when the day is done the junk is still there. The useful items are literally given away. The next day, a trip to the local dump is in order. Some items may be donated to charities like the Salvation Army. A small percentage of those items, including clothing, gets used. Unless the clothes are cleaned and in mint condition, they end up in the rag bin.

A huge percentage of new consumer goods are charged either with mainline credit cards or store credit cards. If the full amount is not paid at the end of the month, the interest kicks in, which is twice as high as the normal bank rate. I know of a number of young people who got into a big financial mess with those credit cards. Buying is so painless, just charge it on the card. The pain comes later. Something like premarital sex. The pain of an unwanted pregnancy or social disease comes later. Every choice we make has consequences, either good or bad.

I kind of strayed from the advertising game. I happen to think many of the bad choices we make are the result of the advertising we are pummeled with daily. In the social, recreational, and commercial areas of our lives, young people are especially vulnerable. Everybody has it or does it, so they must have it or try it as well. It's a sad picture, but one that will not change in the foreseeable future.

There is also a positive side to advertising. It tells us where to find the things and services we really need. It also creates jobs, not only at ad agencies, but also for people working in manufacturing and in the service industries. Real estate ads, although grossly overblown, present us with a choice of where we want to buy and at what price.

I am always wary of a 'for sale' ad that does not state the price. To me, that indicates the advertiser hopes to talk you into a purchase even if the price is too high. We own a few buffalo, so I usually scan the ads in the *Western Producer*. There are dozens of buffalo-for-sale ads. Only a few list the price. I never phone an ad that does not list the price, whether it is real estate, buffalo, or anything else.

CHAPTER FIFTY-ONE

FRIENDS

We all have friends, at least I hope we do. A friend is a person who sticks with you through thick and thin. It is someone to share your life with, without betraying your confidence. We dearly love one another, although not in a sexual way. Next to God and family, friends are the most precious people in our lives.

There is an old saying that is true: "They who would have friends must be a friend themselves." Some people find it easier to have friends than do others. However, if people are too gushy when meeting someone new, the friendship sometimes evaporates as fast as it has started. New friends are good, but the old adage still holds, "There is no friend, like an old friend."

Nothing hurts as much as being betrayed by an old friend. Fortunately, this does not happen often but, when it does, it can devastate a person.

We learn early in life that some people are fickle. By the time young people are in junior high school, friends are the most important thing in their lives. Some of those friendships forged in school last a lifetime. Others just melt away like the snow. Still others just fade out of your life. Often those faded friendships are rekindled when you meet that person twenty, thirty or fifty years later.

The Bible says, a friend sticks closer than a brother does, although some brothers will stick together no matter what.

Friends may be defined in many different ways such as: old friends, new friends, close friends, good friends, fair-weather friends, loyal friends, business friends, and groups of friends, which consist of a number of people – often church groups, service clubs, lodges or any other social group that has a mutual interest.

The test of friendship is when someone has a major upset in life. It may be poor health, a financial loss, death in the family, or any other fate that often befalls the human race.

A true friend will stand by, no matter how much heartache and tragedy you experience in life. I speak from experience. Believe me, it warms my heart when friends stand by through all of those adverse circumstances.

Many people have been saved from committing suicide or giving up on life, when someone befriended them, and encouraged them when all was doom and gloom.

May each one of us treasure our friends. It helps us to enjoy our life's journey, even when the going is tough.

Love is friendship set to music.

When we lose a friend, we die a little.

Having money and friends is easy. Having friends and no money is an accomplishment.

Chapter Fifty-Two

REPUTATION

Every person has a reputation, good or bad. Some people might fall somewhere in between, they may have a reputation of being rather bland.

A reputation is something that evolves over a period of time. In my lifetime, I have observed that a person's reputation often is greatly exaggerated. Sometimes somebody does a good deed or two and word gets around about this act of kindness. From then on, even if that person is only an average decent citizen, their reputation continues to be embellished in the coffee shop or other social gatherings.

On the other hand, if a person makes a mistake and does something dishonest or mean, their reputation becomes bad even though it was only an isolated incident. When I was the livestock manager for a large packing house firm, I had a number of cattle buyers working for me. I always told them to guard their reputations by never stealing or lying. I said to them that it takes a lifetime to build a good reputation, but it only takes five minutes to lose it if you are caught telling a lie or stealing. Negative stories about one's reputation spread much faster than positive ones. That is why it takes a long time to build a good reputation and only a short time to ruin it.

Often we cannot see ourselves as others see us. As we get older, we have a tendency to tell a lot of stories. I am no exception. We must be careful that we do not tell too many tales that are not factual. I know of some people who relate stories that are way off base and, in some cases, outright lies.

One man told me that, when he was a young man, he played ball in the major leagues. What he did not know is that I have two complete baseball encyclopedias that list every player who ever swung a bat or pitched an inning of ball in the majors. His name is not in there. Obviously, he lied to me. After that, I took every story he told with a grain of salt.

Some people have the reputation of being windbags. They seem to delight in telling all kinds of exaggerated stories, usually involving themselves or friends. A man told me a story about a wealthy man who took ten thousand dollars worth of one-hundred-dollar bills and scattered them in the wind in a large group of people, just to watch them scramble for the money.

It so happens that I personally know that wealthy man. In fact, I did a lot of business with him. In my opinion, he was far too conservative and frugal to pull such a stunt. I do not think the man who told me the story was outright lying. He was only repeating what some windbag had told him. It pays to check out a story that we've heard before repeating it to someone else.

I would say that ninety percent of a good reputation is true and has been well earned by the recipient. Here are some of the traits of a good reputation: honesty, integrity, hard working, kindness, intelligence, up front (in other words, telling it like it is), being a good husband or wife, good neighbor, generous, loyal, easy-going, considerate of others, compassionate, modest (I have a little problem with that one), thoughtful, raconteur (storyteller), good parent, and a number of other attributes that make for a good person of good reputation.

Some categories for a bad reputation are: dishonest, thief, windbag, selfish, tightwad, greedy, ungrateful, lazy, devious, incompetent, schemer, cheater (in marriage and other things), ignorant, stubborn, a gossip, bad breath, plus a number of other character traits which make us a person with a bad reputation.

In the area where I grew up, there were a couple of young men about eighteen years old. They were average, decent rural boys. They had never been in trouble with the law. One day, temptation overtook them and they broke into a building where a number of coyote pelts were hanging on skin stretchers. They stole and proceeded to sell the pelts. In short order, the Mounties investigated the crime and found the culprits. They arrested the boys. At the trial that followed, the young men were found guilty. If my memory serves me correctly, they were sentenced to six months in jail. They got out early for good behaviour. When they got out, they resumed their lives as before.

After a few years, they both got married and raised fine families. Never again did either one of them get in trouble with the law. But, in the eyes of some people, their reputation was shot. I was only a child of about six or seven, but I heard adults discuss the case and it left a great impression on me that crime does not pay. Every time I saw one of those men, all I could think of was those coyote pelts. This was a mistake that they made in their youth. Maybe they did it on impulse or a dare but I am sure it affected them for the rest of their lives. Both of these gentlemen passed away a number of years ago.

In the business world, reputation is everything. Good reputation makes for good business. With a bad reputation, chances are you won't be in business for long. In commerce, just as with private individuals, a bad reputation gets around fast. In the cattle industry, ninety-nine percent of people are honest but, like in any human endeavor, a few people cut corners or pull shady deals. Most of these people do not last long. Their reputation does them in. I am referring to cattle dealers and order buyers.

In the purebred cattle industry, reputation is important. If you build a good track record of producing good seedstock, your cattle will bring premium prices based on good reputation.

Fast food outlets thrive on good reputations. If you doubt that, ask any kid between two and ten where they want to go for lunch. Nine times out of ten they will say MacDonald's. Why? Because MacDonald's has built up a worldwide reputation that they cater to kids. Of course, this is wise strategy since parents or grandparents always accompany kids. My wife and I have often taken our grandchildren to MacDonald's. Frankly, I am not a great fan of MacDonald's but, I will admit, that it is a good place for kids, including the playhouse.

Other professions and businesses also strive to have good reputations. One of those industries is construction or building contractors. People will always look for a house that is built by a reputable builder. Some houses have shoddy workmanship. We had a house like that once. The window screens did not fit, the floors squeaked, the fireplace kicked back smoke. Worst of all, the electric stove was not grounded until we had lived in the house for two years. The electrician who fixed it said we could have been electrocuted from this faulty installation. Whenever I contacted the general contractor about these problems, he shrugged it off by saying the subcontractors were responsible for those mistakes and shortcomings. Almost without exception, those subcontractors were out of business. I guess the general contractor had accepted the lowest bids. Those subcontractors were desperate for business, hence their low bids and poor workmanship. This gave them a bad reputation, which put them out of business.

I know of one town where they boast that their spring water is the best in the world. In fact, the Queen of England even had some of the water shipped to England. I often drank this town's water from the tap. It is good but, in my humble opinion, no better than the water at a lot of other places. However, once the good water reputation has been entrenched for a number of years, the public believes it and has the confidence that it is the best water in the world.

In another town, there is an ice cream shop that claims to have the best ice cream in western Canada. Decades ago that was probably true, but these days there are dozens of ice cream stores whose ice cream is every bit as good. But, because of a long history of praising that particular ice cream, it has achieved the reputation of being the best ice cream in western Canada. On weekends, and especially hot summer days, people line up for this special ice cream and pay two dollars and thirty-five cents a cone.

I am sure that most of us think of ourselves as having a good reputation. We claim very few of the bad things that give us a bad reputation. If the truth were known about each of us, the result would be that we possess some of the traits in each category. We should strive, on a daily basis, to attain having a good reputation. Here is a quote from an unknown wise sage:

"There's so much bad in the best of us and so much good in the worst of us that it does not behoove any of us to talk about the rest of us."

CHAPTER FIFTY-THREE

LOVE AND HATE

It has often been said that love and hate are closely related. I do not agree with that statement. What I do know is that they both are powerful emotions in the human race. That is where the similarity ends. Hate seeks to destroy not only the person to whom the hatred is directed, but also the person from whom the hatred comes.

The Bible mentions both love and hate. There are several things we may dislike or even hate, but we must never hate other people. The thing we may hate is wrong doing, but not the wrong doer, those people we should love. This is hard for us to do. Communism and fascism are two systems that we should have a strong dislike for, bordering on hate. The Bible says we should hate sin, but not the sinner.

When it comes to love, there are dozens of passages in the Bible on that subject. Every one of those verses which talks about love are positive. Here are a few of them.

You should not take vengeance, nor bear any grudge against the sons of your people, but you shall love your neighbor as yourself. Leviticus 19:18

You shall love the Lord and your God with all your heart and with all your soul and with all your might. Deuteronomy 6:5

A friend loves at all times. Proverbs 17:7

I say unto you who hear, love your enemies, do good to those who hate you. Luke 6:27

I say unto you, love your enemies, and pray for those who persecute you. Matthew 5:44

For God so loved the world that He gave His only begotten Son that whosoever believes in Him shall not perish but have eternal life. John 3:16

Husbands, love your wives, and not be embittered against them. Colossians 3:19

Older women likewise are to be reverent in their behaviour, not malicious gossips, nor enslaved to much wine. Teaching what is good that they may encourage the young women to love their husbands and to love their children. Titus 2:3-4

As you see by the above scripture references, the Bible covers a wide range of things that we should love. They are God, love in marriage and family, our neighbors, our enemies and, maybe most important, God's love for us. "God is love."

There are numerous passages in the Bible that mention love including *love of money is the root of all evil.* Timothy 6:10

Let us take an objective look at love in our society today. Love basically breaks down into seven categories. God's love for us, our love for God, love in marriage, love of family, love for neighbors, friends and enemies – in other words, for all our fellow human beings – and love for our country.

Godly love is often referred to as agapé love. It is something we, as God's creation, can hardly fathom. God's love to us echoes back in the love we have for other people. I have noticed that people who have no time, let alone love for God, have little capacity to love others. Much of today's love between men and women lacks depth and commitment. It is shallow, with sex being the main motivation. Often when a young man or woman meet, they become infatuated with each other. This temporary infatuation is mistaken for real love. When this fascination with each other evaporates, they split up. Sadly, this split often comes after they have been married for a year or two.

I am not a minister, marriage counsellor or psychologist. I am an ordinary person who has had a lifelong interest in human behaviour and developed a philosophy about much of what makes us tick.

If young people approach a relationship, which can lead to marriage with a big dose of common sense, much heartache and regret would be prevented. Our problem today is that Hollywood and the film industry in other studios portray a distorted picture of love. Many movies on the big screen or on TV convey the messages that love hinges on the beauty of a woman and virility of the male – a hunk. Usually, to make the picture more exciting, they throw in a bunch of jealousy, which erupts into violence. On the soaps, there is a lot of mate switching. I have never watched a complete soap story on TV. I have had a few glimpses, now and then, and every time the scenes displayed infidelity. The personal lives of those actors and actresses are in shambles. Most of them have been married anywhere from two to five times and a few of them up to seven times.

When a new romance blossoms between a celebrity couple, the news media shows pictures and writes about how madly in love they are. A few years later the relationship ends in divorce. For the past three decades, this practice has spread into the general population. Today, it is difficult to meet people who are fifty years old and younger who have not had at least two marriages. Why?

I think the so-called celebrities who have become role models for society have bombarded us with that lifestyle.

By now, some of you reading this may be questioning my love for my fellow men and women. Let me assure you that I am not condemning people who have married several times. We have many friends and relatives who have been remarried. Most of them are good people and I love them. However, I still think it is unfortunate that we humans find it so hard to be compatible with our partners. When real love prevails, we can overcome.

In every day conversations, we use the words love and hate on a regular basis. Here are a few examples of what we might say: "I love sailing. I hate wind. I love Chinese food. I hate liver. I hate horror stories. I love mystery movies. I hate most politicians. I love my country. I hate cold weather. I love snow. I hate getting up early. I love getting up early. I hate cabbage rolls. I love cabbage rolls."

There are hundreds of things in life that we express in terms of either love or hate. When those two terms are too severe, we say 'like' or 'dislike'. My nephew, Loran Harder, uses the expression, Love conquers all. I think he is right.

I Corinthians 13 is often referred to as the love chapter of the Bible.

If I speak with tongues of men and angels, but do not have love I have become a noisy gong or a clanging cymbal. If I have the gift of prophecy, and know all mysteries and all knowledge, and I have all faith, so as to remove mountains, but do not have love, I am nothing. If I give all my possessions to feed the poor and if I deliver my body to be burned, but do not have love, it profits me nothing. Love is patient, love is kind, and is not jealous, love does not brag and is not arrogant, does not act unbecomingly, it does not seek its own, is not provoked, does not take into account a wrong suffered, does not rejoice in unrighteousness, but rejoices with the truth. Bears all things, believes all things, hopes all things, endures all things. Love never fails, but if there are gifts of prophecy, they will be done away; if there are tongues, they will cease; if there be knowledge, it will be done away. For we know in part, and we prophecy in part; but when the Perfect comes the partial will be done away. When I was a child, I used to speak as a child, think as a child, reason as a child. When I became an adult I did away with childish things. For now we see in a mirror dimly, but then face to face: Now I know in part, but then I shall know fully. Just as I also have been fully known. But now abide faith, hope, love, these three, but the greatest of these is Love. I Corinthians, Chapter 13.

The foregoing scripture is a comprehensive overview of the role love should play in our lives.

There are two more types of love. They are a mother's love and puppy love. Nearly all pre-teen and young teenagers (twelve to sixteen) experience this puppy love when they have a crush on someone from the opposite sex. It afflicts both boys and girls. In some cases, one of the parties does not share the same feeling. But most of the time they share the same "pit-of-the-stomach," giddy feeling for each other. Their little romance consists of sly winks, walking home from school hand-in-hand with the chivalrous boy carrying both his and her books. In the evenings and weekends, they may go to some social events such as the movies, ball games, even church. In church, they have to act proper because some of the elders might not approve of their actions. These evening and weekend dating activities depend on the strictness of the parents. Many parents put limits on the son's or daughter's dating habits. They insist they go in groups and have an evening curfew anywhere from nine o'clock to midnight. The exact time depends on the age of the young person. A twelve-year-old may have to be home between nine and ten o'clock. Those from fourteen to sixteen, between ten o'clock to midnight. Some of those puppy-love couples grow up and get married. However, about eighty-five percent of these young romances evaporate like a morning mist. Some young people have three or four little romances before they mature and, as young adults, really fall in love. I hope that I did not repeat too much of what I wrote in the chapter, Courtship and Marriage.

A special category of love is a mother's love. Of course, most fathers also dearly love their children. However, a mother's love for them often supersedes a father's concern.

I mentioned a mother's love for her children in the chapter about women. I will say it again, that the average mother will stand by her children though thick and thin, through the good times and the bad times. My wife is concerned for each of our children, every waking hour of the day. I love them and am concerned about their well-being, but my wife, like most mothers, goes the extra mile. She never forgets their birthday or anniversary. Their well-being is always on her mind.

People that I enjoy talking with are those who have a lot of common sense and wisdom, along with compassion and love. Unfortunately, few people have all of these attributes. When I visit with these folks, it is like a fresh breeze. It gives my spirits a lift. This may give you a desire to be such a person yourself. If you are such a person already, keep up the good work.

Love is of God. Hate is of Satan. I sure feel comfortable having God in my corner in this battle called life. I know God can defeat Satan (the devil). He did it at the cross when they crucified His Son, Jesus Christ. The victory came when God resurrected Him from the grave. Jesus is alive and well. He lives in the hearts of millions of people today. Next Christmas and Easter, stop and reflect what Jesus did for each one of us.

CHAPTER FIFTY-FOUR

CRITICISM AND PROTESTS

In a democracy, criticism is a necessary part of the process of a free society. Unfortunately, these days it has gone overboard. What starts out as criticism often ends up as a rash of protests, demonstrations and, in some cases, strikes. Many of these protests have become violent.

There are a wide range of protests, including anti-government policy and legislation protests and a whole array of environmental concerns. Some of them are real but the large majority of them are bogus. They include water conservation, tree huggers, greenhouse gases, endangered species and a host of other causes. A lot of blame is placed on big business, such as logging, the oil industry and mining. Lately, agriculture has been added to the list.

Recently, there were huge protests against the World Bank. The protesters blame them for keeping the poor nations of the world in poverty when, in fact, the World Bank has helped many of those countries. It has also forgiven a large number of loans.

On social issues we have the radical feminists, pro-abortion and anti-abortion protests, as well as the pro-homosexual and anti-homosexual folks, plus a lot of other causes.

The protest groups are getting larger and larger. They actually are anarchists. When anarchy reigns, society is in danger of disintegrating. We see that today in many countries, especially Africa.

What bothers me is that the percentage of people who participate in these lawless demonstrations is relatively small. The majority of people are not that radical, even though they sometimes agree with a cause to a certain extent.

Some of these groups are only politically motivated. Someone, whose only mission in life is to stir up people's emotions, whips mobs into a frenzy. On the top of this list, we have a number of high-pressure union bosses who incite their membership into strikes, some legal, others not legal.

Strange as it may seem, I believe in most of these causes, but the key phrase is 'radical' or unreasonable. A small number of people blow everything out of proportion and almost make a mockery of what could be a worthy cause.

One example is the tree hugger. To them, every tree is sacred. I love trees, but they are a renewable resource if properly managed. Old growth forest is a big issue with tree huggers. I have been told by folks, who have spent all their lives close to old growth forests, that it is not as idealistic as the protesters say. Trees, like people, eventually die. Some old growth forests are a mess with rotten logs all over the place, and some trees are in danger of toppling over because of old age and inner rot. There are some areas where those old trees seem to be in pretty good shape. My guess would be that a forest fire wiped out the trees in that area one hundred and fifty to two hundred years ago.

My suggestion is that some knowledgeable forest people be delegated to select a few modest-sized areas of old growth forest and set it aside so that interested people can see what old growth forest looks like. I know this is already being done, but the radicals want to stop logging in huge areas. This type of activity leads to confrontations and possibly bloodshed in the future. When people are deprived of their livelihood things get ugly.

If the curtailment of logging increases to the point where it ceases, we may have to go back to building our houses and other buildings from stone. If that were to happen, it would not take long for protest groups to organize against using so much rock and stone because it disturbs the landscape and the environment.

If building from wood and rock were both no-nos, what can we use? We cannot live in tents made from hides and skins. The animal rights people would throw a fit. All I can figure out, is that mankind would be back to living in caves. Then again, the trouble with living in a cave is that it too could disturb the natural environment.

There would not be much of a litter problem since, without wood pulp, there would be no paper, boxes or cartons. With no oil, plastic would also be absent. There would be no animal or chicken bones, since hunting and killing animals would be prohibited.

Since everyone would only be consuming food from plants, there would be little refuse, except for feces, which are biodegradable. No flush toilets wasting water. Not even bathtubs or showers. To rinse off the cave dust, we could go outside in our birthday suits in the rain to rinse off in the natural way. For a bath, we could jump into a lake or stream, provided it didn't disturb the fish.

For furniture we could drag in a few boulders, just like the Flintstones. Heat would be a problem. Some of the deeper caves may be warm enough. However, most caves are shallow, just an opening in the side of a hill or mountain. There would be a few skins around to cover up with at night, but there would not be nearly enough to go around. The only skins available would be from animals that died from natural causes.

Eventually, people would have to move to the temperate and tropical zones of the world. If available caves in these areas became scarce, folks might have to sleep on the ground in the "old growth jungle."

Once all the people have vacated the more frigid areas, over half of the surface of the planet would be void of people. In this empty landscape, old growth forest and animals would flourish, providing fires from lightning storms, tree rot and animal diseases did not decimate this pristine world. There is also the danger of too much animal feces and bird droppings continuing to radiate greenhouse gases, so the greenhouse effect would carry on. And the hole in the ozone layer would continue to enlarge. Is the above what the radicals want?

Whatever they want, one thing is certain, they are out to change civilization, as we know it today. For the time being, we may be able to avert such a drastic change in our lifestyle if we go along with some of their ideas. One change we could make is to double up in our housing needs. Today, there are many large houses that only have two or three occupants. If another family moved in, we could suspend new house construction for another thirty years. The same could apply to cars. Make it against the law for a car or van to have less that four people in it. That way we could cut gas consumption by about seventy percent. Many big trucks could be eliminated as well since there would be less fuel, paper, lumber and other related goods to haul.

The radical animal rights people, along with the endangered species fanatics, are out of hand. So I decided to join them. This permits me to submit my personal list of species that some day might be endangered. I thought that by putting these plants, animals, birds, and insects on the list now, it might make us more aware of them so we can take precautions to protect them before it is too late. Here is my list:

Canada thistle, chickweed, wild oats, gophers, rats, mice, mosquitoes, bed bugs, house flies, flying ants, starlings and magpies. If you agree with my choices, I urge you to send your support to the authorities in Ottawa and Washington. I am sure they will dispatch your message to the front runners in this great crusade to ensure these plants and creatures have a place in future generations.

What about critics, other than environmentalists? Criticizing is one of the things we humans indulge in. Criticism is cheap. We do not have to worry much about how to fix the problem we are criticizing. Case in point: what I just wrote about radical environmentalists is criticism in a satirical manner. But I hope it conveys the message that it is better and more civilized to criticize these radical protesters and demonstrators with a pen, rather than with billy clubs, tear gas, pepper spray, rubber bullets, or live bullets.

Some people delight in criticizing other people. No matter how good a person is, they still find fault with that individual. Sometimes that criticism borders on gossip or jealousy – it is easy to criticize someone whom you may be jealous of.

The critic always uses the excuse that he or she is trying to help the person overcome their shortcomings. Extreme criticism in a marriage relationship can be destructive if either the husband or wife always finds fault with whatever the partner does or says. This also rubs off onto the children. As they get older, the children will side with either mom or dad. If the parents do not agree on how to handle discipline, the children will always stick up for the parent that is most lax in enforcing rules.

Another area that is sometimes critiqued, sometimes called reviewed, is the arts - books, plays, movies and musicals. They are supposed to be beneficial – maybe not for the work already done or performed - but for future productions and endeavors.

If there is a consensus among a number of critics, it may be fairly accurate and valid. However, if it is just one person's critique or opinion then often it is offbase. For instance, if I was given the job of critiquing Stephen King's or some other novelist's works it may rate zero. On the other hand, the people who write interesting books on history, geography, and some philosophy would get high ratings from me.

I shudder to think how some of the book critics in New York would rate the books I have written. My score with them would probably be zero.

I firmly believe we must make our own choices in all areas of life and not be swayed by someone else's opinion or critique. At the same time, be open-minded to other people's ideas and opinions if they make sense in your life.

CHAPTER FIFTY-FIVE

PAINT AND COLOR

Something that each one of us encounters every day is paint. Our surroundings would be pretty dull without paint. Not all paint comes from paint stores, or should I say color. Nature has an incredible amount of color.

Everywhere we look there is color. Who can resist the beauty of a sunset or a rainbow after a rain shower? Trees and plants, many of them flowering types, have every color imaginable. There are also beautiful meadows of green grass and golden fields of grain. Animals and birds also come in all colors. Some, like male peacocks and numerous other birds, have a delightful variety of colors - parrots, bluebirds, blue jays, redwings, blackbirds, or snow swans to name a few.

Animals come in all colors as well. Some examples are zebras, skunks with their two stripes, snow white polar bears, deer and rabbits whose color in the wild changes with the seasons.

I think paint as we know it today had its origins in what man beheld in nature. The most primitive tribes in the world used paint made from berries, plants, and roots. Even Mother Earth supplies some of that material in the form of red, brown and black dirt.

When the white man arrived in North America he was greeted by Natives who were very colorful in the clothes and robes made from furs and hides, plus their head dresses made of bird feathers. When these folks went on the warpath they painted their faces and bodies with a large variety of colors. Like I said, the paint was made from plants and berries. Red was the predominant color.

In the modern world color and paint play a huge role in our everyday lives. Every type of consumer goods we can think of is painted. Houses, offices, buildings, cars, trucks, vans, buses, furniture, clothes (dyed), books, virtually everything our eyes behold has color in it.

Our modern society is not too far removed from the paint colors that more primitive people used hundreds of years ago, especially women. They use lipstick, rouge, eye shadow, and colored nail polish. Or how about hair? I dare say seventy-five percent of all women, between the ages of fifteen and ninety, dye or color their hair, or at least tint it. There are a great number of colors to chose from. I have seen a woman with at least half a dozen different hair shades in a ten-year period. In the old days, platinum blonde was the 'in' color. These days, brunettes and redheads are more common. Black is quite popular as well. One color that is not from a bottle is mousy brown. The reason is that a large percentage of people are born with that color of hair. In old age, most hair turns gray and eventually white. I hope my wife does not get too perturbed with this, but the truth is that I have no idea what the real color of her hair is. I have no problem with women dying their hair. I know that hair can make a big difference in a person's appearance. So why not dye hair in a color that a woman thinks suits her?

Incidentally, many men also dye their hair. These days many teenage boys have colored hair.

What would our world be without art? I am referring to paintings by amateurs and the old masters. Most people like paintings. There are very few homes that do not display some pictures. There is a great variance in the colors that different artists choose. Some like bright colors, others more subtle, subdued colors. I like both types of pictures, although I lean more towards the subdued colors.

Beauty is in the eye of the beholder. This really applies to art. Some of the abstract art we have today does not turn me on. I like to look at a picture and know what I am looking at. Before cameras were invented the only way to reproduce a scene from life or a person required an artist to paint it. I think that is why artists from hundreds of years ago were very good at painting portraits of people.

Today, there are thousands of artists who are excellent at painting the world that surrounds us. But in my opinion, there is only a small percentage that are good at painting the faces of people. Cameras have pretty well taken over that little chore.

In spite of having been around for almost fifty years, color television is still a mystery to me. How can the picture, let alone colored ones, appear in my living room from thousands of miles away? We know it is bounced off a satellite, but color transmitted through the air? No use wracking my brain about it. I have had it explained several times. Maybe I am a slow learner, but the mystery remains.

Cameras that take color photographs are a little easier to understand. But they're still a mystery to me.

Color has a great impact on our moods and well being. Color can cheer us up or depress us. Did you ever walk into a room that is painted black? I have and I must say it is depressing. I like black horses, hair, shoes and dresses, but not black rooms. I like purple but not as a hair color.

I read once that researchers found that different colors affect people in different ways. They said that pink has a calming effect on people. My favorite color is green. My wife likes red. Most people have a color that they prefer over the other colors.

The paint business is an enormous industry. It spans all national, ethnic, religious, or cultural differences. I know of no people on the face of the earth that do not like the colors that paint provides.

Do you like painting rooms in your house? Many do not, including me. However, I must say that once a paint job is finished, there is a satisfaction in having a freshly painted room. It cheers you up. Men, keep that in mind the next time your wife asks you to do a little painting.

CHAPTER FIFTY-SIX

FOOD AND RESTAURANTS

If there is one thing that is universal for every living creature including man, it is food. Without food, life cannot exist.

Daily, this is demonstrated in our new media. Worldwide, millions of people starve to death every year. Many more are permanently damaged from malnutrition. Much of the famine is caused by overpopulation, drought and most of all by wars and rebellions.

I am of the firm belief that this old planet has the capacity to feed three to four times the population that's in the world today. A large portion of the world's land is ideal and some has been devastated by bad agricultural practices in the past. I personally saw millions of acres of good land in Colombia producing little or nothing. That is the case on every continent and island in the world. This includes Canada and the United States, although in North America it is not as widespread.

In the United States, millions of acres are out of production under a federal government program. The government pays people to idle the land for ten years.

What about road allowances? I have no idea how many millions of acres alongside our roads produce nothing but weeds and some grass that goes to waste. In Japan, I noticed every foot of ground, right to the side of the road - gravel or paved - is farmed.

I know academics and scientists who disagree with my assessment of the world's food production capabilities. They do agree with me that education, education, education, is the most important equation on how to teach the world's farmers to properly utilize their land.

The variety of food is enormous. Every country and region produces a range of foods. Food can be broken into five main categories: meat, such as beef, pork, mutton, chicken, turkey, eggs, and a number of wild game animals and fish – which is a category of its own that I have lumped in with the meat. Pasta products are made with grains. This category comes in dozens of different forms. When all is said and done, the truth is it is all made from dough. The third category is dairy products. This is a versatile, interesting group. There are least twenty sub-categories of products. Milk, of course, is the most important. A few others are butter, cottage cheese, yogurt, cream, ice cream, and a variety of cheeses, buttermilk and other products.

In North America, cows are the main producers of dairy products. However, this is not the case in a number of other countries of the world. In Africa, Asia, the Middle East, and parts of Europe, goat milk is more common than cow's milk. Some medical people claim that goat milk is healthier. Sometimes, infants are put on goat's milk because it agrees better with their digestive systems. In some countries, people milk sheep, camels, water buffalo and probably a few more that I am not aware of. I never heard of anyone milking a whale but they are mammals, as well.

In Mongolia, mare's milk is used extensively. It is a large part of their diet. I tasted it once and it is quite sweet. But I still prefer cow's milk on my cereal.

Let's not forget mother's milk. It launched most of us on our life's journey. Today, doctors recommend breast feeding. Mothers need good nutrition to produce adequate milk for their infants. The problem is in the third world this food is not available to the mother, so their babies are malnourished and many die. The United Nations, the Red Cross, the Mennonite Central Committee and a number of other relief agencies make an effort to get food to these famine-stricken areas. Often it does not go to the people who need it the most. I have read of instances where some of that food – mostly grain sacks – was highjacked at the port of entry and sold by ruthless thugs for high prices. The relief agencies have tightened up the rules so there is more food going to the people for whom it was intended to help.

I am thankful every day of my life that I was born in Canada. I remember the depression of the 1930s, when barrels of apples from Ontario and salted codfish from Atlantic Canada were shipped to Saskatchewan. However, we always had lots of wholesome food. I never went hungry.

Category four is vegetables, which grow in every area of the world except the Arctic and Antarctic and some desert areas. There are too many vegetables to mention all of them. A few of the mainstays are: potatoes, tomatoes, corn, beans and peas. A popular and healthy vegetable these days is broccoli. Unfortunately, that is one of the few vegetables I do not like, although I eat it for health. Former United States President George Bush, Sr. does not like it either.

Category five is fruit and there are even more varieties of fruit than vegetables. Different types of fruit grow in every region of the world, from the tropics to the far north where certain berries grow.

I am not a nutritionist, but I do know these five categories of food give us a balanced diet. Meat has protein, minerals and other useful nutrients. Pasta has carbohydrates for energy. Fruit and vegetables have vitamins. Dairy products, rich in calcium, are needed in our daily diets.

To supplement these five categories and to enhance tasty dishes we have salt, pepper, sugar (including honey) and a variety of herbs and spices.

From the beginning of time, food has played a big role in every society that has existed. It started with Adam and Eve in the Garden of Eden. I have no idea what fruits and vegetables were in that garden but the Bible tells us about one apple tree from which Adam and Eve were forbidden to eat. Just like human nature today, they disobeyed and ate an apple from that tree. We have suffered the consequences ever since. Adam blamed Eve. Eve blamed the serpent. Maybe that is why most people don't like snakes.

Later on in the Bible, a wide variety of foods are mentioned. Meat was a large part of the food supply, along with different grains and vegetables including leeks and onions, and plenty of fruit. Some that come to mind are pomegranates, apples, olives and figs.

In biblical days and later in the Middle Ages, many feasts were held on a regular basis. This was a special form of fellowship. Some were religious feasts; others were to celebrate weddings and other social events. This has not changed much in the past five thousand years. Today, they are called receptions or banquets, and in Texas and other places, they are called barbecues.

Ancient kings loved feasts. At those feasts all the finest food that the kitchen staff could provide was served in ornate rooms. There was a lot of debauchery, which the dictionary describes as an extreme indulgence in sensuality, an orgy, seduction from virtue or duty.

Many was the young maiden who lost her virginity, perpetrated on her by the king and his buddies. These feasts could last up to a week or until they ran out of virgins. The wine flowed freely.

To this day, food is still front and center in most social events. Besides banquets, receptions, and barbecues, there are thousands of restaurants, from small diners and greasy spoons to fast food and family restaurants. There are also a number of fancy eating establishments where dining costs a king's ransom.

In large cities all over the world expensive restaurants exist in large numbers. Celebrities flock to the most exclusive restaurants they can find. I think the theory is, and it is probably right, that the riffraff and common person will not be there.

The tastebuds of people around the world vary as much as do facial features. My wife and I have been married for fifty-four years and the food we like differs greatly. She likes cabbage rolls, I don't. I like tongue, she doesn't. She likes sweet rolls, I do not. I like shrimp, she does not. She loves onions, not me. In spite of these differences, we still share a lot of food that we both like and enjoy.

It is quite astounding what some people enjoy as food. Jackie (Kennedy) Onassis sometimes flew in unborn lamb from Greece. You read that right – unborn. In China, smoked dog meat is a delicacy. They also enjoy cat meat and duck eggs. In Borneo and a number of others countries, all rodents and insects are eaten on a regular basis. They tell me that bugs have a lot of protein. That is one way to balance your diet.

Snakes are eaten in most countries of the world. The closest I have come so far is catfish and eel. They are not really snakes, they just look like them. Someone told me he enjoyed rattlesnake meat. Not appealing to me. All I can say is that I would rather bite into a rattlesnake than have one bite into me.

This world has a lot of rich people. Even the poorest of nations have a small group of extremely rich people. If no one else, then at least the dictator and his friends are wealthy. Like I said the rich and famous have to display their wealth in one form or another. One way is the restaurants they patronize and the food they order. In Canada and the United States, foreign names for food are the choice of discerning rich people and celebrities. Here are a few examples: tournedos Rossini, veal scaloppini, stifado, Tara mosalalta, sushi, cannelloni, salsiccia dicasa, melanzane moussaka, and camberetti grisglia. There are hundreds more. The names of the dishes I mentioned originate in France, Italy, Greece and Japan. A number of other exotic dishes come from China, Pakistan, Spain, and a host of other Asian and European countries.

After being served a meal that consists of five courses such as Tara mosalata, caviar, pheasant under glass, quail brochette, and moussaka, you can top it off with a five-hundred-dollar bottle of wine and a cup of cappuccino. The bill, including the tip, may amount to two thousand dollars for four people.

Not all 'in' food is expensive. In New York, and many other locations, bagels are popular. I actually like bagels even though they taste like a bun failure. Pizza is another popular food that is relatively cheap. There must be a lot of profit in pizza. Airdrie, Alberta, a small city close to us, has no less than ten pizza places.

Eating out has become popular in North America. It is estimated that approximately forty percent of all food is now served in restaurants. Who prepares all this food? The chefs. Where do the chefs come from? They grind them out at technical schools.

There is a limit to how many ways meat, pasta, fruit and vegetables, and dairy products can be prepared. It seems to me the chef school solution is a large variety of sauces made from a variety of herbs and spices. They pour this sauce over a certain dish, often pasta, and give it a fancy name.

In my opinion, the salads served in many restaurants are a disaster. It looks to me like they went to someone's backyard and stripped a bunch of leaves off a dozen different types of trees. No thanks. I will stick to lettuce, tomatoes, cucumbers, radishes, green peppers and celery.

I have eaten in a number of countries. Some places I enjoyed the food even though it was foreign to me. In some places I could hardly choke it down. In China, the vision of Fido flashed through my mind. In France, I am sure we ate horsemeat, not exactly my favorite. In Fiji, it was fish with heads - I hate those eyes staring at me. English kidney pie does not turn my crank either.

In my opinion, England (except for kidney pie), Holland and Germany have the best food in Europe, although I am not a big fan of German sauerkraut.

I think the reason I like North American food is because we have a mixture of ethnic backgrounds which has developed into a unique selection of dishes. My wife still cooks a few dishes that our ancestors brought over from Europe one hundred and thirty years ago. The other day, I counted over fifty recipe books in our house.

I have attended a few independent publishers meetings in the past ten years. What always astonishes me is the number of cookbooks published every year. Many of them end up on the best seller list. Whenever I browse in a bookstore I notice racks full of recipe and cookbooks. I will never write a cookbook but I will share a few recipes from my ethnic background. My parents were born in Canada, but my mother made many of the dishes that her parents and grandparents brought over from Europe.

Chicken Noodle Soup

Cut a fowl or frying chicken into serving pieces. Cover with cold water and bring to a boil. Skim off the scum that comes to the top. Simmer slowly for 1.5 to 2.5 hours. Add salt to taste.

Spices: 20 whole pepper corns, four or five bay leaves, small sprig of parsley, one onion - finely grated, four star anise. Add spices one hour before serving. Pour over egg noodles. Your delicious soup is ready.

My mother made her own noodles. These days, we buy them at the supermarket.

Cheese Pockets (perogies)

Dough: one cup milk, one tsp. salt, four egg whites, flour to make dough soft. Cut dough into round pieces.

Filling: one package dry curd cottage cheese, one package wet cottage cheese, one tsp. salt, four egg yolks. Blend well.

Place four tbs. of filling on dough round. Seal edges well. Drop into boiling water and boil for eight minutes. Serve with cream gravy. Can also be fried in butter after boiled.

Cracklings (meat crumbs)

Cracklings are made from medium ground pork. The portion of pork used is the side from which bacon is made. It has a mixture of lard and lean. The lard is necessary. It serves the same function as in potato French fries (this is raw, not cured pork).

Put on medium heat, boil in a large pot for about two to three hours or until cracklings become slightly brown. Strain the lard off through a wire mesh strainer. Put cracklings in jars for future use.

They are usually served for breakfast. Take whatever amount you and your family need. Put in frying pan. Heat for several minutes. Then once again strain whatever lard remains. Put cracklings back in pan. Add a few tablespoons of water. This neutralizes them so they are not a bit greasy. A good way to eat them is to take pieces of bread and squeeze a small portion of crackling in the bread and eat with your fingers (like they do in India). Use salt and pepper according to your taste.

I went into a long explanation on how to prepare and eat them. It is important. A few times I have had them at someone else's house. They were not good (too greasy).

Other dishes I grew up with include home-cured ham, headcheese, summer sausage, plum mousse, potato soup, cabbage borscht (which I dislike), cabbage rolls (which I also dislike), Roll Kucken (something like deep fried fritters), zwieback (double-deck buns), homebaked whole wheat bread from home-ground flour.

There are dozens more but, if I keep writing on this subject it may develop into a cookbook, which I said I would never write.

There are several hundred countries in the world and each country and ethnic group within each country have their favorite foods and recipes. Children from an early age learn to like and appreciate the food their parents provide for them. When they grow up and immigrate to another country, they hang onto the food that their tastebuds enjoyed. Beauty is in the eye of the beholder. So is how we perceive food. It is all in the tastebuds of an individual.

From Old Testament days to the present, Jewish people were forbidden to eat certain foods unless it was Kosher (blessed by a rabbi). Some Jewish folks these days do not strictly adhere to those rules. However, Orthodox Jews do. In the New Testament, the rules were relaxed, as stated in Acts 10: 10-14.

And he (Peter) became very hungry, and would have eaten: but while they made ready, he fell into a trance, and saw Heaven opened, and a certain vessel descending unto him, as it had been a great sheet knit at the four corners, and let down to earth. Wherein were all manner of four-footed beasts, of the earth, and wild beasts, and creeping things, and fowls of the air. And there came a voice to him. "Rise Peter, kill and eat." But Peter said, "Not so, Lord; for I have never eaten anything that is common or unclean;" and the voice spake unto him again the second time, "What God hath cleansed, that call thou not common!"

That Bible passage makes it clear that anything that grows, plant or animal, can be eaten, with the exception of poisonous plants.

Most of us, in our modern western society, still abhor eating certain animals or birds. A few that I would not be fussy to eat are dogs, cats, horses, rodents, hawks, eagles, crows or any bird of prey. I am also a bit squeamish about eating bear, rabbits or, for that matter, most wild game with the exception of buffalo and small portions of venison, elk and moose. Antelope taste too much like sagebrush.

In the past few years, coffeehouses have become in vogue. Not the old coffeeshops where there was only traditional coffee. These new coffeehouses feature a variety of different coffees and blends. It has become fashionable to go for a cup of cappuccino or some other exotic blend. I still like plain old Colombian coffee, with a little cream and no sugar.

The prices charged for this new coffee are unbelievable. Recently, we were in a middle-class restaurant, not upscale. There was Milano, Irish, Dreamy Eyes, Italian, Spanish, Monte Cristo and Imperial. The price was $4.95 for a small cup. I am told that is peanuts compared to prices in some of the trendy cafes in New York or Europe.

In the depression of the 1930s, coffee was five cents a cup. Would you believe, as recently as 1988, coffee in Kit Carson, Colorado was ten cents a cup and they gave refills. Then it was raised to twenty-five cents a cup. In 1999, when we sold our ranch, it was still twenty-five cents.

It is interesting how coffee became such a national drink in most places of the world. In North America, all our coffee is imported, as it is in Europe.

A large portion of our supply comes from Brazil and Colombia. In countries like Great Britain, Japan and India, a lot of tea is consumed. I have to confess I am not much of a 'tea granny'. When we are guests at someone's home and they serve tea, politely I will drink it with a little sugar and no cream.

I have a complaint about seniors menus in restaurants. To be blunt, they are kind of phoney - they pretty much border on a ripoff. Smaller portions are featured for very little less money. Smaller portions should be available to all patrons, not just for children and seniors.

A true senior's discount is when you may order anything on the menu and are given a ten to fifteen percent discount at the cashier's till. Better still, no discount for anyone, just smaller portions at a more reasonable price should be available to everyone.

I know my opinion on this issue will not endear me to people who operate restaurants but, then again, not many businesses, including restaurants, are run on a common-sense basis. The whole criteria is profit. Since I profess to be a free enterpriser, I will put up with whatever menu these establishments put in front of me. My wife and

I visit one restaurant which gives seniors a thirty percent discount. I think that is going too far but, then again, that's free enterprise. Maybe they like seniors better than most people do.

I have barely scratched the surface concerning food and restaurants. Thousands of books have been written on the subject. We are fortunate to live in North America where food is plentiful. That is not the case for over half the world's population. I hope those of you who live in urban areas appreciate the farmers and ranchers who produce this food, often at a loss. The markup on food takes place after it leaves the farm gate.

Most people enjoy dining out once in a while and there are thousands of good eating establishments. The two areas, to me, that are important are: good food, at reasonable prices, and good service, with a smile. Based on these principles, I have selected four people whose restaurant operations meet my standards.

Hank Biesbroek owns the Smitty's Pancake franchise in Cochrane, Alberta. The food served is the same as in all other Smitty's restaurants but the difference is, you are served with a smile. Hank is a great host, whose good manners and smile have rubbed off on his staff. Hank is well-informed and he is an avid reader.

Gail Rau owns the Express A&W franchise on the south side of Airdrie, Alberta. For sheer enthusiasm and friendliness, she has few peers. You may only be in the restaurant for a 'Momma' or 'Poppa' burger, but she treats you as though you were buying a $100-dinner of lobster, caviar and pheasant-under-glass. Gail has a radiant smile for everyone. I know her husband, Rod, admires her spunk. He is in the cement business.

Paul Lappas owns and operates Paul's Pizza and Steakhouse in Airdrie, Alberta. He greets and talks to everyone entering his restaurant. To me, Paul is an example of how owners should run a business. His staff makes and serves excellent food, at reasonable prices. Some folks eat at Paul's on a regular basis, three to four times a week. Paul also says a farewell to his customers.

Leo Sheftel is a legend in Calgary. He is widely-known as one of the best hotel proprietors and restaurateurs in the business. We have patronized his restaurants at the Highlander Hotel (now Days Inn), the Blackfoot Inn and, most of all, the Carriage House for at least twenty-five years. Top quality food is served including excellent bread and buns, which are baked in their own bakery. Leo strolls from table to table, for brief chats with the diners, many whom he knows on a first-name basis. He is everybody's friend. He has been in customer service since he was thirteen years old. His love for satisfying people far exceeds anyone's expectations. Leo has met people from all over the world. I have reserved rooms in his hotels on a number of occasions for American friends visiting the Calgary Stampede. Leo finds the hospitality industry interesting, exciting and rewarding. It was fitting that the Calgary Convention and Visitors Bureau named him Mr. Hospitality for the city of Calgary in 1998. Photo courtesy of Leo's daughter, Sheila.

CHAPTER FIFTY-SEVEN

BOOTS AND SHOES

All through history, footwear has been of utmost importance. Man, unlike animals, has a tender foot so, from the very beginning, he sought and developed protection for his feet. In the old Biblical days, the footwear was sandals. The sole of those sandals protected their feet from the hot sand, also from pebbles, stones and thorns. Even today, in many primitive cultures, sandals are still the footwear of choice (weather permitting). Many folks in third world countries also walk barefoot (again, weather permitting). I remember a number of children walking barefoot all summer. This was in the depression of the 1930s. Their feet became so calloused, they could walk over almost anything without complaint. Of course, when winter came, they had to wear shoes.

There was a period in our history between 1860 to 1960, when styles in footwear were important to people. In order to be considered a lady, one would wear spike heels and the higher, the better. For men, high quality oxfords were the sign of a gentleman. Before the turn of the century, laced or button shoes were the order of the day, especially for women.

In China, women had their feet bound as young girls so the foot would not grow. Small feet and small shoe sizes were what all upper class ladies wanted, even if it crippled them. This preoccupation with shoes changed in the early 1960s for two reasons. One was the hippie movement; the other was the accelerated movement of women's liberation. That generation decided that being comfortable with shoes was more important than to be up-to-date with whatever style was in. Men just tagged along. Up until that point, I always wore oxfords for dress wear and cowboy boots at other times. Since then, I wear cowboy boots seven days a week. If they fit properly, they are the most comfortable shoe or boot there is.

As for the general public, there is a wide variety of footwear. In other words, anything goes. They are all in style. So-called "running shoes" seem to have the inside track. From little kids to young people, older folk and yes, senior citizens. The residents in nursing homes all wear them.

Have you ever noticed that ninety percent of the running shoes that people wear are dirty? Sometimes they are well dressed, but the dirty runners kind of mess up their appearance.

There are shoes for every occasion and occupation. They are made from a variety of materials such as various leathers (the most common one), felt, canvas, plastic, cloth, rubber, and even paper as well as the glass slippers that Cinderella wore. Steel is also used in the toes of industrial and miners boots. There is an old saying that an army is only as good as the boots its soldiers wear. What would a cowboy be without cowboy boots? There are also roughneck or lumberjack boots and just plain work boots. The Eskimos wear mukluks, the Indians, moccasins and many Russians wear felt boots. There are also many shoes related to sports such as golf, baseball and football, which have cleats. There are bowling shoes, basketball shoes, and boots with blades attached (called skates). There are ski boots and mountain climbing boots; hipwaders for duck hunters, and plain old rubber boots.

In every day footwear, we have men's oxford dress shoes, ladies high heels, low heels, flat heels, and ladies clunkies with massive heels, some low, some high. Within all these types of shoes there are names like pumps, slip-ons, Hush Puppies and overshoes.

Shoes come in a large variety of colors and designs. As already mentioned, many kinds of skins and leathers are used such as cowhide, horsehide, bull hide, elephant hide, water buffalo, deerskin, elk skin, snakeskin, sheepskin, alligator, ostrich, eland and others.

There are a number of sayings pertaining to shoes:

He died with his boots on.

His shoes will be hard to fill.

Those boots are made for walking.

You never know until you have walked a mile in his moccasins.

He got booted out.

If only these shoes could talk.

I will trade horses with you, but only if you give me something to boot.

In the old days, the village cobbler was an important man in the community. Some actually made shoes, others just repaired shoes. Their importance faded since we are now in a "throw away" society.

I liked one of my dad's sayings: "I complained because I had no shoes, until I met a man who had no feet."

Shoes and boots must fit. Many is the person who buys footwear that does not fit. I have seen people with huge blisters. Pinched toes are also common. Some ladies buy shoes that are too tight because they want to wear a small size. Again, that is not as common as it used to be. These days, people are more inclined to wear what fits them, no matter how large they are.

The type of shoes or boots we wear tells us quite a lot about what type of person we are. I have observed that, male or female, wear the kind of footwear that reveals, to a large extent, what their interests in life might be and the lifestyle they prefer.

When I autograph books in a public place, I can pretty well tell who is a potential book buyer by looking at their shoes. Different books for different folks. My books have kind of a western tinge to them, *Cows, Cowboys, Cattlemen and Characters, Round up of Memories* and *Cattle Call*. If the person wears cowboy boots, chances are they will buy a book. If they wear dress shoes, they may also buy a book. However, if they wear running shoes or clodhopper work boots, they seldom buy a book. Of course, there are exceptions to the rule.

If my books were about sports, mechanics or technical subjects, many of those 'young bucks' wearing running shoes might buy one of my books.

Imelda Marcos, who was the first lady in the Philippines, has over three thousand pairs of shoes. In 1999, a museum was established in the Philippines, to feature two hundred pairs of this lady's shoes. The country hopes to draw many tourists to this museum. Personally, I know of many other sights in the world that I would rather see.

CHAPTER FIFTY-EIGHT

CAMPS AND CAMPING

Camp implies a temporary home away from home.

There are a large variety of camps, such as Boy Scout, Girl Guide, army, church, family, internment, nudist, plus individual camps where people set up a little pup tent in the wilderness or transients camp beside a road.

Today, we have campgrounds all over the world, including youth hostels for backpackers. Several of our sons have stayed at hostels overseas.

When we think of camping, we usually visualize tents. However, there are also camper trucks, trailers and motor homes. These modern-day campers have all the conveniences of home, including heat, air conditioning, tables and comfortable beds. So is that really camping? What it amounts to is that you transport your home to some crowded campground, along with hundreds of other jaded folks who are looking for a little peace and quiet, only to find yourself parked beside people who decide to party most of the night.

Camping has been around a long time. Four thousand years ago, when one million Israelites left Egypt, they camped in the desert for forty years. I am sure that was the largest, longest camping trip in the history of mankind. Every day, manna fell from heaven to feed those people. The manna was probably quite bland, but it kept them alive. No wonder that many of those people murmured against their leader, Moses. They longed for the leeks and onions of Egypt. How soon they forgot that they had been slaves in Egypt.

Finally, after forty years, they were allowed into the 'Promised Land', a land that flowed with milk and honey, as the Bible puts it.

My wife and I have been involved in dozens of camps including: Young Peoples, Boys Brigade, church camps, family camps, as well as our own family campings. Conducting a camp can be an exhilarating experience for young and old. At camp, many young people have made commitments to follow Jesus and become missionaries and other worthy occupations. Some people may think these are spur-of-the-moment decisions, but I know that when hundreds of these young people grew up, they became exactly what they had decided or felt called to do while sitting around a campfire in some remote wilderness area. Some of the young people from the camps which we conducted became doctors, nurses, teachers, missionaries, ministers, dentists, carpenters, electricians, plumbers and farmers. In other words, useful caring citizens. I never visited any of these young people in jail. I did have a few boys from Boys Club in jail, but they were not at camp.

There is something about an open campfire that brings out the best in people, whether it is Scouts, Girl Guides, Christian Service Brigade, or family camp. There is camaraderie about the singing and storytelling around a campfire that cannot be equalled anywhere else. I think we feel closer to nature when we are outdoors, away from the various distractions we have these days.

Have you ever noticed how good the food tastes at camp? Be it wieners, beans, or any other ordinary food, it all tastes great. And how about hotcakes (we used to call them flapjacks) and bacon in the morning, with the sun just peeking over the trees?

The best fish I have tasted was at a boy's camp in the mountains southwest of Calgary. Some of the boys went fishing early in the morning. They came back with a fair catch, just as we were about to prepare breakfast. Fish for breakfast did not really appeal to me. I had learned as a camp leader you need to be flexible, so I said, "Sure guys, let's fry those mountain trout for breakfast." Well, let me tell you, that was the best fish I ever ate.

In a large part of the world, people live their entire lives in kind of a camping atmosphere. In most of those countries the climate is mild, often tropical. They do not necessarily live in tents, although some people do. Sometimes, they have straw huts or small wooden shelters with a thatched roof. Much of their food comes from the forest, both meat and vegetation. If they happen to live close to a river, and most of them do, or close to the ocean, then fish becomes a large part of their diet. Temporary buildings and tents permit people to move to wherever the best food supply is.

It is a laid-back lifestyle that is foreign to people like us, who think we have to hustle-and-bustle to keep up our so-called modern lifestyle. I am not an expert on third-world countries, but we have visited at least ten countries where the lifestyle is simple - the two of them were in the remote backcountry in Colombia, South America and the Fiji Islands.

The early west in North America (Canada and the United States) had a lot of camping that was out of necessity, not for pleasure. When people started a ranch or a homestead, they often lived in tents to start with, until such time as they got around to building something a little more permanent. Up to that point, it actually was camping. Sometimes they built a little soddy (a building made from sod).

After a farm or ranch site was well established, there still was some camping done. Many big ranches had camps that they called 'line shacks', primitive shelters where a line rider (cowboy) would spend most of the summer and often part of the winter. His job was to watch the cattle and treat them when necessary. They had what was called 'a drift fence' that ran for miles. This stopped the cattle from straying too far from the ranch. The line cabin was usually close to that fence, about twenty to thirty miles from the home ranch headquarters. Can you imagine what a lonesome life that was for the cowboy assigned to that duty? Approximately once a week somebody from the home ranch would deliver some food to the line cabin. There was no refrigeration so that food consisted of flapjack flour, salt, sugar, salted pork, coffee, beans - anything that did not spoil in the heat. Sometimes, they brought a special treat that had to be consumed the same day, such as a vegetable or some dessert.

In the old west there were many itinerant riders, sometimes called drifters. They consisted of cowboys out of work, some too lazy to work, some just riding long distances to new locations such as from Texas to Montana or New Mexico to Wyoming. There were also many outlaws and rustlers who inhabited that vast region from Texas clear into Canada.

Harry Longbough worked for the Bar U Ranch in Alberta for several years. Nobody knew that he was 'The Sundance Kid' wanted for murder and robbery in the United States. He behaved himself pretty good in Canada.

These various types of men camped outdoors every night. They tried to find a stream or spring with a few trees for shelter and wood that they needed for their campfire. If they were rustlers or other riffraff running from the law, they were careful where they built their fire. A fire on the open plains could be seen for miles. They usually built a small fire in a secluded place in the hope that no nosey rancher or lawman would find them. I would not call that relaxed camping, but it was camping nonetheless.

Some of the world's most famous campers are the Bedouins of the Middle East who move their flocks and herds to wherever the best grass is. They have special tents, often made from goatskins or other skins. Whenever the grass becomes scarce, they move on. They welcome strangers into their tents for goat milk cheese, mutton and some other dishes made from their herds and flocks. I am told that there are a lot less Bedouins these days, although there are still some clinging to that lifestyle. The oil business in those countries is to blame for the urbanization of the people. In Mongolia, they also practice following their flocks and herds to where grass is. The Mongolians are excellent horsemen.

I have been to cow camps, boy's camps, family camps, and also to a one-person camp (me), but I have never been to a refugee internment, army or nudist camp. Let's face it, camping is fun.

This is a little story about camping that actually happened not far from our place. There was a rancher who had a nice, scenic place. He had one problem. People often set up a little camp on his property. They did not really camp but, more or less, built a big bonfire to roast wieners and marshmallows. This was usually accompanied with a lot of drinking. In the morning, there was a mess of beer and liquor bottles, along with other litter. Since it was summertime and the grass was green, the fire hazard was not great.

One evening, he noticed a car stop at a clump of trees in his pasture. He decided to take action. He rode in a big circle, and then approached the little party that was in progress from the side where the trees were. Some distance away, he tied his horse to a tree. Silently, he snuck up to where the people were. He managed to get the license number of the vehicle. Quickly, and silently, he retreated to where his horse was tied up. No one had noticed him.

The next morning he went to where these people had been. What he saw was a big mess. A week later he loaded his pickup truck with some dry wood, a little gas to light the fire, along with some other rubbish, including empty bottles.

He had discovered who these people were from the license plate number.

He drove down the back alley where these people lived. There appeared to be no one looking out of the back window of the house. Quickly, he stacked up the firewood, poured on a little gas, and threw a match on it. It burst into flames, and then he scattered some litter and bottles around the fire.

After a few minutes, the occupants of the house rushed out. When they saw a man sitting in a folding chair, not too far from the fire, they shouted at him, "What are you doing?" "Oh," the rancher calmly replied, "I am the owner of the ranch where you had your bonfire and party last week. I am here to repay your visit to my place." Needless to say, they were speechless. When the reality of the situation sank in, they knew that they did not have a leg to stand on. The rancher doused the flames and cleaned up the mess (maybe they helped him, I am not sure) then he told them, "Next time, you folks want to have a little party in the country, whether at my place or someone else's place, ask for permission. Usually, permission will be granted, providing it is not in the fire hazard season and you clean up the mess before you leave."

The majority of city people who go to the country for a picnic and have a little campfire, do respect the landowner and ask permission. Most people have a yearning for the great outdoors. They wish to experience the primitive things that their ancestors lived with each day.

No matter what luxurious houses or apartments we live in, or how many gadgets or sophisticated computers we have, camping will be around into the foreseeable future. Camping may have more therapeutic value for uptight jaded folks than pills from a bottle or sessions on a shrink's couch.

The Friesen family camping in Kananaskis Country, west of Calgary, Alberta.
Courtesy of Graham Friesen.

CHAPTER FIFTY-NINE

WHAT'S IN A NAME?

In our society, names are important. In a mixed national background, like we have in North America, we are not too name-conscious. However, for some reason when we are introduced to someone, it crosses our mind as to what nationality the person's ancestors are. For instance, if a person's name is Wong, Chen, Singh or Yip, then we know they are not from Eastern Europe. On the other hand, if their names are Zwozdesky, Gudzowaty or Yaskowitch, we know they are not from China or India. If the name is Rasmussen or Nielson, we can be pretty sure they are not from Ireland. By the same token, if their name is Graham, Marshall or Smith, we can be sure they are not from Denmark.

I think the Natives have a good system of naming their babies - Back Fat, Bear's Paw, Beaver, Big Bear, Big Lake, Black Elk, Black Kettle, Black Wolf, Blue Weasel, Calf Robe, Crazy Horse, Crow Child, Curious Antelope, Day Woman, Deer Foot, Dodging Horse, Falls Down, First Dog, Flying Cloud, Four Bears, Fox, Good Stoney, Grey Mouse, Grey Owl, Hawk, Heavy Breast, Lame Buffalo, Little Dog, Long Elk, Morning Star, No Heart, Never Laughs, Night Bear, Old Yellow Woman (this name also applies to men - I know a fine gentleman named Vincent Old Yellow Woman), One Spot, Pointed Arrow, Pound Maker, Prairie Rose, Rolling in Mud, Red Cloud, Seven Arrows, Silent Tongue, Sitting Bull, Shot-on-Both-Sides, Spotted Calf, Poor Eagle, Standing Eagle, Star Light, Three Suns, Three Stabs, Tail Feathers, Thunder Bird, White Elk, White Shield, Walking Buffalo, Weasel Head, Wolverine, Yellow Robe, plus hundreds more. Some names are not flattering, but always descriptive and practical.

Many of the immigrants who came to America from Europe changed their names. I personally know a number of folks who changed their names, and there are basically two reasons. One was if their name had twelve to sixteen letters, it was often hard to pronounce. They shortened their name for practical purposes. The second reason was that up until fifty years ago, it was better to have an Anglo-Saxon name than one from Continental Europe. A number of my Jewish friends also changed their names. A few that come to mind are Smith, Kerr, Green, Hanson and Pearce. In the old days, nearly every movie star had a changed name. Are you aware that Dyan Cannon used to be a Friesen? Bob Dylan was a Zimmerman? John Wayne was a Morrison?

Scores of actors and actresses changed their names. One singer's career was going nowhere. He changed his name to Englebert Humperdinck, not exactly an Anglo-Saxon name and, almost immediately, his career took off. He named himself after a German composer who died in 1520.

Here are a few other people who changed their names. Pele, the world's most famous soccer player from Brazil, was born as Edson Arantes Do Nasimento. Marilyn Monroe used to be Jean Baker Mortenson. Cassius Clay, the world's heavyweight boxing champion, changed his name to Mohammed Ali after he embraced the Muslim religion. Golda Meir, a former Prime Minister of Israel, was Golda Mabovitch. Greta Garbo was Greta Lovisa Gustafsson. Rita Hayworth's real name was Margarita Carmen Cansino.

One of the most interesting names in the world is that of the Sultan of Brunei. He is reputed to be worth fifty billion dollars. He owns a palace with over seventeen hundred rooms. His official handle is His Majesty Paduka seri Baginda Sultan Haji Hassanal Bokiah Muizzaddin Waddaulah. How would you like to be saddled with a name like that? Of course, the fifty billion dollars could cushion such an inconvenient name a bit.

The longest name that I am aware of is that of a village in Northern Wales -
Llanfairpwillgwyngyllgogerychwyrndrobwillllantysiligogogoch. Try to pronounce that name. If you don't believe that the names exist look it up in an atlas. Wales also has several other interesting names such as Aberdaugleddau, Machynileth, Caer, Philly, Rhaandiromwyn,

Dolgella, Aberystweyth and many other strange sounding names. The Welsh people are just as proud of their heritage as the Irish and the Scottish people are. That leaves the English who think the universe spins around them as far as Great Britain is concerned and maybe it does since - they have the biggest population, the biggest city (London) and the monarchy, Buckingham Palace, where the Queen resides, and parliament. I got a little sidetracked, now back to names.

These days, there seems to be more pride in ancestral names. Consequently, not as many people, including actors, change their names.

Each generation conjures up a set of new first names. They also recycle a number of old names, many of them from the Bible, such as Sarah, Naomi, Jake, Luke, Joshua and Mark. Another trend is what I call unisex. The name applies to either sex such as Francis, Gene, Stacey, Mitchell, Taylor, Alexandra, Clem, Bobby and dozens more. I even heard of one girl called Charley. I also know several men called Beverly, a name usually given to females.

In the old days, many cultures had only one name. This included most people mentioned in the Bible. People were identified by their trade or profession: Simon, the tanner; Peter, the fisherman; Luke, the physician; and Isaiah, the prophet.

In Scandinavia, it was common for the son to receive his father's first name as his last name. For example, Peter's son became Peterson, John's son became Johnson, Ole's son became Olson, Carl's son became Carlson, and so on. It was also common in those counties to give yourself a new surname. My brother-in-law, of Norwegian ancestry, was born in Canada. He went to Norway for a visit, and found it interesting that his Norwegian cousins had different surnames even though their fathers' names were all Carlson. His name was Otto Carlson.

I knew a gentleman by the name of Hans Hindbo. He came from Denmark as a young man. One day, I asked him about his name. He said, "Oh, I was not born with that name. When I came to Canada, I decided to change my name to Hindbo." It was the name of his parent's farm.

It is surprising how a name often fits a person's personality. Babe Ruth does not sound masculine, but we all know he wasn't a pansy. Or how about Hitler? It sounds evil, but only because the man was evil. Churchill sounds dignified. Bill Gates sounds like money. Wayne Gretzky personifies hockey. If it weren't for Wayne, the name Gretzky wouldn't stir up any great emotions.

Caesar makes one think of power, Stalin of cruelty and enslavement. It is estimated that he was responsible for twenty million deaths. He was born Vissarionovich Dzhugashvili. In 1917, when he was thirty-eight years old, he changed his name to Stalin. He died in 1953 when he was seventy-six years old. So, for thirty-eight years, he had the unpronounceable name and for thirty-eight years he was Stalin.

Jesus stands for forgiveness and love. If we live long enough we all begin to fit the name our parents hung on us. I feel quite flattered by the confidence my parents had in my future when they gave me the name Leonard, which means lion-hearted. I have not always lived up to it, but I have given my best shot to be brave as a lion.

CHAPTER SIXTY

ANGER

Anger is experienced by every individual at one time or another. With some people, it is a daily occurrence. We all have different levels of anger.

Anger is an emotional outburst. It often is confused with hate, which actually is quite different. Many people who have a bad temper or become angry easily often also have a great capacity to love, whereas hate is more deep-seated and constant.

Some people get angry quickly and then get over it just as fast. Others stay angry for a long period, which then may develop into hate.

Uncontrolled anger has caused a lot of havoc in our society. Every year, thousands of people are murdered by someone in a fit of rage. Someone who exhibits his or her anger injures many more.

Countless marriages go on the rocks, because spouses cannot control their anger. Sometimes children are severely punished because of a parent's frustration and anger.

I have known my share of angry people. Fortunately, not many of them directed their anger at me.

I know one man who became angry when he received an unpleasant phone call. He jerked the phone off the wall, threw it on the floor and jumped on it, smashing it to pieces.

I know of another person who committed suicide in a fit of anger. Because of anger, many people commit irrational acts when their brain is not functioning normally.

There are a number of names for anger such as mad, ticked off, irate, violent, annoyed, hot-tempered, wrath, enraged, irritated, furious. Call it what you will, it still boils down to anger.

There is also such a thing as righteous anger. This happens when we encounter harsh treatment of people, often children. Sometimes the action may be perpetuated against animals. Sometimes governments come up with unjust laws and rules. Whenever we are up against these things, I think our anger is justified. However, we must keep it in check, so it does not get us into too much hot water.

Even Jesus approved of righteous anger. He demonstrated that when he drove the moneychangers out of the temple.

Because we are human and all have emotions, anger will always be with us. Oh, I almost forgot to mention that I have a bit of a temper myself. Not too outrageous, but it's there. My weak point, when it comes to anger, is when I think I am falsely accused of some action or deed. I also get angry at all the rules and regulations with which we are saddled.

It definitely is not wrong to get angry once in a while. The secret is to control our actions when we do get angry. Another good idea is to forget and forgive real or perceived injustices done to us. We must also practice some tolerance when it comes to other people's actions. We all have plenty of shortcomings ourselves.

There are all kinds of programs to overcome various addictions, including anger management courses. If anger rules your life, it might be a good idea to take that course.

Chapter Sixty-One

PROFANITY

In today's society, swearing has become so common that we have built up an immunity to it. In the old days, it was usually only men who swore. These days, nearly as many women swear as do men.

Why do people swear? There are a number of reasons why it becomes a habit. Young people as they grow up hear their parents and others use profane words. An even greater influence is when peers use swear words. It makes young people feel grownup, just like smoking does.

Once you develop a vocabulary that includes a lot of swear words, it becomes a habit that is hard to get rid of. Some people only swear when they are angry, others swear all the time. I know of one man whose conversations were laced with words that made those listening to him cringe. One day, he was describing one of his friends. He said, "He is a good son-of-bitch."

Many people who swear a lot seem to lack knowledge of words to describe what they are trying to convey, so they use swear words to fill in the blanks. Some men think that swearing is macho. Some swear to mock the existence of God. Fortunately, those people are in the minority. Most people who swear a lot give little thought as to why they use phrases like: Oh, my God, Jesus Christ, Go to Hell, God damn it, or any other words pertaining to the Bible. These words, in themselves, are good but in the context they are used become sacrilegious. Often, they are used in conjunction with other swear words, including the common phrase of f - - king. By now, you must think that I am a holier-than-thou person. This is not the case. I use my share of slang words, but I do avoid using words that I feel are not honouring to God. I think that our English language, or any other language for that matter, has enough words in it to explain or describe any situation that arises so that we don't need to resort to using questionable words.

I have written a magazine column for twenty-six years. In all those years, I managed to write on a number of topics without using words of questionable defamatory meaning. When you are searching for a meaningful way to express yourself, it is not a bad idea to pick up a dictionary and look for appropriate words. Have you noticed that most dictionaries omit and ignore swear or curse words, at least in the context of how they are used? They even avoid most slang words.

Writers such as Margaret Atwood, Farley Mowat and hundreds of others use foul and vulgar language throughout their novels. They pose as sophisticated, worldly-wise intellectuals, who disregard God and those people who do not appreciate that kind of language. Unfortunately, a large portion of our population is numb to such vulgar statements. Consequently, they read these books, which puts the authors on the best seller's list.

God's name is used in dishonor, not honor. They talk about being 'pissed off', or 'who gives a shit'. Other paragraphs use the 'f' word a number of times. Not only is the language low-life, but so is the story. The plot usually centers on the bizarre, involving cheating, immoral living, intrigue, and murder. No wonder our crime rate is high – people, young and old, fill their minds with this trash. Even if only a small percentage of people make that trash a reality in their lives, it amounts to a lot of people ending up in court, jail or hospital emergency wards. Some become murder or suicide statistics.

Often, what comes out of our mouth indicates what kind of person we are. I have known decent, law-abiding citizens who swear a lot. In my humble opinion, if they cleaned up their language their acceptance by friends and family would be even greater. Intelligent, well-adjusted individuals do not have to use foul, vulgar, dirty language to express themselves. Be honest, do you really enjoy visiting with a foul-mouthed person who uses a swear words in conversation?

I am sure you don't, even if you swear a little yourself. I challenge each of you to cut down on your profanity. It will build your self-esteem and others will appreciate you more.

CHAPTER SIXTY-TWO

ADDICTIONS

What is an addiction? The dictionary suggests it is a pathological weakness, a habit in our life that is hard to overcome.

Everyone has an addiction of some sort. Not all addictions are bad but, in reality, most are not good. Countless lives have been destroyed by bad addictions.

An addiction usually starts slowly. Young people sometimes just want to experiment with drugs or alcohol. Initially, it gives them a lift so they do it again. Before they know what has happened, they have become addicted.

One of the most common addictions is liquor. It starts with a social drink. Then it becomes a regular social drink like three or four times a week. After several years, it's daily drinking. The amount of alcohol consumed varies with each individual. Some drink only a toddy or two. Others drink a number of glasses each day. At this point, they are alcoholics, craving a drink so much that nothing can stop them from indulging.

I have been around and worked with people who had a serious drinking problem. Almost, without exception, they denied that they had a problem. The ones who finally admitted that they had a problem usually overcame their liquor addiction but it was always a struggle. Seldom did counselling by friends do the trick. Often, it was after the individual joined Alcoholics Anonymous (AA). Sometimes it was a spiritual turnaround. God can cure any addiction which we may have if we give it over to Him.

These days there is a big drive against smoking. I am in favor of that. However, in my opinion, excessive drinking does far more damage than smoking. Yet, about the only thing we ever hear or read about drinking is, do not drink and drive. That is good, but it does not address all the damage that liquor does to society.

We all know what liquor does to a person's life. I think it bears repeating over and over until the message sinks into our minds that drinking is a no-win situation at all times. Briefly, here is how liquor addiction impacts people:

1. It affects health. Millions of dollars are spent annually on medical bills for a number of health problems as a direct result of alcohol.
2. It costs a lot of money, liquor is not cheap.
3. It breaks up families, when one spouse, or both, comes home drunk regularly.
4. It causes family violence. Often, the wife and children are beaten when the husband/father is in a drunken stupor.
5. Each year drunk drivers worldwide kill thousands of innocent people.
6. People make fools of themselves in public when they are full of booze.
7. Often when a person is drunk, a jealous streak surfaces. This sometimes ends up in barroom brawls.
8. In the days before women's liberation and birth control, many young women lost their virginity and sometimes became pregnant by someone they met at a party. He would be relatively sober, but he made sure she had lots to drink. I once knew a man who specialized in seducing drunk, young women while he remained sober.
9. Even people, who drink a fair bit themselves, do no want to associate or be with someone who is considered a chronic drunk. Cities, around the world, harbor thousands of people on skid row and in flop houses who, at one time, were normal young people who thought they could handle liquor, until liquor had such a hold on them that they lost their jobs, family, and friends and were left to live out their lives in the gutters and back alleys. How tragic.

In spite of all the things I mentioned, society still endorses drinking as socially acceptable, provided you don't overdo it.

Unfortunately, five to ten percent cross over that line to where they become alcoholics and another fifty percent drink excessively.

Rich people can cover up their alcohol problem much better than poor people can. A poor person who is a drinker often, in fact nearly always, loses his or her job. From there on it is all downhill.

I am sure my tirade against drinking will hardly make a dent in anyone's drinking habits. But if even one person sobers up after reading this, I consider my opinion on the drinking problem a success.

The Bible has over one hundred verses which mention drinking. Approximately ninety percent of them condemn excessive drinking. The verse that is often quoted is when Jesus turns water into wine at a wedding feast. Some scholars claim it was nonalcoholic. I think it was real wine. Even if it was, the scriptures make it abundantly clear that strong drink is not good. The following verses back up that statement.

Proverbs 23:21 states that *a drunkard will come to poverty*. Joel 1:5 says, *Awake ye drunkards and weep and howl, all ye drinkers of wine*. Galations 5:21 says, *Envyings, murders, drunkenness, revellings, shall not inherit the kingdom of God*. Romans 13:13 says, *Let us walk honestly, as in the day, not in rioting drunkenness*. Ephesians 5:18 says, *Be not drunk with wine where in excess, but be filled with the spirit*.

There is another story in Genesis that is rather hard to understand. It tells about Lot having sex with both of his daughters. They both become pregnant. The story says that the girls got him drunk with wine before performing sex acts with him.

We know that morality cannot be legislated. Prohibition in the United States did not work. The purveyors of liquor went underground. It is a matter of educating our young people and that is easier said than done. At this moment, we are going in the wrong direction. In the United States, thousands of college students congregate in Florida during spring break. It turns into a week-long party with thousands of gallons of liquor consumed. These are the educators, business leaders and politicians of the future. If this is not a picture of the Roman Empire before its disintegration, I don't know what is.

Booze is a multi-billion dollar business. With that kind of money at stake, lobbying to keep the liquor flowing is all the greedy purveyors do. There are liquor stores, bars, restaurants and nightclubs that sell every drop possible. Of course, governments collect mega-bucks from the sale of booze. They give lip service to the, 'if you drink, don't drive' slogan. If the truth were known, ten times more drunk drivers could be caught if the police checked every car that leaves a drinking establishment on any given night. I could ramble on about drinking, but I think you get the message.

How about the addiction of smoking? We have known for years that smoking is unhealthy, but it is a fairly recent development where smoking has hit the headlines as a no-no. It is also claimed that second hand smoke kills as well.

Smoking, like drinking, starts slowly. Many kids, including myself, start puffing on a few cigarettes in the early teens. By the age of eighteen, they are addicted smokers. I smoked until I was twenty-three. Then I quit cold turkey. I know many other men who also quit between the ages of eighteen and forty years. It is a difficult habit to break. These days most businesses are smoke-free. That's why, even on a cold winter day, we see people, huddling on the sidewalk beside a building, dragging on a cigarette.

At the Foothills Hospital in Calgary, I often observe thirty to fifty people, many with oxygen tanks and some in wheelchairs, puffing away on the sidewalk alongside the hospital. I often wonder if they realize how foolish they look being a hospital patient trying to get better and abusing their body by smoking.

Recently, I heard that the authorities are considering passing a law that will prohibit people from smoking anywhere on hospital property.

I think eventually that smoking in our society will diminish because governments seem to have the will to warn people of the dangers of smoking. I wish they would take the same stance on liquor.

Gambling is another addiction. I mention gambling in another chapter, so I won't bore you too much about it here. I will say that this addiction is just as hard to break as drinking and smoking.

Maybe the worst addiction of all is drugs. They are deadly. If you don't believe me, take a stroll on some of Vancouver's streets. The sights there, and in hundreds of other cities, are so revolting that I think every young person, from the age of ten to sixteen, should have an escorted tour to witness how horrible life is for people who are hooked on liquor and drugs.

There is also sex addiction. I have read of some sad cases where an individual could not control his sexual impulses and desires. This resulted in him committing some horrible sex crimes against women and children. These crimes are reported in our newspapers almost every day. I am told some women are sex addicts as well. I do not feel too qualified to discuss this subject in detail.

We have mentioned the addictions of alcohol, smoking, drugs, gambling and sex. How about some other addictions, some of which are good?

My wife says I am addicted to cattle. Weakly, I deny that, but I must admit I find it hard not to be involved in cattle one way or another. Some people must have a dog or two, other people need one or even a dozen cats. I'm not sure addiction is the right word to use for the love of animals, including horses. But if they are something people desire and must own and enjoy, it is an addiction.

Some people are addicted to having a bunch of relatives around at all times; others could care less if they ever see a relative, except for their parents, spouse or children.

Some women are addicted to shopping. Their motto is, 'I will shop till I drop.' This can result in huge credit card bills. I have heard some horror stories about how a 'clothes horse' lady absolutely cannot control herself when it comes to purchasing shoes and clothes. If she has a good job and makes good money, or if her husband is rich, then everything works out. If, however, she is not so well off, it can cause a lot of friction in a home when the bills start piling up.

A lot of men have a sports addiction, often playing golf or watching every hockey, baseball, basketball and football game on the 'boob' tube. I mention more of this in the Sports chapter.

Some people are addicted to helping other people, even when that help is neither needed nor solicited. If they cannot help in some way, they feel guilty.

One good addiction is if spouses are addicted to each other. This results in a good marriage. They operate as a team. They compliment each other and overlook some weaknesses in their partner. Family, friends and neighbors all benefit from such a blissful union.

We can also become addicted to certain foods. I have this problem. I can eat beef two to three times a day. I also like crisp bacon for breakfast. I know that these are addictions, because if I don't have beef at least once a day, I feel deprived. Many folks become addicted to coffee or tea. Some to soda pop. These food addictions are habit-forming but not really dangerous, unless you over indulge, which I do occasionally. So you see, I'm not perfect either.

An addiction is any habit we acquire that is hard to break. Like I said at the outset, every human who has ever lived has experienced and addiction of some sort.

There is no addiction known to mankind that we cannot overcome with God's help.

CHAPTER SIXTY-THREE

MISTAKES

Life is full of mistakes, some small, some big. None of us can boast that we do not make mistakes. Sometimes mistakes are made because of ignorance or wrong judgment. Often they are the result of our impulsive nature. We neglect to count to ten before making a decision. Major things like moving to another location could take several days or weeks, and still be a mistake. We are prone to see mistakes in other people, but are often in self-denial about our own mistakes. Some people find it difficult to apologize for their mistakes, even though the mistake may have been detrimental to someone else.

We learn from our mistakes, especially children. Remember when you were in elementary school, and the teacher gave your class a test? When you got your paper back, the correct answers had a tick beside them with a black pencil, and the wrong answers had a red X beside them. It was those questions where you made a mistake that caught your attention. With a little guidance from the teacher, you researched the questions until you had the right answer. You had learned from the mistakes so that in future exams you had fewer red X's. We learn by doing.

As adults, mistakes may go something like this. You plan to go on a little trip, but the weather isn't good. There is a fair bit of snow. You happen to have a comfortable car and a four-wheel-drive truck. You decide the roads won't be too bad, so you take the car. About five miles down the road you are hopelessly stuck. You made a mistake by not taking the truck. Some mistakes may be life threatening. On another occasion, you may go to an outdoor sporting event such as a football game or a rodeo. You forget about the weather and do not take warm clothing. You sit and shiver, because you made the mistake of not wearing proper clothes.

You may run out of gas, because you made the mistake of not looking at your gas gauge (it happened to me once). Sometimes, on a farm or ranch, a person will go through a gate and leave it open because they plan to come back through it in half an hour. Meanwhile, the cattle or horses discover the open gate and scatter all over the country, maybe even causing a serious accident when a vehicle hits one of these stray animals. A costly mistake. There are dozens of other mistakes we make every day.

An area where our mistakes can have grave consequences is in our social life. These days, everything is described as choices. Young people are especially vulnerable to wrong choices, such as choosing with which friends they wish to hang out. Wrong friends will pull them down in a hurry. I know of some young people who came from good homes yet, for some reason, they chose to hang out with the wrong crowd. This led to drinking, drug addiction and, in some cases, robbery and murder.

Although the bulk of the kids who turn out bad come from dysfunctional homes, the mistakes of parents and grandparents are often repeated by their children.

It is also a huge mistake to marry the wrong person. I think that every teenager at fifteen years of age (by eighteen, it is usually too late) should attend a seminar on who and what type of mate they should choose in the future. I know of dozens of marriages that turn out to be a disaster. The sad part is that it was obvious they were not meant for each other. The seminars should be based on New Testament principles.

Sometimes a young woman makes the mistake of allowing herself to be carried away by a persistent, persuasive young man. Often the man is at least ten years older than she is. The result is an unwanted pregnancy. Often she makes a second mistake and gets an abortion.

Another area where people often make mistakes is how they manage their finances. I dare say that, in our free democratic society, eighty-five percent of people do a poor job of money management. They make a lot of mistakes on their investments. I know from experience. Sometimes we are too cautious, other times too reckless. I mention some of those wrong choices in the "Money" chapter.

History records major mistakes in military operations. Over the past three thousand years, these mistakes cost the lives of millions of young men and women.

Some mistakes were made by heroes, others by tyrants. In World War One, Winston Churchill was First Lord of the Admiralty. He dispatched a number of battleships to sail through the Dardenelles, by Turkey. The channel was thirty-eight miles long and narrow. In fact, in some places, it was barely wide enough to let the ships through. The enemy sank three ships and badly damaged two others. There were 213,980 casualties, a large number of them fatal. This was a colossal mistake and blunder by Churchill. This happened in 1915. Twenty-five years later, he lead the Allies in the Second World War, which made him a hero.

Hitler, along with his strategists had conquered a large portion of Western Europe in the first two years of the Second World War. Then he got ambitious and invaded Russia, where he also had some good success, until the Russian winter closed in on the German army. The same thing happened to Napoleon a hundred years earlier. This little mistake cost the lives of several million German and Russian soldiers. The Germans also captured about six hundred thousand Russian soldiers, who were released after the Germans were defeated.

Another military mistake and misadventure was when the Allies, nearly all Canadians, were ordered to sail across the English Channel in every type of vessel available, and some were basically old tubs. Their mission was to gain a beachhead at Dieppe. The Germans learned of the plan, so they riddled the Allies with machine gun bullets before they could even land. Several thousand were killed. That was a major mistake by the people in command.

Then there was the battle of the Little Big Horn. What a mistake that was by General George Custer. Maybe I sound a little callous, but I am on the Indian's side on that one. Custer's mistake wiped out his whole unit.

There are hundreds of other battles where mistakes were made. The sad part is that usually the people who made the mistakes remained alive. It is the young soldiers who paid the price.

A mistake that millions of people make is in their lack of concern about the hereafter. They live for the moment. This can lead to addictions and debauchery. In another chapter, I mention that addictions such as drugs, alcohol and prostitution often start slowly. Nobody expects to end up on skid row, but they often do. A childhood friend of mine ended up in skid row in Vancouver, where he died a relatively young man. Like I said, every one of us is vulnerable to mistakes. The secret is to think of the consequences before we make the wrong choices.

The other side of the coin is that, if we have never made a mistake, we have done nothing. So let us accept the fact that we will make mistakes. We must be humble enough to admit them and make a correction.

CHAPTER SIXTY-FOUR

WEATHER

Weather is probably the most-often discussed topic in our conversations. I don't think that a day goes by that we don't mention the weather. Good or bad, weather impacts every aspect of our lives. It dictates the activities we plan for on a daily basis. If we have plans to travel by car to visit family or friends or maybe a business trip, the trip is sometimes terminated before it begins. Why? Because suddenly a blizzard blows in, or maybe torrential rains wash out roads and bridges. If you do brave the elements and decide to travel in bad weather, you risk losing your life.

There are countless stories about people getting killed because of icy roads or accidents on washed out roads. There are even stories of some people getting stuck in the snow and freezing to death. TV, radio and newspapers have daily weather forecasts. In spite of all the satellites and computers, they often miss the forecast by a country-mile. Once in a while, they are dead on. When that happens, they sure let you know how correct they were on their forecast.

There are some other ways the weather impacts on our work and sports activities. Golfers want dry weather and sunshine. So do ball players and most other sports enthusiasts. Skiers want snow (lots of it). Sailors need wind, but not a storm. The average urban person wants nice dry, warm weather. The farmers and ranchers like nice weather as well. However, their livelihood depends on adequate moisture, so they look for rain (that includes me).

Worldwide, there is a tremendous variety of weather and climates. It is quite startling when one considers that on the same day somewhere on this planet, the following weather takes place at the same time:

- 60° below zero (Fahrenheit) in Antarctica;
- 130° above zero (Fahrenheit) in Death Valley, California;

- 75° above zero (Fahrenheit) in New Zealand; and every temperature between 60° below zero (Fahrenheit) and 130° above zero (Fahrenheit) somewhere in the world.

On that same day, some places have torrential rains, which cause severe flooding and many people lose their lives. In the same period, other areas of the world suffer severe drought resulting in total crop failure. This, in turn, causes famine and malnutrition. Thousands of people die from this every year. Even animals starve to death.

Over the centuries weather related deaths exceed the loss of life from all the wars and vehicle accidents combined. These death include famine, drowning in floods, freezing to death, being struck by lightning, car accidents on icy roads or foggy weather, sun strokes, mud slides caused by excessive rain, and snow and rock avalanches. Then there is the wind. With the exception of famine, it causes the most deaths.

I am taking the privilege of reprinting a column I wrote in June 1992. It was also featured in the book, *Cattle Call*.

"Today I am going to write about something we talk about almost every day, but can do little about. We are talking about w-i-n-d. Webster's dictionary simply says it is a movement of air. Not being a meteorologist or a scientist, I am not going into what causes this air movement.

"Like many who were raised in Western Canada, I certainly know what wind is. Wind, in its various forms, has caused more deaths, property damage and environmental devastation than all the earthquakes, volcanic eruptions and fires combined. Over the centuries, thousands of people have lost their lives at sea in shipwrecks, which were caused by wind. The wind has flattened buildings, uprooted trees and destroyed crops.

"Let's look at the names given these winds, from the gentlest to the most severe: completely calm, slight breeze, gentle breeze. Then comes high wind, which can be broken into categories such as thunderstorm, rainstorm, dust storm, sand storm, hail storm and snow storm (blizzard).

"Lately, we have heard a lot about El Nino, which caused our weather in North America to be extremely mild this winter, while the southern United States has been drenched with rain.

"Now we move into the big time winds, starting with a relatively harmless whirlwind, then onto a twister, cyclone, tornado, and finally hurricanes and typhoons.

"The last always start at sea and are usually referred to as tropical storms. They are very dangerous because of the rain they discharge. They also cause high tidal waves, which, in Bangladesh alone, have killed hundreds of thousands of people.

"Many of us have never experienced wind in the extreme forms. Most of us have read and heard accounts by people who experienced first hand the destruction of a hurricane or a tornado.

"Most of my wind experiences have been more annoying than devastating, although a friend of ours lost sixty head of cattle in a blizzard. Those cattle were grazing our winter wheat in Colorado. We saved all of ours because they were able to be behind shelter. His cattle were on the open plains.

"We have also been wiped out several times by wind-driven hailstorms.

"As a young person growing up in southern Saskatchewan, I can remember lighting lamps at two in the afternoon because of dust storms. I also remember pitching loose hay or straw when the wind was really howling. Sometimes in winter it was twenty or thirty below but the cattle had to be fed, wind or no wind.

"Wind also causes problems for the ladies. It is hard to maintain a good hairdo in a windstorm. What about those skirts? Maybe that is why we see so many slacks being worn these days. Hats can be a problem for both men and women.

"I have an uncle who will be one hundred and four years old on June 17. My wife and I visited him two years ago. His main topic of conversation was wind. He brought the topic up a number of times, expressing his dislike of wind. He used to farm on top of the river brakes of the South Saskatchewan River (now Lake Diefenbaker). I guess, over the years, wind just got the best of him.

"Is there anything good about wind? There certainly is. Isn't it nice to sit in the shade when it is hot and a gentle breeze caresses you?

"We need wind to pollinate our crops and plants. How about at haying or harvest time? After two weeks of rainy weather, we all wait for a nice warm wind to dry out the swaths. Wind also blows away a certain amount of pollution. It blows away flies and mosquitoes from our livestock, giving some relief. Or how about the rain it blows our way when needed?

"It can also be harnessed to generate electricity with wind charges. I foresee the time, in the not-too-distant future, when this form of energy will play a larger role than it does now. It is cheap, clean, and we will never run out of wind.

"On our ranch in Colorado we water our cattle with windmills. In a ten-year span, we had a problem with lack of wind on four occasions.

"What would people who love to fly hot air balloons do without a breeze? Or how about kids flying kites? It is all possible by wind.

"I feel strongly that our weather forecasters do not put enough emphasis on the wind factor. Their main concern seems to be temperature and precipitation. Once in a while they do mention wind, if it is really going to be strong.

"Twenty degrees below zero with a thirty-mile-per-hour wind is cold. Twenty below zero, with little or no wind, is relatively easy to take. Twenty below zero, plus fifteen inches of snow, spells a bad blizzard.

"We do need wind, just like we need fire, water, and all the other things the Lord has put on this old planet to keep it ticking." - End of column.

Lifestyle and well-being depends a lot on the climate of the area where people live. It is a well-documented fact that people who live in moderate to cold climates are more advanced and industrialized than what folks are who live in hot tropical countries. By that, I do not mean northerners are smarter. But as the saying goes, necessity is the mother of invention.

Because of the frigid weather it is imperative that we prepare for winter. This entails shelter, heat, and food. This has resulted in many inventions and developments in order for us to survive the winter.

In hot climates, with no cold winter weather, there is no urgent need for these precautions. They live from day-to-day. Their food is home-grown in fields and gardens, as well as the jungle. Extensive fishing and hunting is also done.

Once in a while, Mother Nature deals them a hard blow, usually in the form of excessive rain or high wind. These storms may blow down their shelters and cause damage to crops, gardens and trees. These storms do not occur often.

The weather subject is so vast it could fill a library. There are incidents that involved myself and several other members of our family. Some incidents could have cost our lives, such as when my brother Nick lost his sense of direction in a fierce blizzard on the Matador Ranch. By five-thirty in the evening, it was dark. As usual, he was riding a green-broke colt. A mature horse, if given its rein, will always head for the homeplace, where they know that some oats are waiting for them. But most young horses will drift with the wind or go in circles. After floundering around for an hour in three- to four-foot drifts in the low spots, Nick knew it was hopeless. Besides, he was getting chilled through to the bone.

He dismounted and led his horse in a fifty-foot circle. Round and round he and the horse went. After about twenty circles, they had trampled out a fairly good path. He kept walking hour after hour with only a few short pauses for a slight rest. Meanwhile, the snow kept on falling. He thought morning would never come. He was getting tired, but he knew there was no stopping until daylight. That walking kept his blood circulating. It was about fifteen below.

Finally, daylight came and, along with the daylight, a slight abatement in the storm. Everything was white. He surmised the wind was blowing from the northwest so, with that assumption, he started to ride in the direction of the river, which was frozen over. After riding for about two miles he came to a fence and followed it. Sure enough, it led him down to the river which he crossed and, an hour later, he was home, very thankful to be alive.

My experience was not nearly as dramatic. It happened one night when I was courting my wife, Edna. Usually I skied or rode to her place. However, whenever we wanted to go to a party, I took horses and a sleigh if the roads were blocked, which was quite often.

On this particular night, we were heading to her place across country. There was from one- to two-feet of snow on the ground. Everything was totally white, but that was not the problem. The problem was that there was a dense fog. You could not see more than two hundred feet in the daylight. In the dark, the vision ahead was nil.

I thought we should be at her place at any time until suddenly I noticed the wind had changed direction. It was not a strong wind, just a breeze. Then it changed direction again. That is when I realized that we were going in a huge circle. I was so disoriented and mixed-up in direction that I had no clue which way we were going. Fortunately, it was not cold. Just me and my sweetheart. It should have been romantic. But at that point, my manhood was in question. Real men don't get lost, so romance was put on the back burner. We drove around for quite a while, until I finally figured out which was east and kept the horses heading in the right direction. Edna did not lose her respect for me. Eight months later she became my wife. That foggy little episode took place fifty-five years ago.

I must mention one more bit of trivia about weather. For years it was assumed that cool, cloudy weather was depressing for people. Maybe it is, but one survey in Denmark proves otherwise. Denmark is quite overcast for most of the winter and even, to some degree, in summer. Italy is sunny a large portion of the year. What researchers found is that Italy has almost twice the suicide rate than does Denmark. It was concluded that, overcast or sunny, weather has little to do with depression, which sometimes leads to suicide. I think the reason for the difference is that Scandinavian people are much easier going and laid back than Latin people who have a more volatile nature, generally speaking. Like everything else, there are exceptions to the rule.

I have rambled on for a long time on the weather topic. Like I said in the beginning, weather is like music. It knows no borders, it is universal. The best we can do is accept the weather in the area we live. Whether it be it sunny, cloudy, dry or wet, hot or cold, we have to roll with the punches. I enjoy all four seasons.

CHAPTER SIXTY-FIVE

HAPPY OR CRANKY?

I never cease to marvel at the wide range and types of people that are in this world. I am not talking about ethnic groups, religious or the various nationalities. What I am observing is this: the nature and character of people no matter what nationality.

Cranky people really turn me off. No matter how nice you treat them, they just kind of scowl and give you curt or abrupt answers to any question or conversation you have with them. Sometimes they do not even bother to answer you.

I am not sure if people are cranky because they are depressed, or depressed because they are cranky. The dictionary defines cranky as, "irritable, peevish, eccentric, queer." Depression is described as, "cast down in spirit, lowered in position, dejection of spirits, abnormal functional weakness, languor, dullness, listlessness." Some people suffer from clinical depression. There is an imbalance in their system. Thousands of dollars are spent each year on psychiatrists, psychologists, and every other type of counsellor (some are quacks) for depression and dysfunctional problems. Sometimes, those shrink sessions are successful, sometimes they are not. Quite often the unsuccessful patients become suicide statistics.

Certain types of jobs can also cause people to be bored. This, in turn, leads to crankiness. People on assembly lines who do the same job eight hours a day, five days a week, for years on end, tend to become disillusioned workers. People in government offices are at risk as well, including those who work for the tax department. They have to deal with the public every day. It puts a strain on them, be it the tax department or any other sector of government, red tape rules supreme.

This often causes the person trying to get a permit or any other activity that involves government to become as cranky as the official with whom they are dealing. Over the years, I have dealt with various governments such as municipal, provincial, state and federal. In nearly every instance I have emerged from that encounter in a defeated manner. Most of these cases involved taxes. Have you every met anyone who enjoyed paying taxcs?

Poor marriage relationships cause stress. This ends up with one or both partners becoming cranky. Inner anger manifests itself into a bleak outlook on life. People develop a sour attitude in nearly everything they do in their daily lives. This results in snapping, angry words at everyone with whom they come in contact. They look negatively at every situation and often have road rage when they get behind the wheel of a car.

Much of this anger, rage, depression or crankiness stems from the bad choices they made. They blame others for everything that goes wrong in their lives. I am getting depressed by what I just wrote, so let's pursue a more cheerful aspect of life.

The story is told about a man in Milan, Italy who was irritable, depressed and cranky, so he decided to see a shrink. The doctor examined him for quite a while. Finally he said to the depressed man, "What you need is to loosen up and laugh. Right now there is a circus in the city. I suggest you go there. They have a clown there by the name of Garibaldi. He is extremely funny and he can make anybody laugh. A good belly laugh is just what you need to loosen up."

The depressed man looked the psychiatrist right in the eye and said, "I am Garibaldi".

There are millions of people with a happy, cheerful outlook on life, no matter how many things go wrong. I like being around people like that. They give your spirits a lift. These people are often referred to as having a sunny disposition. They are eternally optimistic. When something does not work out, they do not throw their arms up in despair. Their attitude is that maybe things will work out better next time. In business this is crucial. Nearly every person who has become successful in business has had a number of setbacks when they first started out. Instead of going into a depression about their failure, they dug in, regrouped and tried again. In the end it worked out well. If they had given up, they would have considered themselves failures. This causes isolation because nobody likes to associate with a cranky loser.

It is unfortunate that some people are born with a negative nature while others are born happy from the first day of their lives. It seems unfair. I have known people who were totally disillusioned with life. Then they had an encounter with God and his son Jesus Christ. From that day on their depression and pessimism almost disappeared.

They still had problems, but they viewed them in a more positive way. They actually became happy people.

CHAPTER SIXTY-SIX

SPORTS AND RECREATION

Sports and games have been part of all cultures and societies throughout the history of this planet. The activities and type of sport varies from country to country. Every nation participates in some sport or game.

In North America, we have gone bonkers over sport. Billions of dollars are spent every year by sports teams and fans. Huge stadiums and arenas and other sport facilities have been erected, often with a good chunk of taxpayers' money. Billions more are spent on the right type of clothes and equipment.

One of the largest gatherings that involves nearly every country in the world are the Summer and Winter Olympics held every four years. They originated in ancient Greece and consist of competition by amateur and a few professional athletes in a large variety of sports and games. The prizes are gold, silver and bronze medals. To receive one of those medals is a great honor to the recipient and the country he or she represents. Those medals can translate into big money for the people who win them. Because of the fame and media coverage, they are sought after for endorsements by large corporations. They also receive good job offers. Some become excellent convention and after-dinner speakers.

The Olympics are riddled with politics. In recent years, bribes and favoritism have tarnished the image of the International Olympic Committee (IOC). Drugs have become a problem as well. A number of athletes have been stripped of their medals for drug use. These days they often test for drugs before competition begins. If substance abuse is discovered the athletes are banned from the games, sometimes for life.

TV networks pay megabucks for the right to telecast the games. Over one billion people watch the Olympics on TV.

The Olympics are only the tip of the iceberg as to what sport is all about worldwide. There is every conceivable sport in which several billion people participate. Most games and sports that people play are for recreation. However, even at a young age, it can become competitive. Many is the parent who has visions of their Johnny or Suzy becoming sports stars when they grow into adults, either in professional sports or the Olympics. Whenever their child plays in a game and they think either the coach or the referee makes a bad decision or call on their child, they are not bashful in telling them so. Sometimes it leads to fisticuffs.

The soccer riots in Europe and other parts of the world are a disgrace. England is one of the worst countries when it comes to soccer hooliganism.

All professional sport has gone overboard. When baseball players receive multi-million-dollar salaries for a season, something is out of whack. This goes for football, basketball, boxing and several other less prominent sports. The top pro golfers also rake in millions of dollars. Tiger Woods received over $500,000 for winning the 2000 Canadian Open.

About the only professional sport where the pay is meager is rodeo. There are a few cowboys who earn $100,000 a year or more. And out of that, they have to pay their own expenses such as travel, accommodation and entry fees. Bull riders, especially, risk life and limb for very little money. In 2000, two young professional bull riders lost their lives after they were bucked off their bulls.

Most men, and many women, like sports, either as a participant or a spectator. My favorite sport is rodeo, except for bull riding. Next is baseball, followed by swimming and golf. Just for fun I will list thirty-two different sports and rate them on a scale of one to ten. This is only my opinion. See how they compare to your likes and dislikes.

- Rodeo − 9 (would rate it ten if it wasn't for the bull riding)
- Baseball − 9
- Golf − 8
- Swimming − 8

- Skiing – 7
- Polo – 6
- Sailing – 5
- Bowling – 5
- Olympic sports such as running, jumping, gymnastics – 5
- Horse racing – 4
- Water skiing – 4
- Tennis – 4
- Ping pong – 3
- Curling – 3
- Amateur wrestling – 3
- Football – 3
- Hockey – 3 (surprise?)
- Volleyball – 3
- Car racing of every type – 2
- Fishing – 2
- Basketball – 2
- Horse jumping – 2
- Boxing – 2
- Trap shooting – 2
- Snowboarding – 2
- Soccer – 2 (my grandchildren don't agree with me on that one)
- Pro wrestling – 1
- Cricket – 1
- Lacrosse – 1
- Handball – 1
- Mountain climbing – 1
- Sky diving – 1

You will notice by this list that sport is not big in my life. In spite of this, I fully endorse and believe that participating in sport is good for people, especially young people. The physical activity is healthy for them and keeps them from getting in trouble on the street or otherwise.

An eighty-eight-year-old friend of mine watches every hockey game on TV. Dave Shantz, another good friend who has passed away, was a rabid sports fan. He watched all sports on TV. His sports channel was on from morning to night. When he was young, he was a good hockey player. Two of his children became world-class curlers. Two of his daughters were good fastball players.

A lot of men and women like to hang out at sports bars. These bars do a booming business. I suspect liquor has as much to do with the patronage as does sports.

Many women are football widows. In other words, when football season is on, their husband is glued to the TV. The wife may as well be on another planet as far as he is concerned. At least she knows where he is.

Every daily newspaper has a sports section, sometimes up to a dozen pages. When the hubby is not watching TV, his nose is buried in the paper checking all the sports news and the scores and standings of each team, including auto racing and English rugby.

In the old days, many sports were played for the love of the game. These days, at least in pro sport, seventy-five percent of it is played for the money. The news is littered with cry-baby athletes, with multi-million-dollar salaries, who want more money. Ticket prices are outrageous. Yet, quite often, the owners lose money, which may result in franchises moving to more lucrative areas.

It is a catch-22 situation. If the players' salaries were cut in half and ticket prices lowered, the crush of people wanting to go to games would increase by thirty percent – a volume of people most arenas couldn't handle. Most arenas are filled to capacity now. I guess, in the foreseeable future, we will have to bumble along like we do today.

Meanwhile, common folk still enjoy whatever recreation or sport they like at relatively low cost.

CHAPTER SIXTY-SEVEN

THE CASH-COW ROAD

Perhaps what I am about to write should not be in this book. On the other hand, I am sure that many of you reading this chapter could tell a similar story about your county or municipality.

We live on a country road called Big Springs Road. For years, this was a washboard gravel road. About five years ago, a cheap paving job was done, which made the road almost worse than gravel. Finally, in 1998, a proper paving job was done.

Guess what? The speed limit remained the same for the gravel, cheap pavement and good pavement. The speed limit is eighty kilometres an hour (fifty miles per hour). Nearly every other road in this area of similar standards has a speed limit of one hundred kilometres an hour (sixty-two miles per hour). Why the difference?

The only logical explanation is that the municipality receives a lot of revenue from speeding tickets. There seems to be a competition between the Royal Canadian Mounted Police (RCMP or Mounties) and the municipal police (County Mounties). They both zealously patrol this road and they also use photo radar. Most people drive about one hundred kilometres an hour. It is a fairly busy road, so the harvest of tickets is substantial. Hence the new name, 'Cash Cow Road.'

I am not sour grapes. I have never received a speeding ticket on this road. I am not endorsing excessive speed but, in this case, the speed limit is too low. It feels unnatural to drive fifty miles an hour on a road of this calibre.

There is a more interesting, but sad, history concerning this road. Seven miles west of Airdrie, Alberta, is an intersection where the Symons Valley Road crosses the Big Springs Road. At this corner there are stop signs for the east and west traffic on Big Springs Road. There are no stop signs on the Symons Valley Road going north and south. The result is a rash of accidents. One Airdrie paramedic, told me that this corner has the most accidents of any location in our municipality.

Our twenty-one-year-old son was killed at that corner ten years ago. Since then, three more have died and a number of others have been seriously injured at that intersection. After our son's death, I suggested that four-way stop signs be placed there. That way, two drivers had to be wrong in order to cause an accident. Of course, nobody paid any attention to my suggestion. In August 2000, they worked on that corner. I am hopeful it will reduce the number of accidents.

Another strange thing happened to this road. The contractor who laid down the new pavement did an excellent job. The road was smooth as silk. Several weeks after his company had completed the job, I noticed someone with a hand-held gadget rolling over the road. In that seven-mile stretch of road he marked fifty-one spots with a white-marking instrument. I asked him what it was all about and he told me that he was testing for slight depressions, as little as a quarter of an inch. We drive down that road several times a day. I did not notice even the slightest unevenness on that road. When he finished marking it, a work crew came along and jackhammered up the pavement wherever he had marked it. Then another crew came along and dumped some asphalt in the holes, which was then rolled over with a compactor. The result was that, what had been a beautiful smooth road was turned into a patched road. Some of those patches are small, maybe one or two square feet. Others are five to fifteen square feet. Most of those patches are pretty smooth, but a few of the bigger ones are rough.

I spoke to the contractor. He told me they deducted $67,000 from his final payment to pay for the patch job. In our opinion, this was not necessary.

I happen to know the reeve (in the United States, he would be the chairman of the county commissioners). He is a good man with a lot of common sense. I do not know the other councillors, but I believe whoever made the decision on the road, made a bad one. Some zealous bureaucrat who used the excuse that they were raising the road to provincial standards probably made it. It is still a good road despite all of the visual and some slightly rough patches. The question is, why relieve a company that did a good job of $67,000? There may be a bright side to this Cash Cow Road. Maybe the revenue from the tickets will lower taxes. I'll believe that when I see it happen.

Maybe by the time this book is published, the speed limit on this road will be raised to one hundred kilometres an hour and a four-way stop put in. Like I said at the beginning, I am sure that many of you, in Canada and the United States, will identify with this kind of bureaucratic activity in your county or municipality.

CHAPTER SIXTY-EIGHT

IGNORANCE

The Funk and Wagnal's dictionary defines ignorance as lack of knowledge, lack of information or awareness, no learning, unenlightened.

I think that of all the things that afflict the human race, ignorance is one of the worst. Over the centuries ignorance has caused major upheavals. It resulted in thousands of disasters from which millions have died. Ignorance causes mistakes. This is especially true in industry, war and politics.

It is sad when people are ignorant. What is even sadder is when people choose to remain ignorant. Education does a lot to dispel ignorance, however, it is not one hundred percent effective. I know of some well educated people who still practise ignorance in many areas of life. Often on a TV trivia or quiz show, there are professional people such as lawyers accountants, doctors and nurses who are stumped by simple questions about history, geography, agriculture and a few other subjects which they learned about in school. But, because those things did not interest them, it faded from their mind. We all have areas of ignorance. My knowledge about physics and science is minimal. The secret is to have the wisdom to know that you are ignorant about some things and seek to improve your knowledge in those areas.

There are few things as disgusting as talking to a person who does not realize how ignorant they are. Such a person talks about a lot of hearsay rather than facts. Their view and philosophy of life is rather limited, no lofty ideas, just way off-base chatter at the intellectual level of a ten-year-old. Those kind of people often pride themselves in how little they read.

You may think I hate ignorant people. That is not the case. I dislike ignorance but not the person. I do feel sorry for them. But, then again, maybe it is ignorance on my part to assume that I am not ignorant as well.

Some pass their ignorance off as being humble. There is a vast difference between ignorance and humility. Some very intelligent, well-informed people are humble. Ignorance can develop into an inferiority complex because they feel intimidated by people of superior knowledge. This, in turn, may lead to anger. Many people who are in jail arrived at that destination via ignorance which erupted into criminal acts and violence.

Ignorance about politics has, over the years, enslaved millions of people, both in democracies and dictatorships. The political candidate who can spout the most rhetoric filled with lies and half-truths often wins the election. Once in power his or her true colors soon show up. When their term in office is drawing to a close they suddenly clean up their image by offering the electorate all kinds of goodies, provided by taxpayer money. Sure enough they get elected again. This would not happen if people were well informed rather than blindly and ignorantly following slimy politicians like sheep.

Ignorance also fills our divorce courts. If either or both spouses are ignorant, big marital problems may develop. A deadly mix is ignorance and alcohol. Many is the woman who got beat up or even strangled by a husband or boyfriend who had limited mental capacity and was fuelled by liquor. The exact opposite of this kind of behaviour is sobriety, common sense and love.

The Bible does not put a premium on ignorance. It is mentioned in a number of passengers. One example is Ephesians 4:18: *having their understanding darkened, being alienated from the life of God, through ignorance that is in them, because of the blindness of their heart.*

Many people are ignorant of what is in the Bible. They choose to stay ignorant by never reading the Bible.

A phrase we often hear is 'ignorance is bliss.' That may be true in some instances, but sometimes that bliss can blow up in your face. One practical anomaly might be if you visited a country where a war had raged several years previous. Now all is peaceful. The countryside's beautiful. You decide to go for a stroll in that blissful environment, suddenly you step on a land mine which blows off one of your legs. So much for blissful ignorance. If you had checked and found out which areas were proven to have old land mines, you would still have both legs. Many people have died from these land mines.

As we know, ignorance of a law is no excuse when we break the law. I think we have too many rules, laws and regulations. In spite of this, we should be informed about what the various laws are. If we wish to break a minor unjust law, so be it. But we should not use the excuse that we did not know it was unlawful. We should not be ignorant of our laws. If we are successful in eliminating ignorance from our lives, life will take on a new meaning. Life is good, may we all seek to live it wisely.

CHAPTER SIXTY-NINE

FIRST NATIONS?

In the February 2000 issue of *Alberta Beef*, I wrote a column, which touched on some Native problems in our society in Canada. Much the same scenario exists in the United States. Here is what I wrote:

February 2000 Column

"Lately I have become a little more controversial when I write a column, than I used to be. I believe in calling a spade a spade, unless it hurts innocent people. All my life I have sided with the Indian people. They definitely got a raw deal from the European white settlers in North America. But do two wrongs make a right? I think not. What is going on today is absolutely wrong. These people were mistakenly called Indians, because the early explorers thought they had reached India. For five hundred years they have been called Indians. However, in the past few decades they prefer to be called First Nations, Natives or Aboriginals. I am a native as well since my parents were both born in western Canada, dad in 1881 and mother in 1884. There are millions of other Canadians that are natives as well.

"The Liberal government in Ottawa got the ball rolling when they created the new self governing territory or should I say, "Nation of Nunavut." There are only about twenty-five thousand people in that vast region of the eastern Arctic. That is about half the population of the city of Medicine Hat. Ottawa poured several billion dollars into that creation. Every cent of it taxpayers' money.

"One sage figured it out, he said, 'we could have moved all those people to fancy condos in Florida, paid all their living expenses and still saved ten thousand dollars a year on every man, woman and child.' Such a move would also appease radical environmentalists and the anti-fur lobby. No more shooting or trapping animals in that region.

"On the other hand, the Canadian government could set up the vacated territory as a huge hunting preserve, charging rich Europeans and Americans an arm and a leg for the privilege to hunt some of that Arctic game. In fact, they probably could get enough money from those hunters to pay all the expenses of relocating all those people to Florida. That way taxpayers could save another two billion dollars. Everyone comes out a winner. Such a move might be a bit of a culture shock for the North Inuit people, but after a few years they would get used to the hot climate, swimming pools and fancy restaurants. They might find a little diversion by hunting some alligators.

"Then there is the Nish'gaa boondoggle in BC. This land area, while not as large as Nunavut, is still larger than the sixty smallest countries in the world. Besides the land, there is a cash payment of two hundred million dollars.

"Now if these were the only two land settlements, we could tolerate this kind of activity. The fact is there are almost six hundred different bands in Canada. There are somewhat less reserves than that, since in a number of cases, several bands inhabit the same reserve.

"All humans are the same no matter what nationality they are, when they see someone get something that they think they should get as well, it's a cinch they will go after it. Can you picture all the land claims that could arise in the next decade? Let us imagine four hundred nations within Canada, each calling their own shots, while still at the federal money trough. Don't say it could not happen, it is already happening!

"At this point it appears that the Indians and Inuit are the only Canadians who can hunt and fish all year on any crown land. Lately, they can cut timber as well on government land. They also have a cushy tax deal. No wonder some of the Maritimers got a little antsy last fall, when the Indians caught a big portion of the lobsters before the season opened.

"Like I said, traditionally I was on the Indians' side, but let's be realistic, it has got right out of hand. British Columbia (BC) has the most bands, one hundred eighty-nine to be exact. The standing joke in BC is that there is not enough land in BC to settle all those claims. It's about fifteen percent short because of overlapping claims. This state of affairs is not really the Indians fault. It is the mixed-up and confused policy of provincial and federal governments that has opened up this whole mess. Most white people would do exactly the same thing if they had the opportunity.

"I know there are many well-educated, intelligent people among the Indians. Some of them admit what is going on is not right, but then what is? There are several million poor white Canadians who also think that society owes them a better living. Couple that with our aging population and the cost to government is staggering. Between the Indians, the poor and the elderly, the tax drain on middle class working people is huge in ever rising taxes to pay for all of this.

"There is another danger and that is, we could become an apartheid country like South Africa used to be. The difference is the Indian folks only make up a little over one percent of our population. The blacks in South Africa are at least eighty-five percent of their population.

"What is the solution? I really do not know. What I do know is if the present trend continues, there will be a tremendous amount of unrest and animosity among Canadians between the ages of twenty to sixty. Those are the people who pay the bulk of the taxes in Canada." - End of column.

This brief analysis about the Indian people did not exactly endear me to them. As we all know, the truth sometimes hurts. Here is some United States history regarding Indians. Incidentally, the word Indian is still used by most American Indians. They are not as socially- nor politically-correct as our Canadian First Nations people.

When the first Europeans arrived on the eastern shores of the United States and Canada, they encountered the Natives. Most interaction between them was peaceful. There were occasional skirmishes, but no major battles. The 'white men' did Natives no social favors. Thousands of Natives died from smallpox and other diseases, imported from Europe. The white men also introduced firewater (liquor) and this also helped decimate Native numbers. Some small tribes pretty much got wiped out. A number of explorers, fur traders and mountain men married young Indian girls and they often had a small brood of children. After eight or ten years, these men would often go back East leaving the women to fend for themselves. Some men stayed and took responsibility for their families. That is why today, we sometimes see fair-skinned or blue-eyed Natives.

As the white settlers slowly advanced westward, the hostilities increased especially in the United States. Indian raids on white settlers became common. At the same time, white settlers were not particular what they shot with their muskets, be it a deer or an Indian.

The Mississippi River was the approximate dividing line of where the problem between whites and Indians exploded into warfare.

The Indians were not to blame. They saw, and rightly so, that the white man was taking over their hunting grounds. It threatened their way of life. The white people called them redskins, savages, hostiles and a few other names that were not complimentary. The fact was the Natives had a different culture, which the white people did not take time to understand. There were some wise people in every Indian band. In fact, the honor that those folks bestowed on their leaders and elders for their knowledge and wisdom puts the white man to shame.

In my opinion, in the technological age in which we live today, the wisdom of older people is disregarded and shunted to the side, often to the detriment of society.

Back to the American west. Countless battles were fought between various Indian tribes and the United States Army (Cavalry). Nearly all these battles took place on horseback. The Indians won a number of those conflicts. In the end, the sheer number and power of the United States military won out. At that point, the Indians were settled on reservations. There were a number of great Indian warriors and leaders who put up a valiant battle. Even the United States military had to admit that Crazy Horse, a Sioux warrior, was one of the greatest battle strategists of that era. Besides him, there was Sitting Bull, Cochise, Geronimo, Red Cloud, Chief Joseph and numerous others. One Indian who was a great leader, but not a warrior, was Sequoya, a Cherokee who developed the Cherokee alphabet.

In Canada, there were also a number of good Indian chiefs and leaders such as Tecumseh, Crowchild, Little Bear and, of course, the great Métis leader, Louis Riel, who led a major uprising in 1879.

I must mention one other terrible event that took place on Sand Creek in southern Colorado, twenty miles south of our ranch.

On November 29, 1864, Colonel John M. Chivington and his troops massacred about three hundred Indians. Approximately twenty-five percent were braves, the other seventy-five percent were old men, women and children. Their chief, Black Kettle, hung out a flag indicating peace. The Colonel and his troops totally disregarded this gesture and proceeded to slaughter them. Today, there is a historical marker at that location close to the little ghost town called Chivington. I think it should be renamed Black Kettle.

Approximately eighty-five percent of the United States Army's 'west division' was used to subdue the Indians. In Canada, that role was left to the North West Mounted Police. There were several other areas in which the United States Army got involved, such as the border skirmishes with Mexico, the California gold rush, the Oregon Trail, the Santa Fe Trail, the Bozeman Trail and other early-day trails. The army also policed some of the civilian forts, where commerce was carried on.

There was much lawlessness in the west. The army seldom got involved in saloon brawls or personal gunfights, cattle rustling and horse thieving. This was left to the local sheriff or marshall. About twenty-five percent of the law enforcement officers were or had been involved in crime themselves. I guess the old adage applied - it takes a thief to catch a thief.

Back to forts. In the southern United States, forts were built with adobe, in other words, dirt or clay. Further north, they were built with logs. In this enclosure the residents were relatively safe. In the walls were small openings which were used for shooting at the enemy. The walls were so thick that arrows could not pierce through, nor could bullets penetrate. One danger was fire. If the enemy, usually the Indians, managed to set the fort on fire, big trouble ensued. Firefighting equipment was about nil. One fort that was burned to the ground by Indians was at Julesburg, Colorado. There were several others as well.

Besides the military forts, there were some civilian forts. They were built for the protection of commerce and travellers. They started out for the use of fur traders and, later on, they became supply depots for new immigrants. Some of the civilian forts were also used by the army. The first forts in the west were built in the early 1800s. Their heyday was from approximately 1840 to 1890. After that, they became relics from the past. I have toured several of these forts. Some have been restored. One such fort is at La Junta, Colorado. It was a civilian fort called Bents Fort.

Following are the number of old Western United States military forts: Texas, twenty-three; Montana, eighteen; Arizona, fourteen; Wyoming, fourteen; Oklahoma, eleven; New Mexico, eleven; California, eleven; Kansas, ten; Colorado, eight; North Dakota, seven; Utah, six; Oregon, five; Idaho, five; Nevada, five; Nebraska, four; South Dakota, four; and Washington, four. This is a total of one hundred and sixty forts.

The number of forts in each state does not correlate with the number of Indians in each state today. The states with the largest Indian populations in the western United States in 2001 are: Montana, Arizona, New Mexico, South Dakota, Oklahoma and Washington.

Canada also had some forts, but not nearly as many as the United States. In Canada, the North West Mounted Police (NWMP or Mounties) and government officials used more persuasion and less force than they did in the United States. The end result was about the same. The Indians in both countries were placed on reserves. At the time, it seemed like the right solution. In retrospect, it was a mistake.

In the past decade, the crescendo of Indian grievances has increased at an alarming rate. There are hundreds of land claims and natural resource disputes. There is also a blatant disregard for Canadian laws regarding hunting, fishing and timber. A current hot topic is claim of Native students that they suffered abuse at their former residential church schools. I have read several articles on what some Indian students said. They stated that maybe those schools stifled their culture to some degree, on the other hand, it gave them an education they would not have received otherwise.

It is a well-known fact that for third world country people and aboriginal populations around the world, education is the key to help lift them out of poverty.

There will always be change in our society. Some of us, including me, long for the past, but change comes whether we like it or not. It is alright to hang onto our past through ceremonial traditions and becoming aware of our history, but we must adjust to the new reality or we will head for upheaval and trouble, even bloodshed.

Over the past three years, a friend of mine, Henry Bridgewater, clipped out one hundred and thirty-one news items concerning Native people. He suggested I put them into a little booklet. Instead I decided to put them into this book. I am only quoting the headlines. They more or less reveal what the article is about. These news items were clipped from a number of newspapers and magazines, some daily, some weekly, and a few from monthly magazines. I am only including forty-one headlines. They paint a gloomy picture for the future unless Natives take drastic action to improve their social behaviour otherwise things could get ugly.

Here are the headlines:

RESERVE CONDITIONS PRIMITIVE

NATIVE TENSIONS RISING

NATIVES AWARDED LAND, CASH IN TREATY

MANY RESERVES MIRED IN DEBT

FEAR IS MAKING A NIGHTMARE OF NATIVE DREAMS

BAD SOCIAL CONDITIONS BLAMED FOR SUICIDE

NATIVES SUE FOR TEN BILLION

NATIVES THREATEN TO SEIZE CASTLE MOUNTAIN (Banff National Park)

FORMER CHIEF CHARGED IN $400,000 KICKBACK SCHEME

LOBSTER DISPUTE HEATS UP!

MOHAWK CHIEF DEFENDS RIGHT TO IMPORT DUTYFREE GOODS

ABORIGINALS BLAST TREATY; PREPARE TO FISH FRASER RIVER
TREATY RIGHTS MOVES TO THE WOODS
ANGRY NATIVES THREATEN TO SHUT WINNIPEG AIRPORT
TIMBER RULING COULD RESULT IN VIOLENCE, SAY NATIVES
AIDS COULD WIPE OUT NATIVE BANDS, REPORT CLAIMS
NORTH AMERICAN INDIANS MOVE TOWARDS POLITICAL UNION
ONE IN FOUR RESERVES BROKE
NATIVE GROUP FILES SUIT TO RECLAIM PORTION OF CITY
NATIVE WELFARE ABUSE RAMPANT
NATIVES BLOCK LOGGERS AT PARK ENTRANCE
NATIVES TO GET MILLIONS FOR ABUSE COUNSELLING
$20 MILLION MORE FOR NATIVE HOUSING
NATIVE FUNDING STILL LACKS ACCOUNTABILITY
CORRUPTION BLAMED FOR SUICIDES
NATIVES SEEK $147 MILLION FROM PIPELINE
ABUSED NATIVES CALL FOR QUICK SETTLEMENT
TOLL ROAD OR NO ROAD: CHIEF
BAND UNDER INVESTIGATION
ARMED PROTEST THREATENED ON RESERVE
NATIVE BAND SETS UP TOLL
TAXPAYERS GROUP WANTS TO FIGHT NATIVE TAX BREAKS
ATTITUDE ON NATIVE ISSUES HARDENING: POLL
NATIVE FISHERMEN BLOCK HI-WAY
NATIVE BANDS HIT $300 MILLION DEFICIT
ABORIGINALS TAKE PROTEST TO STREET

Now for a few positive headlines:

LISTEN TO NATIVES, SAYS NAVAJO JUDGE
BUSINESSES SHOULD REALIZE ABORIGINAL POTENTIAL
EDUCATION, JOBS KEY TO NATIVE FUTURE
TIME FOR A NEW DIRECTION

Giving Natives more money is not the solution. It would cause a severe backlash from the rest of the population. In my opinion, education and integration are the answers. It will take time, but it can be achieved. History tells us that, worldwide, when cultures have integrated successfully, the secret was for each group to retain its historic past, special days and a written historical record. But otherwise, blend into the society in which they live. The nomadic lifestyle with millions of buffalo roaming around is gone forever but it will live on in folklore, stories, songs and written records.

I am proud of my cultural background even though these days, my way of life and social activities are far removed from my forefathers (and foremothers).

There are thousands of well adjusted, educated Native folks. Keep on encouraging your people. They can be restored to the proud, noble people they were before the rude intrusion of the white man.

We can not roll history back two hundred years. We must live in the present.

The following editorial appeared in the *Ottawa Citizen* Mach 28, 2001 and is reprinted with their permission.

How much is enough for Nunavut?

Nunavut was created so that its residents could be proud and self-reliant, rather than ashamed and dependent. It doesn't seem to be working. Since it became a full-fledged territory on April 1, 1999, Nunavut has received an average of $581 million in yearly transfers, more than $92,000 annually for each household. Apparently this not enough. Faced with a $12-million budget deficit, the government of Nunavut is considering a court challenge, alleging that the failure to provide an even larger sum is a violation of Inuit constitutional rights.

Nunavut was always a controversial idea, promising self-government to the Inuit but at the expense of southern taxpayers. Politicians and bureaucrats who spend other people's money may be held to account by the electorate. In Nunavut, little of the money is raised from local sources, some ten percent, much of that from taxing the incomes of those whose salaries are funded by federal transfers. When recruitment is completed, Nunavut will have an estimated sixteen hundred bureaucrats, the highest ratio of bureaucrats to population in the world. Ironically, but predictably, the surfeit of public employment has not primarily benefited the Inuit - some sixty percent of the jobs have gone to outsiders, many positions remain unfilled.

Nunavut's twenty-seven thousand people (five thousand more than Brockville, Ontario) share nineteen MLAs and ten government departments. Self-government has proved to be no panacea for the economic and social problems that have long characterized the region. Employment levels remain low, massive social problems persist. Nunavut has the highest level of violent crime in Canada

The idea that government rather than the private sector will generate economic growth is quintessentially Canadian but misconceived, here as elsewhere. Instead, the new territory has fostered dependency and gathering sense of entitlement. Consider the recently announced program to educate lawyers. Students will be admitted without the normal qualifications and education will be delivered in the territory. Even if the program succeeds, Canadians who are paying for their own education may be less impressed that this program will pay students a whopping $50,000 a year.

Nunavut's premier, Paul Okalik (currently Nunavut's only lawyer), has expressed his disappointment with the failure of the federal government to increase funding: "We need our fair share." The Canadians who are funding this arctic experiment might be puzzled as to what share is "fair." Okalik says he sometimes asks himself: "Why the hell am I Canadian?" Well, if you weren't who would you sue for endless handouts?

The suggested court action is apparently based on the demand that in addition to the existing transfers, the federal government provides a parallel flow of funds, similar to those going to status Indians. How much would be enough? Would a transfer of $150,000 a household foster independence? Does Nunavut's first premier really want to extend to his constituents the dubious benefits of the paternalistic Indian Act?

Instead of threatening lawsuits, Nunavut should trim its burgeoning bureaucracy and encourage the private sector. Even if the economic future of Nunavut will depend on the efforts of other Canadians, it should seek to train its inhabitants to compete in the wider labor market, not just the courtroom. That's the route to real personal independence. - End of column.

CHAPTER SEVENTY

POSITIVE AND NEGATIVE

I am not an electrician. But I do know for electricity to work there has to be a positive and negative connection. A good example is that for a car battery to function both the positive and negative connections must be hooked up.

In the human race, we have both positive and negative people, and most of us have some of both characteristics in us. If we have too much of either one, it may get us into real trouble. For instance, if we become too positive, we sometimes make bad decisions. Positive people who totally neglect to look at anything negative are fair game for con artists. They also fall into the trap of thinking they are invincible.

I knew a man once, who thought he had an invention that would revolutionize the way a certain business would operate. In the end, his positive invention was a flop. If he had considered both positive and negative aspects of his invention, he may not have proceeded with it and saved himself from bankruptcy. In another chapter, I write that we should never say can't. But there are times when we have to be realistic and know that some things will not work and cannot be done. We must only come to that conclusion after considering all aspects of the situation.

Sometimes, when people are too positive they come across as 'know-it-alls'. These folks turn most of us off. It is almost impossible to win a discussion or debate with an extremely positive person. They maintain they are always right and often they are, but not always. To be honest with you, I am somewhat afflicted with being too positive.

Another way to describe positive and negative people is an optimist or pessimist. We are all familiar with the old saying, when a positive, optimistic person looks at a glass of water, they say it is half full. When a negative, pessimistic person looks at the same glass, it appears to be half empty. When they behold a rose, the optimist will say, look at the beautiful flower, the pessimist will say, look at all those thorns.

Negative people are not all bad. They are needed in a democracy, when some difficult decisions are made. Without the criticism of negative people, many wrong things in government would never be challenged. They also avoid some of the pitfalls in business that positive people might fall into. As a whole though, I do not enjoy associating with negative people. I am always afraid some of that negativity might rub off on me. I would sooner make some mistakes and be positive than to make very few mistakes being negative.

When a married couple approaches situations differently, one being positive and the other negative, problems can develop. We know that opposites attract and this quite frequently happens in marriages. To begin with, it is fascinating to both partners but, when the real tests come, it often creates great conflict. The positive person may want to go into a certain business. The negative partner opposes it. If they go ahead with the venture and it happens to fail, the negative partner will never let the positive one forget they were warned not to go into that business. Many marriages have failed because of business failures. Sometimes, the new venture is a great success. When that is the case, the negative partner will soon find something else to be negative about.

In my humble opinion, it would be a much better world if we could all achieve an eighty percent positive attitude and twenty percent negative one. That twenty percent might just prevent us from getting into trouble in our marriages, business ventures and our interaction with society in general.

The secret to controlling our negative impulses is to have the ability to turn our negative thoughts into positive action. That's much easier said than done. But it can be done if we let our common sense prevail. One of my favorite sayings is, when life hands you a lemon, make lemonade.

Incidentally, I still do not know exactly how a battery works.

CHAPTER SEVENTY-ONE

WHERE WILL YOU SPEND ETERNITY?

Beside the gate, as people leave our yard, we have a sign that says, Where will you spend eternity?

Have you ever pondered that question? Many people have. Unfortunately most dismiss that thought from their minds. They somehow think that God will take care of them.

He will, but it is up to you to make that deal with God. The Bible states clearly if we accept and receive Jesus Christ into our hearts as Saviour and Lord we will spend eternity in Heaven.

Some people who claim to be atheists dismiss the thought of eternal life as a fable. Sad to say they will be in for a big surprise when they leave this earth.

You will have noticed throughout this book I referred to and quoted from the Bible a number of times. As stated in my introduction, the Bible is the greatest blueprint there is of how to live our lives. Those of us who claim to be Christians are no better than anyone else in this world. We are sinners, saved by grace.

God is not a respecter of persons. In God's sight, we are all equal. God is color blind when it comes to people. God loves everybody that was ever born. However, we must love Him back. This is the catch that trips up a lot of people. Many people never pray or go to church. They often swear using God's name in vain. They cheat and lie, yet somehow expect to enter the pearly gates.

When I mention going to church, let me explain. Going to church and fellowship with other believers is good. However, just going to church does not necessarily make you a Christian. You have to have a personal relationship with God and his son Jesus Christ.

In John 3:16, we read: *For God so loved the world, that He gave His only begotten Son, that whosoever believeth in Him should not perish, but have everlasting life.*

I left my personal strong belief to near the end of this book. When you close the cover I want you to take an assessment of your life and settle the question, Where will you spend eternity?

The Friesen family in 1999. From left, Graham, Melody, Dee, Edna, Leonard, Ward and Leland. Not pictured is youngest son, Trent, who was killed in a motor vehicle accident May 28, 1990. Leonard and Edna's eldest son, Leland, passed away January 23, 2001 following a battle with cancer.

CHAPTER SEVENTY-TWO

CATTLE CALL COLUMNS

In the *Cattle Call* book that I wrote I published one hundred and ninety-two selected columns written from 1975 to September 1997. Incidentally, it was Dorothea Schaab who suggested the name *Cattle Call* for my column.

I am taking the privilege of inserting twenty selected columns in this book. They were published in *Alberta Beef* from September 1997 to October 2000.

I will reprint one column that appeared in the *Cattle Call* book. It was the September 1997 column. The reason I am doing this is because it brought such a great response. Another magazine with a circulation of fifty-five thousand reprinted it with *Alberta Beef* magazine and my permission.

September 1997

Every night on the TV news, there is bickering, terrorism, even war, by countries that are trying to split up or redraw their border lines. Some want to gain independence from the rest of the country. Canada is no exception. We are familiar with the Quebec situation.

Our neighbor to the south has an interesting history. They started out with thirteen states (New England). In 1803, the United States purchased the Louisiana Territory from France for a total of $27,267,622 including interest at final settlement. This territory included thirteen states all the way from Louisiana to Minnesota.

Texas, California, Arizona, New Mexico and southern Colorado (south of the Arkansas River) were annexed from Mexico (actually Spain). There were only a few battles fought over this large land acquisition. One of those battles was the Alamo at San Antonio, which the Texans lost. They won several battles later on and eventually gained their independence. A short period after, they became part of the United States of America.

In 1846, the Americans outmanoeuvred the British and got possession of the Oregon Territory, which included Washington, Oregon, Idaho, parts of Montana and southern Alberta and British Columbia. At the negotiations, the 49th parallel was declared the border between the United States and Canada. All we got was a little chunk of Alberta and southern British Columbia.

In 1868, the United States purchased Alaska from Russian for $7.2 million.

Now, it's time again to do some 'horse-trading', actually land trading, between Canada and the United States. Canada will deed to the United States the following provinces: Ontario, Quebec, Nova Scotia, New Brunswick, Prince Edward Island and Newfoundland. In return, the United States will give us North Dakota, South Dakota, Montana, Wyoming, Idaho, Washington, Oregon and Alaska.

The number of square miles in the swap would be almost identical. Canada would give up 1,250,585 square miles and the United States would give up 1,100,500 square miles. The population of the Canadian provinces going to the United States is approximately twenty million people. The population of the American states becoming part of Canada is approximately twelve million.

The new Canada would have a population of approximately twenty million (eight million western Canadians and twelve million new American Canadians). At this point, the population of the United States would approach the three-hundred-million mark, still only twenty-five percent of the population of China.

Now, for the advantages to both countries. For starters, it would settle the salmon fishing dispute once and for all. The salmon would now all belong to Canada. However, all the fish from Florida to Newfoundland would belong to the United States. That would settle another argument over fishing territory.

We would get the timber in Washington, Oregon, Idaho and Montana. The Americans would get the timber in Northern Ontario, Quebec and Atlantic Canada.

Following are some benefits for Canada. We would be rid of Ottawa with the new capital being, 'the exciting city of Calgary.' Gone would be Jean Chretien, Sheila Copps and Allan Rock. We may even throw in Lloyd Axworthy, even though he's from Manitoba. The Americans could use him to negotiate with Cuba.

The United States could set up a puppet government in Canada, using all those Liberal MPs from Ontario. This would only be temporary. In four or five years, they would completely melt into the United States orbit.

Canada would have only one major league baseball team, the Seattle Mariners. The United States would inherit two more major league teams, the Toronto Blue Jays and the Montreal Expos.

Canada would now be home to three of the largest rodeos - the Calgary Stampede, Cheyenne Frontier Days and the Pendleton Round-up. With Montana, North and South Dakota, and Wyoming in our camp, we could lock up the saddle bronc title at Las Vegas every year - provided the Etbauer boys moved back to South Dakota.

Another advantage would be that the anti-grain and cattle lobby in the northern states would disappear, since they are now part of Canada.

The United States would inherit a large skilled labor force in Ontario, also a number of factories. Both sides of Niagara Falls would now be in the United States. The Americans are nuclear experts. They would have those seven nuclear reactors at Pickering, Ontario up and running in short order. They did at the Three Mile Island malfunction.

Then there is Quebec. I think the Americans would soon shape them up. They did in Louisiana. The Quebecers need a little discipline. Those who refuse to fall in line would be exiled to Louisiana, where many French folks have lived for several centuries. They are Americans and don't talk about separation.

The other alternative for difficult Quebecers would be to settle them in Northern Quebec. This might prevent the Natives from taking over that area. Somehow, the state of Ontario and the state of Quebec has a nice ring to it.

Atlantic Canada could be turned into a classy playground resort for rich Americans. Many vacation there already.

Since this realignment is solely my idea, it is only fitting that I be elected the first President of the New Republic of Canada. If elected, I will make a lot of promises, like all politicians do in present-day Canada and the United States. We will have an elected senate, three from each province. We will abolish the Goods and Services Tax. (GST). Meanwhile, Sheila Copps, now an American, can handle any GST proposed by zealous congressmen in Washington. We will have a free vote in our congress, here in the new Canada. We will retain the Mounties, but no turbans. We will scrap all the present and proposed gun laws. We will rid ourselves of the metric system. The United States will continue to be our biggest trading partner with much of our beef being shipped to Quebec, USA. Gone will be biculturalism, bilingualism and transfer payments (the United States will look after Quebec).

Since it is now a republic, Canada will no longer feature Her Majesty on our currency and stamps (even though she's a nice lady). The coins could have my picture on them as the father of this new republic. The paper money could have the pictures of some of my fellow cattlemen on it. I suggest we put the pictures of some famous Canadian women on our stamps.

We will decrease the government by sixty percent and lower taxes by sixty percent. We will give the provinces more power. Even though we're a republic, we'll continue to call them provinces. The province of Montana sure sounds good to me. I love Montana. The people are friendly and they have good ranches, good cattle and no sales tax.

We must get the ball rolling as I'm getting on in years. History tells us that many world leaders are people in their late-seventies and eighties. My target date for this land swap is 2002. I will only be seventy-six years old at that time.

I sure hope we can pull this off without a shot being fired. We are no match for the Americans when it comes to guns.

Can I count on your vote?

You may have noticed I try to vary the topics I write about. I think you all know that I am not a socialist. I am a free enterpriser. Lately, I've questioned exactly what is free enterprise?

In the old days much of the world, including the United States, had slaves. The society of that day claimed to operate their farms, plantations and businesses under a free enterprise system. Free for whom? Obviously the owners of the slaves. The white folks often bought slaves at auctions. The slave went to the highest bidder. Was that free enterprise? I think not. The slave had to work hard for no pay except food and some substandard housing. He had no chance to participate in the free enterprise system.

Then there is communism. It took over Russia in 1917 and many other countries years later. The true fathers of communism were Engels, Marx and Lenin. The goal was to make all men equal. The state would own everything and everyone would share equally and enjoy the good life.

We all know the result of that system. The only people enjoying the good life were the party bosses. There were no elections, no freedoms and no material wealth for the masses. In other words, the system was a giant flop.

So much for slavery and communism. Let's turn our attention to today's multinational and large domestic corporations. Tell me how much freedom does the average employee of the monolithic corporations have? Virtually none. They do have the option of quitting their job, which sometimes lands them on welfare. The slogans and practices of these large companies are teamwork. It sounds good on the surface but how good is it for the average employee?

The name of the game is control. With today's computers and the team concept solidly in place, every employee must follow the rules. This takes away the initiative to think for yourself. Not much different than slavery or communism. There too, the rules had to be followed. The benefactors were the slave owners and the communist bosses.

In large corporations the beneficiaries are the upper management people – the managers, presidents and CEOs – and they only represent a small percentage of the workforce. They receive large salaries, often five to fifteen times more than the average slave -oops - I mean employee.

The advantage to the company with the team concept is that when someone quits, the company hardly notices. Just like a baseball player leaving a team, the game goes on and sometimes it even improves. This stops a lot of employees from leaving.

There is one good aspect to this system and that is that these corporations have made big profits in the last few years and about half of all Canadians own shares in those companies through mutual funds, pension plans or outright share ownership.

I know we can not go back in time to smaller companies and individual business enterprises, although there are sill a number of them operating these days. But to stay alive they more or less have to play by the rules of the big boys.

I feel very fortunate to have been my own boss for the past twenty-three years. I don't have to look over my shoulder to see if the boss is there to enforce the 'company team rules'.

You rural folks still have a lot of freedom in your decision-making and lifestyle. But how much say have you got when it comes to the sale of your commodities, or the cost of your fertilizer, fuel, machinery and other input costs?

Almost none. Between big government and big business, they have us on the ropes, but not knocked out yet.

I hope some of you wise people out there have a solution as to how to stem this tide before we all go down with the ship. That would be the end of free enterprise.

December 1997

These days we hear a lot about isolated cases of E.coli in our food supply – especially meat. It has also appeared in apple juice and strawberries. E coli is a bacterium that can occur when meat and other food is not handled properly in a sanitary manner and not properly refrigerated. When people eat this food, it can make them quite ill. Once in a while, a few people might die. Several years ago, three people died in the United States. Compare that to the thousands of people who die every year in traffic accidents, and from murders, drug overdoses, AIDS and other causes.

Ever since the Mad Cow Disease in Great Britain, and those three E.coli deaths in the United States, the urban media has had a field day by trotting out these cases at least a few times a month. People hear and read this, so they think meat is a dangerous food, when in fact it is almost one hundred percent safe.

There is a much greater chance of being struck by lightning or hit by a piece of debris from outer space than to die from eating meat. The problem is many scientists, bureaucrats and urban media people are vegetarians. They jump on any opportunity to give meat a bad reputation.

I like fruit and vegetables but wonder how safe they are. We all know that millions of gallons of herbicides and insecticides are sprayed on orchards and vegetable gardens every year. In my opinion, fruit and vegetables are one hundred times as dangerous to eat as meat. In spite of that, I still eat them along with 'safe' meat.

I like medium rare prime rib and steak, but have always demanded that my hamburger will be well done – no rare ground beef for me. Roasts and steaks come from young healthy cattle whereas hamburger is usually made from older cows and bulls. They too have to pass health inspection but I want it well done before I eat it.

Fortunately, we still have some common sense dietitians, home economists and medical people who recommend we include lean beef in our diets. Our teeth and digestive systems are designed for eating all food, including meat.

In the animal world there are carnivores and grazers. A lion or a wolf would not survive long on forage. Moose, deer, and elk could not exist on meat. Then there are bears, hogs and some other animals that eat both meat and plants. I guess we humans fall into that category.

I maintain more effort must be put into teaching our young people the facts about healthy diets. If we fail to do this, our meat consumption will take a drastic drop in the next ten to twenty years.

Just recently, my wife and I heard a minister from Seattle tell what he thought was an amusing story. Here is what he said:

"A group of young people were putting on a skit. A number of them were standing around visiting, when a teenager walked into the room eating a hamburger. In a matter of seconds he fell to the floor as though he were dead. Immediately, the other young people gathered around him and started to sing and chant E.coli! E.coli! E.coli!"

I saw no humor in this little skit. I saw plenty of brainwashing that caused them to put on a skit like that. The intense pressure and hysteria that radical animal rights people, vegetarians, and extreme environmentalists are subjecting our industry to is shameful.

Wishing you all a great Christmas with family and friends and a happy and prosperous New Year.

P.S. Remember to enjoy 'safe' roast beef on New Year's Day.

February 1998

We are reminded nearly every day that this is the information age. We belong to the global community via the Internet, E-mail, and the old-fashioned telephone and are littered with voice mail. There's fast travel, international sports events, student exchange programs and stock gyrations that reverberate throughout the world.

Despite all of this activity there appears to be a vacuum in our school curriculum. I am told that social studies (history and geography) are no longer taught past grade nine. I know of grade twelve students that cannot name all the provinces in Canada, let alone the capital cities. The whole focus in school seems to be on science and technology which are important. But, in my opinion, every generation should also know some history as well as the basic geography of the world.

Several years ago, the *National Geographic* magazine did a geographical survey of grade twelve students in the United States and the results were appalling to say the least. The bulk of the students received a failing mark. One question was, "Where is Toronto?" Only twenty-five percent knew it was in Canada. This, in spite of Toronto having an NHL hockey team, the Blue Jays baseball team, and an NBA basketball team. Some thought Toronto was in Italy.

We Canadians pride ourselves in being more informed about our country and other countries in the world than the Americans are. If the present trend in education continues in Canada we will sink and be on par with the Americans.

Some universities have set up reading programs for first-year students. I read recently where the reading skill of grade twelve students today is on the same level as the reading skill of grade eight students fifty years ago.

Now, if we used Chinese alphabet characters, I could understand why our reading skills are lagging. But plain old English is simple, even though we have a lot of unnecessary letters in our words. One example is phone – why not fone? Or night – why not nite? Physical – why not fizical? Lamb – why not lam? Citation – why not sytation? Plus hundreds of other words that cannot be sounded out but have to be memorized by sight.

Often foreign languages use several words to describe something whereas we only use one word. Or sometimes it's the other way around and they use one word where we may use three or four to say the same thing. Following are a few German words where one word does the trick:

Staatssicherheitsdienst – In English, it means state security service.

Schrebergartenkolonie – In English, this is a garden colony.

Knoblauchfressor – means a garlic eater.

And then there's vergangenheitsbewaltlgung. In English – coming to grips with the past.

I think we should come to grips with the past in educating our young people in a more practical way than we are doing at present. I am all for advanced education in many disciplines but let us build a firm foundation on the basics, which we use every day of our lives.

Knowing how to read intelligently, knowing what is going on in the world, and knowing history will enhance our lifestyle whether we are scientists, doctors, carpenters or cattle people.

P.S. Some schools may still teach social studies past grade nine. I know for a fact that some do not.

June 1998

In the last three or four columns, I have taken rather a harsh view of things that I see as wrong in our industry and in society in general. I have been told that any columnist or writer who does not criticize some things or situations is doing his or her readers a disfavor. People must be made aware of things we can improve.

Today, I am extending an olive branch. I am not apologizing for anything I have written in the past, but in this column I will take a softer view of life. This is not New Year's or Thanksgiving Day, when we all pause to reflect on how our life or attitudes shape up. But it is spring, the time of new life in the plant and animal world – and in our hearts. I am going to list what I think we should be thankful for.

1. **Eyesight**. I thank God nearly every day for good eyes. With our eyes we can see the beauty of nature, including sunrise and sunset. We can also enjoy looking at good cattle. And most important of all, we can see family, which includes watching grandchildren grow up. We can also read, drive a car, and many other things. We must never take our eyes for granted.

2. **Family** is something that we all enjoy. There may be rough times, but in the end they are the ones that stand by you when it really counts. A good wife is also a great blessing (I have a good one).

3. I am thankful **to be Canadian** despite all the flaws in our governments at all levels. Nearly every day on the news we read or see poverty and turmoil that three-quarters of the world's people live in on a daily basis. Let us appreciate the tranquillity and peace we enjoy in Canada.

4. **Freedom of the press and speech**. At times I feel it's a little shaky but, so far, so good.

5. **A sound mind** – maybe not brilliant but adequate. Let us make good use of the talent and ability we have.

6. **Good roads and vehicles** that do not have a flat tire every one hundred miles or so like cars did fifty or sixty years ago. I also appreciate four-wheel drive pick-ups.

7. I am glad **to live in Alberta** where we have some of the best cattle in the world and a free enterprise spirit.

8. I also enjoy the **friendships and acquaintance of cattle people** and a few other folks as well.

9. I like **the United States** as a friend and neighbor. We sometimes are a little hurt because they seem to know so little about Canada. We are in Colorado right now and everything is great. By the time you read this we'll be back in Alberta.

10. I like **cattle auction markets** even though I do not go to many sales myself any more. All the owners and staff have been very accommodating and nice to me. I have two sons who are cattle buyers.

11. I enjoy **good food**, especially beef. I do not eat as much as I used to. I have lost twenty-five pounds in the last three months. But I feel good and beef is still a big part of my diet.

12. **Freedom of worship**. I am so thankful that in Canada we have so much tolerance. Much of the world's problems are over religion. But a true belief in God and his son Jesus Christ coupled with life will not cause strife but rather harmony.

One little incident I must tell you about – A few days ago I went to the Federal Express office in Calgary to pick up a parcel from Arizona. The lady at the counter checked their records and told me the parcel wasn't there. This was at 11:30 in the morning, so we drove home. Our daughter phoned and told us that Federal Express had phoned her at 10:45 that morning saying we had a parcel to pick up. We live approximately fifteen miles from their office at the airport. So I got in the car and went back to fetch the parcel.

Needless to say, I was a little irate. I told the lady I was not very pleased about such sloppy business communications. She disappeared into the back to get the parcel. I was going to tell her this is the last time I will ever have anyone send us a parcel with Federal Express.

But while she was gone I noticed someone sitting in a wheelchair about six feet from me. His brother or friend had wheeled him in. He was a young man about twenty-five or thirty years old. He was the most crippled, twisted individual I had ever seen, and he even had one hand missing. His head was held in an awkward position yet he had a good look on his face, you could tell someone loved him.

Suddenly my little inconvenience seemed like nothing. When the girl arrived with my parcel I was courteous with her and thanked her instead of saying unkind words to her. She was actually a very nice person (she was not the same lady that told me there was no parcel).

I have gone into a lot of detail but hopefully we will take stock more often in our lives and act accordingly. You will catch a lot more flies with sugar than you will with vinegar. A kind word accomplishes much more than a harsh word.

I am not of the same religion as Mahatma Gandhi of India but I admire him. He achieved a lot without violence. Gandhi once listed the seven deadly sins: wealth without work, pleasure without conscience, knowledge without character, commerce without morality, science without humanity, worship without sacrifice and politics without principle.

July 1998

As you may have noticed, I often refer to the neighbors to the south of us. We are so interlinked with them that it impacts our life on a daily basis. The areas are financial, cultural, intellectual, social, sports and entertainment.

Often when I talk to my American friends I get the feeling that, as a Canadian, maybe I should not operate in the United States.

What they appreciate even less is the grain, cattle, and hogs that Canada exports to their country. Most rural Americans do not like North America Free Trade Agreement (NAFTA). They see it as a threat to their livelihoods.

However, they like to quote how many farm products they export every year. Some of them do not understand two-way trade, "What's good for the goose is good for the gander".

When I tell them how many Americans live in Calgary, involved in the oil and gas industry, they can hardly believe it. I also tell them about the United States based companies operating in Canada. Here is a partial list of those companies.

Esso (Exxon), Texaco, Amoco, Gulf, Chevron, Cargill, Iowa Beef Packers, Safeway, WalMart, Costco, Sears, 7-11, Hallmark Cards, McDonald's, Dairy Queen, Arby's, A&W, KFC, Perkins, Dennys, Red Lobster, half-a-dozen pizza companies, Ford, Chrysler, GM, John Deere, Case, General Electric, Midas, Mr. Lube, Western Atlas, Baker-Hughes, Century 21, Kodak, Time, Readers Digest, Sports Illustrated, a number of appliance companies, dozens of TV programs and most movies.

In the food area, there are hundreds of items that come from the United States, including fruits and vegetables.

Like I already stated, I am only scratching the surface. Our daughter is a schoolteacher. Recently, she told me that a large number of the text books in our schools come from the United States.

Canada is by far the biggest trading partner with the United States. Japan comes in a distant second.

By now you may think that I am anti-American, but that is not the case. The reason I mention all this United States activity in Canada is to make the average American aware of the fact, so they may better understand Canadian trade and involvement in their country.

Every time we are in the United States (which is quite often) I do my best to explain to my American friends that there is very little difference between us. Sometimes it falls on deaf ears. However, those Americans that have been to Canada do understand us a little better. Those that fly into our northern lakes or mountain areas to fish or hunt big game return home knowing very little about Canada except that the fishing lodges and hunting guides cost a fortune.

In the September 1997 issue of *Alberta Beef*, I wrote a column suggesting we redraw the border between Canada and the United

States. I got a lot of response from that article, all of it positive. I doubt whether that will ever happen.

What I think will take place is that within fifty years Canada and the United States will be one country. I won't be around to see it, but like the prophets of old that is my prediction.

August 1998

The human race has always faced periods of great volatility in areas such as health, wealth and weather. To mention all that has transpired in the last five hundred years in the above mentioned areas would fill a library. I have approximately a six hundred word column to just touch on these subjects.

In the matter of health we had the Black Death plague in the Middle Ages, the flu epidemic of 1918 and polio in the 1950s. Those three sicknesses caused millions to die worldwide. Then there were numerous Small Pox outbreaks and TB, which claimed millions more.

Today, we have AIDS, hepatitis C, plus several other new diseases. TB and diabetes are also on the rise. In spite of this our life span has shown a huge increase in the past one hundred years, thanks to modern medicine and good nutrition (including beef).

However, ninety percent of us will die before we are one hundred years old. In the light of history, one hundred years is but the blink of an eye.

Every person on earth seeks some material goods, or wealth, whether it is a street person looking for a handout or a multimillionaire hoping to add a few more million to his net worth.

Every generation produces some billionaires. In the past it was the Rockefellers, J.P. Morgan, the Rothchilds, the Duponts, plus dozens of others. These days it's the Walton family (Walmart), Bill Gates, Ken Thompson, and hundreds more.

But wealth, like health, can be very illusive. Many people that make it big end up dying in poverty. Others produce offspring who contribute nothing to society. A few family dynasties have been established that carried on for generations in an honorable and useful fashion.

Someone said to me one day, "Leonard, did you ever meet a person, worth $10,000,000, who was happier than one who was worth $9,000,000?"

Actually, I haven't. Someone else said, "You never miss money until you haven't got any."

The weather affects every person on earth, either for good or bad. This past year or two the weather has been wild. The meteorologists blame it all on El Nino. That may be true but history tells us that weather has always been unpredictable.

Over the years, millions have been killed or maimed by tornadoes, hurricanes, tidal waves, snow storms, floods, and fire caused by extreme drought and lightning.

The property damage is almost beyond calculation. In the past two years we have had tornadoes, hurricanes, ice storms, floods and huge fires in Australia, Indonesia, Florida, California and several other states. Here, in Canada, fires have claimed thousands of acres of forest in British Columbia, Alberta, the Northwest Territories, Ontario, Quebec, Saskatchewan, Manitoba and the Maritimes – in other words, all of Canada.

Large areas have suffered severe drought, including northern Alberta and northwestern Saskatchewan. In Texas, the drought is so severe that Governor Bush asked the federal government to declare all two hundred and fifty-two counties in the state a disaster area (this could affect our cow market).

Health, wealth and weather relate very closely to each other. We can do nothing about the weather except to protect ourselves from it to the best of our ability. Health is not entirely in our hands either. When our time on earth is up we are gone. Wealth may or may not come to us. I have come to the conclusion all we can do is accept what life hands us and make the best of it until we meet our Maker.

Did you know that Canadians have invested $320-billion in mutual funds? I sure hope they do not decide to bail off that mutual funds bandwagon all at the same time. If interest was to rise to twelve or fifteen percent in the next few years that's exactly what would happen. We had twenty-two percent in 1984.

I admire Gordon Thiessen for holding interest rates down. It's not often that I praise a bureaucrat. Thiessen has done a much better job as the Governor of the Bank of Canada than his predecessor did.

I will be publishing two books on October 11, 1998.

Round-up of Memories is a four hundred and thirty page hardcover book containing two hundred and thirty pictures. There are fifteen chapters, with each one being a story in itself. Connected together, they tell a story about people and cattle as experienced by me.

The other book is *Cattle Call*. It has three hundred and seventy-five pages and contains one hundred and ninety-two selected columns that I have written over the past twenty-three years. They are opinions and philosophy, and many of them are as relevant today as they were the day I wrote them.

Next month I will tell you how to obtain copies of these books.

November 1998

We live in a very sophisticated and highly computerized age. One of the "spin-offs" of this is the measurement of everything we do. Measuring things has gone on since the beginning of time, but only in the past two decades has it taken on a major role in people's daily life. The Bible mentions conducting business by weights and measures. It also talks about "the measure of a man". Since then man has been able to measure the distance that the sun, moon and other planets and galaxies are from this planet that we live on.

I do not like today's invasion of privacy. It is not that most of us have any sinister things in our life that we wish to hide. Freedom of speech, religion and what we do in our private lives are things that I treasure. If we wish to share areas of our life with other people, that's our business but, with computers and the Internet, much of that privacy is washed away.

With a touch of a button the banker knows every bit of our financial activity for the past ten years. At the auction markets, a touch of a button reveals exactly how many cattle we have bought and sold in the last ten years. If you check into a hotel, their computer tells them exactly how many times you have stayed there and it even has your credit card number. Or, how about the border between Canada and the United States?

Back to measurement. At large corporations (smaller ones too) the performance of every employee is measured. You either measure up to the standard they have set or you are gone. That sounds good on the surface, but it takes its toll on employee morale. It is not pleasant to be "under the gun" all the time. Employees all have strengths and weaknesses, on the computer their weakness shows up big time, even though the areas where they are strong far outweighs their shortcomings. Is this fair? I think not.

In the beef grading system everything is measured. I know this is necessary, but not to the degree it is done today. If the measurement falls a little short, there is a large price discount. When that discounted beef hits the dinner plate it is just as good as the beef that measured up better. Why the big price discount?

I know that weights and measures are an absolute necessity in conducting business. I also know computers are here to stay. They are a great tool for business. For customers and consumers they can be a "pain in the butt", especially when you stand at the counter for fifteen minutes, while the new girl punches the computer system, trying to figure out how it works. In many ways, our society has benefited from the use of computers. They are the tools that spawned globalization. Good or bad? The jury is still out.

If the United States Federal Reserve Chairman Allan Greenspan makes one little pronouncement about the economy or interest rates the stock markets worldwide plunge down or go up sharply. If this planet holds together, it will be interesting how history will record the era we live in. A hundred years from now maybe people will all be clones, so everyone will measure up the same. Many people may be living on another planet. Eating beef will seem as strange to them as cannibalism of a hundred years ago seems to us.

It is a sad commentary on today's society that, to a large degree, reading books has gone out of style. There are still some people who like to read especially older folks. One of the reasons is that people have no time to read because they are too busy. I have had hundreds of people tell me that at our autographing sessions and they really mean it. They absolutely feel there is no time left in their daily schedule. My reply to that is we can make time for something that is important to us. In my lifetime I always took time to read. I felt it was very rewarding and I do not consider reading a waste of time.

I suspect the biggest reason for people not reading much these days is the dominance of computers in our schools, businesses and homes. What little spare time is left is used for looking at TV and videos. In Airdrie, Alberta there are four or five video stores and only one bookstore, which struggles to keep the door open. The town of Brooks and surrounding area is home to fourteen or fifteen thousand people. Would you believe there is not a single bookstore in that town. They did have two bookstores but both closed in the past year. I could mention many other centers with populations from one thousand to six thousand people with no bookstore. Fortunately, some drug stores have a small book section.

I think this lack of interest in reading by young people is dangerous. Writing and reading has been the cornerstone of human history for thousands of years. Our whole education system was built on knowledge and wisdom that good reading material provided. One of the contradictions in our society is that today more people are writing books than ever before.

Even though smaller centers lack bookstores, the large urban centers have huge bookstores such as Chapters and others. The problem is unknown self-published authors write a number of those books. Most of these authors never recover the money it costs them to publish those books (some of them are good books). What happens is a few big name authors dominate the books that are sold? Some of those books are excellent reading but many are pure garbage. A lot of them are fairy tale fiction similar to many programs on TV, videos and in movie theatres. In my opinion this segment of society operates at a mindless shallow level.

I am sure by now most of you think I am writing this with a sour grapes attitude. Let me assure you that is not the case. The books I wrote are selling well (thanks folks). In the last three months I talked to several thousand people at our autographing sessions and in bookstores. The conclusion that I have come to is we face a brave new world, which many of our young people are not equipped to deal with. Suicide is now the second leading cause of death among young people. Three young people have committed suicide in Airdrie in the last month. I know this is a biased opinion but I believe the healthiest environment for young people is in rural areas where people make their living farming and raising livestock where they have good schools and churches along with community centers, 4-H and sport programs. To me that is Utopia.

Over the years I have noticed that kids from that kind of background nearly always turn out to be good citizens not clogging our court system or living off welfare. The percentage of families that have that kind of lifestyle is shrinking each year. Those of you still on the land hang on, you are the most fortunate people on this old planet.

To stay informed on the cattle industry keep on reading *Alberta Beef* magazine.

April 1999

I like old stories from a bygone era. One place where those kinds of tales abound is in the coffee shops all over the west (maybe the east as well). In most rural areas there is a coffee klatch in the local restaurant. It is where the older men, as well as a few younger men and women gather on a regular basis to relate and swap stories, some old, some new. Many of these stories have been told a dozen times before and each time they are told they are embellished a little more. Over a period of time, fairly insignificant incidents that happened fifty years ago, have blossomed into major episodes. They often involve courtship, fights at dances, buck-offs, a skirmish with the law, near fatal accidents or odd incidents that occur in every day life.

We make history every day. As the decades go by, the mundane things that we experience today become interesting bits of history in the future. Whenever a newcomer joins the coffee klatch, he or she is immediately bombarded with some of those stories. Everyone present is anxious to impress the newcomer with their best tales. Some folks are good storytellers, others are too long-winded and detailed.

There is nothing as boring as a long account with all the minute details and very little punch line at the end. I would much sooner listen to three brief versions of different incidents, than one long, boring story. This spinning of yarns with some truth interspersed goes on at other places as well, such as auctions marts, cattle conventions, bull sales, house parties and anywhere that people congregate.

There is an endless supply of jokes, anecdotes and stories by people who are involved in various areas of life. There is rodeo, horse racing, fishing, boxing, and wrestling, hockey, baseball, golf and many other sports. Other topics could include logging, miners, truck drivers, factory workers (usually pretty dull), farming, ranching, cattle feeders, cowboys, steer jocks, teachers, world travellers, an odd preacher, a few doctors, lawyers and veterinarians. One vet that was an excellent storyteller was Dr. Larry Sparrow. If you met him every day for thirty days or more, he had a new joke or story each time.

All the people involved in the above occupations have interesting and often funny incidents that they can recall. Some are worthy of writing a book about their life's experiences. I have read a number of books and short stories about most of the occupations I have mentioned.

The Native people are also great at telling stories and folklore, handed down to them from generation to generation. Until the last three generations all this history was oral – not written, therefore accuracy may be a little suspect. However, in a general sense the activities and exploits of their ancestors contain more truth than fiction even ten generations later.

I still remember stories my dad (1881-1963) told me about my great-grandfather (1832-1910). He was born one hundred and sixty-nine years ago. One reason I enjoy writing books is that events are recorded in print. If this old world stands another one hundred and sixty-nine years, great-grandchildren will have some idea of what happened in today's society as well as their own family five generations ago.

For thousands of years ancient scholars have recorded history. It was written on parchment scrolls, wood or stone. For centuries linguistic experts have been deciphering hieroglyphics often found in caves, monuments or ruins of ancient cities. They tell us stories of what went on in that civilization thousands of years ago. In the 15th Century, a German named Johann Gutenberg developed the first printing press. From that point on it was much easier to record history. In the centuries that followed, masses of people learned how to read as well.

In the electronic age we live in today, computers have taken over much of the knowledge we used to glean from books. Now, a lot of this knowledge is stored in computers, including the Internet. This is progress and it will not be stopped. It has streamlined big and small business operations. Without computers space exploration would still be at ground zero. It has made us almost completely dependent on the system, to the point where we have lost a large part of our privacy and independence. A smart hacker can get all kinds of private information about companies and private individuals. Just the other day, a hacker boasted that he could find out how much money anyone has in the bank. I rather doubt that, surely the banks would safeguard that information.

What bothers me is that someday most of the present historical facts could be lost if a major computer virus wiped everything out including the Y2K bug (I think they will solve that one). Even after the year 2000, an unforeseen malfunction could take place in the 21st Century. I encourage you to take paper and pen and record your little niche in history for posterity. You may wish to put it on tape or in a computer. That's OK. But by all means get it into print so it will be preserved for future generations.

Rodeo cowboys are some of the most admired athletes in our rural western society. However, this does not extend to the urban press and media. They often completely ignore the feats of these men and women. Newspapers in places like Calgary, Houston, Cheyenne and some other cities give good coverage during the time a rodeo is in their city. But, once the rodeo is finished in that location the coverage goes back to almost nil. As for Denver, the rodeo coverage at the annual stock show is non existent (at least the rodeo portion).

Most of us, who are rodeo fans, know how rodeo got started and how it has developed into the precision performance that it is today. It is difficult to understand why the sport has such a low rating with the average urban dweller. You may not agree with me, but if rodeo had the fan support that other major sports enjoy, the corporate sponsors would fall over each other like they do in mainline sports including tennis, golf and team sports.

The prize money in rodeo is a pittance compared to other sports. Michael Jordan (in 1998) made as much in salary, bonuses and product endorsements in a year as the combined income of the top two hundred rodeo contestants. On top of that, the cowboys pay their own expenses including entry fees.

In the United States, only the top fifteen cowboys (including Canadians) in each event go to the National Finals in Las Vegas. In Canada, only the top ten in each event go to the Canadian Finals in Edmonton. At both the National and Canadian Finals, the payout is fairly good, but is still small compared to other sports. There are only a few cowboys who make more than $100,000 annually.

In other sports, they make multi-millions including signing bonuses. Why? To me, rodeo is ten times more exciting and interesting than watching people run back and forth on a basketball court or skating all over a hockey rink chasing a little black puck. There are several reasons why rodeo is the orphan on the sports scene:

1. Lack of regular coverage by the media. It seldom appears in the sport section of the big daily papers or in TV sportscasts.

2. The absence of big corporate sponsors (there are some but not nearly enough).

3. Lack of understanding by the average citizen as to what the sport of rodeo is all about.

4. Radical animal rights people mount a constant propaganda campaign in the name of cruelty to animals. This rubs off on many urban young people, especially young women. The fact is rodeo stock is treated very well.

5. Every large urban center should have at least six rodeos a year (bull riders only events have proved to be fairly successful in the last few years).

6. This may sound strange, but I suggest raising the price of professional rodeo tickets substantially. Anything you get free or cheap usually is not appreciated. The price of tickets to heavyweight boxing matches or any major league sports are astronomical, yet people flock to those games in droves. Corporations and small business people purchase many of those season tickets in blocks.

7. Most rodeo cowboys are too taciturn (silent). They need to have more interaction with the fans.

I will never forget the day, while at the Calgary Airport, that I sat next to a bronc rider from Texas. I tried to strike up a conversation with the individual as I saw him ride the previous day. I got an indifferent and icy reception. So much for public relations (it was not Monte Hanson). I had the same experience on the deck of a hotel swimming pool in Medicine Hat. This time it was one of Canada's top calf ropers (not Marty Becker). I must hasten to add there are a number of individuals and rodeo committees who are good ambassadors and promoters of rodeo.

One example is Jack Daines from Innisfail, Alberta. Jack is a tireless promoter of rodeo. Every June, at the Daines Rodeo Ranch several miles north of Innisfail, the Daines family puts on one of the best rodeos in Canada. They feature the top bucking stock in the country, supplied by seven or eight rodeo stock contractors. I will never forget the day Duane Daines drew the rank bucking horse from the Vern Franklin string called, Airwolf. Somehow Duane lost the buck rein, which of course disqualifies the contestant. But in spite of this, Duane kept right on spurring the horse and put on a good ride to the whistle. Two years ago Glen O'Neil scored ninety-five points on Airwolf to tie the record in Canada. He won the saddle bronc event. Last year Denny Hay scored eighty-six points on the Calgary Stampede horse, Zippy Delivery, to win the event.

The Daines rodeo has a number of company and corporate sponsors. As the rodeo announcer, Jack gives all the sponsors a good plug interwoven with his wit and interesting comments on the action taking place in the arena. Another good feature about this rodeo is the family camping that is provided. All the facilities have been upgraded each year. For the last three years this rodeo has been voted the best in Canada by the top twenty cowboys. The prize money ranks number five in Canada, the payout to the cowboys is $140,000. If you have any doubt about my word on the caliber of this rodeo come, see for yourself. It all happens on June 17 to 20, 1999. See you all there.

A rancher told me that today to be a successful rodeo cowboy, you need to be married to a career woman with a high paying job, who does not mind sharing her money with her husband and staying home alone for periods of time. It also helps if your parents own a good ranch.

There are several positive things going on in rodeo today. One is all the rodeo schools. Another one is the amateur rodeo circuits, as well as college and high school rodeos. At these events I suggest holding the ticket prices at the present level, similar to what they do in other sports. In all sports there is a huge jump in salary when they move from the minor leagues or from amateur ranks to professional.

There are hundreds of amateur rodeo contestants that will never make it to the Pro ranks, but that is life. Thousands of aspiring hockey and ball players never make it past the midget or junior level either. Even if you did not make the Pro's it was fun to give it a try. The main thing is that everyone should have an equal opportunity to prove themselves in their chosen sport including rodeo.

The *Canadian Rodeo News* monthly paper does an excellent job reporting on rodeo and about the people involved in rodeo. This publication basically only reaches people that are associated with rodeo, plus some interested fans. It is similar to my column in *Alberta Beef* magazine. I often exhort and encourage people to eat more beef (the world's finest food). But folks who already are committed beefeaters mostly read this column. What we need in both rodeo and for the benefit of adding more beef in our diets is for the urban media to take up those causes in order to reach the masses of people in this country.

The Calgary Exhibition and Stampede does a super job advertising and promoting their annual shows with the result a large number of people - Canadians, Americans and overseas visitors - attend. Of course, the show includes many other activities besides rodeo. I know some people attend the Stampede but do not go to the rodeo.

There are a number of top quality rodeos in the four western provinces. I cannot name them all in this column. I do think that the Ponoka Stampede merits mention as they do a bang-up job. I like rodeo so anything I wrote in this column is done in good faith. Some of you may not agree with my assessment and suggestions, but that's democracy, we are free to express our opinions. My wish is for rodeo to gain a higher profile, which will help it to prosper and survive.

June 1999

I like reading. Since January 1, 1999 I have read seventeen or eighteen books, one of those books (a gift from my daughter) happens to be a huge volume. It contains seven hundred and eleven large pages of fine print, almost a million words. The average four hundred-page book has from one hundred and fifty thousand to two hundred and fifty thousand words, depending on the size of the print and how many pictures it contains. The book I read is called *Our Times, The Illustrated History of the Twentieth Century*. The senior writers of this huge book are Kenneth Miller, Kevin MacIley and Harold Itzkowitz. Other writers are Stacey Barstein, Jonathan Danziger, Dana Dogar, Rebecca Hughes, Sydney Johnson, Toni Kamins, Daniel Lazare, Nancy Ramsey, Gregory Root, Elizabeth Roxte, Stephen Williams and Lillian Jordan.

Besides all those writers there were another seventy people involved in creating this masterpiece. Included were researchers, editors and design staff. The editorial advisory board is people who are on staff at Columbia University, University of California (Berkley) and Harvard University. As you will notice, these are high profile academics.

I have not yet read every word of this book, but I have read a large portion of it. It is very informative and interesting, especially for a history buff like myself. However, I am distressed by what this book does not contain – I will explain that a little later.

Due to copyright laws, I cannot make any direct quotations from this book without written permission. I can mention people and events that are listed on its pages. It covers all the major events, such as wars, famines, earthquakes, floods, tornadoes, fires, space exploration, motion pictures, inventions, sport and Olympic events, and medicine, including AIDS. It also names thousands of people who were the movers and shakers, as well as the villains of our society. It includes people from all over the world, although the bulk of the events and people are from the United States. Canada gets little coverage.

The following are areas of life that mention people. The number one spot goes to actors (hundreds of them are named). Next are writers (most of them are spinners of fiction). In third place is every sport except rodeo. Then politicians (most of them American), in fourth place are musicians, followed closely by artists. Next are filmmakers and then singers. Other categories of people mentioned are astronauts, architects, archaeologists, composers, criminals, cartoonists, fashion designers, engineers, educators, financiers, journalists, labour leaders, corporate leaders, philanthropists, poets, playwrights, photographers, military people, religious leaders, shrinks, sculptors, world leaders, lawyers, physicians, jurists and a number of others.

Remember, this is a book about what went on in our world from 1900 to 1994 (this book was published five years ago. I just received it recently). Here is why I am disappointed by what the book does not mention! Cattle: zero, Horses: zero, Farming: zero, Ranching: zero, Rodeo Cowboys: zero. In other words, there is nothing in this book about agriculture or any of the people involved in that industry – the pioneers who ranched and homesteaded this great continent do not warrant any recognition.

It is an utter disgrace how low on the totem pole rural communities and agriculture in general have become in our urbanized society. Ninety-eight percent of academics do not give a hoot about agriculture. All we do is supply food for the whole world. This is done at very affordable prices. Often the product leaving the farm gate is sold for less than the cost of production. The main reason that food costs are fairly high in stores is because of all the middlemen who get a slice of the pie. Even after those mark-ups, food is still cheap compared to most other things we purchase, such as cars, trucks, and other consumer goods.

I guess you could call me an activist when it comes to how agriculture is viewed (mostly ignored) in our society today. I am not advocating strikes or major protest movements, but we must find a way to gain higher more favorable media coverage in urban areas. For example, the *Calgary Herald* has no farm writer on staff. I sound like a broken record when I lament the sad state of affairs we face in agriculture today. I know there are very capable organizations and people working on this problem. Keep it up – my hat's off to you!

PS: I wish to thank every one of you folks who bought one of my books, where the proceeds went to a worthy cause such as Stars Air Ambulance, underprivileged children, hospitals, accident victims and a number of other worthy causes and projects. I donated approximately $4,000 worth of books over the past three years. They generated about $20,000 in proceeds. In other words, the books brought an average five times their value. A few brought over a thousand dollars each. Again I say a big thanks to all the cattle auction markets and your patrons for this generous support for people who are less fortunate and in more need than the rest of us are.

August 1999

The "catch phrase" of the '90s is globalization. With all the technical advances in communication, transportation and jet plane travel our world has shrunk. The result is a tremendous boost in world trade in all goods and commodities. If there is a drought in Brazil, it affects us. If Europe and Asia have huge cereal crops, it impacts on us. A few years ago, when the Asian economy fell out of bed, it had big repercussions in North America. Even the interest rates in Japan, Germany and other countries affect us.

The exchange of manufactured goods and commodities between countries is quite astonishing. What makes this possible is relatively cheap transportation on huge container ships and enormous oil tankers. Great Britain used to be the kingpin in world trade. They used small sailing ships and later on modest-sized steam ships to conduct this trade. Now, the whole world has joined the frenzy of exchange of goods.

It always surprises me when I look at the labels of where things are made. Places like Japan, China, India, Korea, Taiwan, Brazil, Portugal, Italy, England, Mexico, Panama and, of course, our largest trading partner the United States, plus dozens of other countries. Just recently I bought a good quality Resistol hat for $50. They used to cost between $80 and $120. When I got home, I took a good look inside the hat. I noticed a small sticker that said the hat was made in Mexico. My first reaction was that I had purchased an inferior quality hat. Then it dawned on me that this hat was made by the United States Company that makes Resistol hats – they owned a factory in Mexico just across the border. The cost of labor was the reason for the cheap hat. The quality of this hat is excellent.

There are hundreds of products made in Mexico, in plants owned by United States companies. The strange thing is this has not hurt the unemployment rate or the economy in the United States.

How does the global economy impact the beef industry? Well, so far, in a positive manner but there is room for improvement. Most of you are aware of an organization made up of major players in the beef industry called the Canada Beef Export Federation (CBEF). These folks do a good job promoting and selling beef to offshore customers. They have been operating for ten years. It is a slow process, but they are gaining ground. In case you missed the story about this organization, their story is written up in the July issue of *Alberta Beef* magazine on page thirty. Incidentally, the export of Canadian beef is not new, in the 1930s and '40s boatloads of live cattle were exported to Great Britain.

On July 1, 1999, the United States imposed a per head tariff of fifty dollars (4.73 percent average) on Canadian cattle going into the United States. They called this an "anti-dumping" duty. This is completely unjust. It breaks the rules of the free-trade agreement. It is the ugly head of protectionism rearing up, similar to what happened sixty-nine years ago, which helped trigger a world-wide depression. No nation can prosper when it closes its borders. History makes that clear – this includes a giant like the United States.

Their economy and quality of life depends to a large degree on their export markets, as well as on their imports such as oil, natural gas, lumber, meat products and cheaply manufactured goods.

There are many glitches in international business such as the Fracmaster disaster in Russia. Several years ago when I read about their involvement in Russia, I said to myself I would not want any part of that company. In fact, I more or less predicted it could turn into a nightmare, which it did – they got wiped out! There is a big difference in trading with another country or investing in it. It is much safer to trade than to invest.

International trade is good. The name of the game is to be alert and somewhat cautious before you invest in "offshore". I speak from experience – Colombia taught me that lesson.

Meantime, let us keep the borders open for exports and imports, that is our lifeline in agriculture – globalization is here to stay. Sorry Mr. Whelan (a former Trudeau-era Liberal agriculture minister), I just cannot agree with your "closed border" policies. He made that statement when he recently retired from his unelected Senate seat. He has offered his services to the government for a dollar a year. I guess he can afford to do that with his large retirement pension. I hope they reject his offer, he needs to be out to pasture for good. I have always said he is sincere in his belief about supply management and marketing boards, but he is sincerely wrong!

September 1999

The name *Cattle Call* implies this column is about cattle and, usually, it is. However, as you know, I stray from writing only about cattle - something like the company Canadian Tire, they too merchandise much more than only tires.

Today, I wish to pay tribute to a very fine gentleman by the name of Grant McEwan. You may have heard or read that on August 12th he celebrated his ninety-seventh birthday. It would take an average good man two hundred years to achieve what Grant did in ninety-seven years.

In his lifetime, he was a professor at the University of Saskatchewan and Dean of Agriculture at the University of Manitoba. He was a Liberal Member of the Legislative Assembly from Calgary (wrong party in my opinion) and a City of Calgary alderman. He was also elected Mayor of Calgary. To top off his career, he was appointed Lieutenant-Governor of Alberta, a position he held for about eight years.

Beside all those academic and political involvements, he had many other pursuits, such as a much-sought-after speaker. I heard him several times and really enjoyed his folksy way of delivering a speech. There was plenty of substance in what he had to say.

He also judged many livestock shows, especially horse and cattle shows. I think he judged hog and sheep shows as well. I have judged the Kamloops Open and 4-H Steer Show on at least five different years (my son Lee has also judged it a few times). The folks at Kamloops really flattered me, when they compared me to Grant McEwan who had judged their show a number of times, several years before me.

Grant has written fifty-five books and I have read most of them. They have given me hours of enjoyment. I like his sense of humor and his grasp of history. I have written three books and some of the inspiration for writing those books came from reading his books. I did not plagiarize any of his material, but I tried to write in his folksy manner, no airs, just down-to-earth stuff.

About a month ago, I went to visit him in the Beverly Nursing Home. He was delighted to see me, although I am almost sure he did not know who I was. I had met him a few times years ago. Over the years, he has talked with thousands of people, most of them more important than me. So I was a vague face from the past.

We had a good visit, but he has a bit of a hearing problem, so to help him hear, he puts on a set of earphones. Then he turns on a little gadget to which a mike is attached. When talking into this mike, he can hear what a person says.

This was on a Sunday afternoon at three o'clock. Guess what he was doing? He is writing another book or attempting to, as he puts it. He was sitting propped up in his bed, with a stack of papers and newspaper clippings on his lap. I asked him what he was writing about. He said, water. I am sure, if the book gets published, it will be an interesting story.

I told him I had always admired him as a great writer and naturalist, as well as an educator and livestock judge. What has impressed me most over the years is his humble, honorable manner coupled with his intelligence. He is a man who considered all men and women equal although not all have the same gifts. He told me his mother always said to him, it is much better to be honest and honorable than rich, he certainly lived up to her advice.

I remember when he was Mayor of Calgary; he usually walked or took a city transit bus. He could talk to kings and queens, or the top academics in the world, or the common man on the street, or the cleaning lady and it was not put on, it just came to him naturally.

When I left he encouraged me to keep on writing, he had a twinkle in his eye. Yes, it may be a long time, if ever, that we will have a man like Dr. Grant McEwan in our midst again.

October 1999

Every once in a while, I like to be controversial. In modern-day society, we have a number of issues that are debated pro and con. One of those issues that are debated is should we share a common currency with the United States. My answer is, yes. Many smart business and money people also say, let's do it.

Paul Volckner, the former chairman of the United States Federal Reserve Board predicts it's inevitable that we will have a common currency with the United States. The euro is a common currency that will be in total use by 2002 by most members of the European Union.

Those Canadians that are opposed to this monetary union with the United States are folks who have a false pride in what Canada is all about. They think it will belittle us if our Loonie became a United States Greenback. That wounded pride would soon dissipate when people begin to realize that if we want to stay competitive in world markets, we have to join forces with the United States.

There could be a few glitches to begin with, but within six months, everything would be back on track, including the cattle market. Like I have often stated, we Canadians are every bit as good at business as the Americans. All we need is a level playing field with a common currency. The goofy border disputes we have these days would disappear (providing we can muzzle a certain newspaper publisher in Billings, Montana).

I still have faith in the average American cattleman when all the facts are on the table – common sense will prevail. No matter how much that publisher rants and raves against Canadian cattle entering the United States.

A lot of Canadian companies already operate with American currency in most of their business transactions. Why not make it official? The same thing applies in Mexico, Central and South America (SA). Years ago when I was involved in Colombia, SA, nobody talked about pesos. Nearly everything was based on United States dollars. In restaurants and small stores the peso was used, but all major business deals were conducted with United States currency.

Once Canada and the United States have joined forces, Mexico, Central and South America could also come on board. That amalgamation would be a little trickier, but with time it could be worked out. The Mexican (and other Latin American countries) pesos have so little value that when those folks trade in their money for United States dollars, the amount of currency they would receive would be very small. However, the United States dollar would buy just as many goods and services as did their larger amounts of pesos.

Volckner also predicts that world currencies will eventually fall into three main blocs – the euro, the yen and the United States dollar. I disagree calling it the United States dollar. I suggest it be called the amero. Maybe the Japanese yen should be renamed as well – it could be called the asio. That would save face in China, Korea and other Asian countries that would share that currency.

Canadians might be hard pressed to suggest a few Canadian statesmen whose faces could appear on some coins or bills of the amero. I am sure it could be worked out - maybe Louis Riel could grace the nickel. The Queen is a nice lady, but many can live without her picture on our amero money.

In the September 1997 issue of *Alberta Beef*, I wrote a column in which I outlined how we should redraw the border between Canada and the United States. I got more comments and calls from people on that column than on any other column I have written in the past twenty-four years. Most of those people agreed with my plan. Unfortunately that realignment will be hard to achieve.

The next best thing would be a completely open border and sharing a common currency. Not only would it be good for business, it could also enhance our self-esteem. No longer would we be embarrassed about our Canadian peso, oops – dollar.

It is no surprise that some of our Federal politicians and a few major banks are opposed to the idea. A small number of loyalists also think it is wrong. I am always proud to be an Albertan but I am not always proud to be a Canadian. Let's get with it before Canada sinks ever closer to becoming a "third world" country.

I know this column will bring two responses; Friesen has lost it – he is out to lunch or, not a bad idea. Which camp are you in?

November 1999

I may get into a little hot water over this column. If I do, it would not be the first time. I am not a political analyst, but as a Western

Canadian, I would have to be awful dumb and ignorant if I could not see what the eastern-based Liberal party has done to us in the past thirty years. It all started when Pierre Trudeau was elected leader of the Liberal Party in 1968. I vividly remember that day. I was at a cattle sale in Walsh, Alberta when the announcement came over the radio. In the weeks that followed, Trudeaumania set in. This resulted in him being elected Prime Minister of Canada. I can proudly state that I never did join in that Trudeaumania. I did not like what he stood for. I had several friends who voted for him that year. A few years later, they told me how much they regretted voting for him.

Before I go into what he did to us, I will state a few good points about him. He is quite intelligent and honest in his opinions. Whenever he did something that the public did not approve of, he just shrugged his shoulders and said, "so what." If the Watergate scandal had occurred in Canada under the Trudeau regime, he would have shrugged it off and would have remained the Prime Minister. It was the lying that got Nixon.

It appears he raised some good sons. Maybe Margaret or a nanny had some input into their lives during their formative years.

Trudeau was the architect of a number of major changes in the way Canada functions as a nation. We all know what those policies were, but we must constantly refresh our memories, lest history records him as a great statesman – which he is not! One of the legacies he left us is the huge national debt. I doubt if our children and grandchildren will live to see that debt eliminated. This is one reason why our taxes in Canada are so high.

Then there was the National Energy Program (NEP) which plundered billions of dollars from Western Canada. Included in this was the formation of Petro-Canada, which cost the taxpayers a bundle. Some people still refer to the Petro-Canada head office tower in Calgary as "Red Square". He also engineered the bilingual and multi-cultural policies, both of which divided the country instead of unifying it.

Another legacy he left us is the metric system. The changeover cost billions of dollars. If we had been in tandem with the United

States on this, we would still be using bushels instead of tonnes, pounds instead of kilos. A quarter section of land would still be one hundred and sixty acres instead of eighty-seven-something hectares.

Trudeau was born with the proverbial silver spoon in his mouth. His father owned a string of service stations in Quebec, which made him a multimillionaire. Consequently, Pierre never did a day's work. This gave him time to visit communist Russia several times. He also became a big buddy of Fidel Castro in Cuba.

Trudeau enjoyed skiing, the theatre and escorting famous and some not so famous women to social events and some not so social. Trudeau surrounded himself with "yes men" and socialists such as Marc Lalonde who was his right hand man in setting up the NEP. Eugene Whelan was his marketing board socialist Minister of Agriculture. How about that mumbling Herb Gray who is still around licking Chretien's boots as deputy Prime Minister. There were also many other Ontario and Quebec MP's with strange political agendas.

Just recently, the eastern scribes produced a program on CTV celebrating Trudeau's 80th birthday. They remained strangely silent on many of the things that he did, which were detrimental to Canadians, especially Western Canadians. Like I always say, history is a great teacher, it helps us avoid mistakes in the future.

We have had Quebec lawyers as our Prime Ministers for the past thirty-one years. With a few short interludes of Joe Clark, John Turner and Kim Campbell. Granted, one of those Quebec lawyers was a Conservative. His legacy was not that great either. Under his leadership the deficit continued to grow. On top of that he saddled us with the Goods and Service Tax (GST), which the Liberals were going to scrap – what a cruel joke that was. I sometimes wonder how Sheila Copps sleeps at night. I guess blatant lying is all part of Liberal policy.

These days the appointed Supreme Court is running the country. They make most of the major decisions rather than the elected members of Parliament. This makes it easy to hand any sticky issue for the court to rule on – a role, which should be carried out by the elected MPs.

We need the Supreme Court but they should be elected and their jobs should be to interpret the laws of the land, not make way off base decisions on their own. The Senate should also be elected and the Governor–General's office abolished.

PS: I am a freelance writer, my opinion is not necessarily that of *Alberta Beef* magazine.

January 2000

So this is the millennium. We look forward to some great times, kind of a Utopia. I am sure the folks a thousand years ago thought the same thing. The reality was quite different. What transpired in the past thousand years is a mixture of success and failure, but overall it is a horror story. History tells us that there were wars and battles fought worldwide, in which millions died. The wars are far too numerous to mention. They range from the Battle of Hastings by William the Conqueror in 1066, to the destruction of Kosovo in 1999.

Besides wars, there were numerous other human disasters. Millions died from the Black Death plague in the middle of the past millennium. Then there were millions that died at the hands of Hitler and Stalin. Pol Pot, the Cambodian monster, also slaughtered several million people. Idi Amin and many other cruel dictators have also slaughtered millions. The above atrocities were not really war, but outright genocide.

The hardship suffered by the masses is hard to comprehend. People worked hard in deplorable conditions for very little pay. Lifespans were very short. Then there was slavery, practised in most countries of the world. The one that we are the most familiar with is the United States. The book, *Roots,* and other books and articles record what a horror story that was. Can you imagine what it must have been like to work from morning to night in the hot sun for no pay whatsoever? If they showed any rebellion they were whipped and often auctioned off like cattle. Sometimes children were sold and their parents never saw them again. One of the reasons the slaves were allowed to get married was so they could produce more future slaves for the owner. The United States is still suffering the backlash from that era.

How about all the natural disasters in the past one thousand years? Earthquakes, floods, fires, tornadoes, hurricanes and mud slides. Untold millions died or were seriously injured in these disasters. Millions more died in sinking ships, train wrecks, collapsed buildings, plane crashes and most of all from motor vehicle accidents. Not a pretty picture, is it?

Now on a more positive note. Creature comforts in the past century have vastly improved. Today we have (at least in the developed countries) good housing with central heating, running water, electricity and phone. Good roads and transportation systems. Good communication networks, much of it bounced off satellites (it is almost too good). Every night on TV we can see what disasters have befallen people thousands of miles away.

Medicine has also made great strides. Even though our health system is in a bit of a crisis these days. I am a testimony as to how successful orthopedic surgery has become. I have an artificial hip and knee. Would you believe they work perfectly? I don't even limp anymore. I am writing this to encourage some of you who may need joint replacement – don't hesitate, just get it done! None of us knows what the future holds, but we know who holds the future – God – trust Him. As we now face the millennium, let us do our part to improve conditions on this old planet. Hate, greed and jealousy are all monsters, which we need to eliminate from our lives. We will never succeed in getting rid of all those things in our lives, but we must try by showing love, kindness and consideration for others. I guarantee this will improve the life of our fellow man as well as our own. How about making that our New Year's resolution. It would be a good way to start the new millennium.

I hope you folks all had prime rib for dinner on New Year's Day. It is also a good idea to encourage your urban friends to eat beef five times a week. We all know lean beef is a health food along with veggies.

I wish you all a Happy New Year.

June 2000

I am glad that in the past few years there has been a renewed interest in our past history pertaining to the cattle industry. Some of the credit goes to the people from my generation. We are the offspring of the pioneers who built this great country, especially western Canada. Our parents and grandparents faced and overcame many hardships in both their farming and ranching endeavors. Now the "baby boomers" are starting to take an interest in their ancestor's activities which includes parents, grandparents, great-grandparents and even great-great-grandparents. There are a large number of people between the ages of forty to fifty-five. This assures me that, even after our generation has passed on, history will be well preserved.

In western Canada our ranching and cattle industry only goes back about one hundred and twenty-five years. This is a very short time compared to other historical events. In Europe, they consider any buildings under three hundred years old fairly recent. Of course, western Canada's history goes back a long way as well, when you consider the Natives were here for many thousands of years. The explorers, trappers and missionaries were also here before the cattle industry was established.

Hank Pallister, my fellow *Alberta Beef* magazine columnist, has written many interesting columns concerning early ranching in Alberta. I do not want to steal his thunder. For that reason I wish to share a bit of history from south of the border – namely Texas. The ranching tradition is very similar from southern Alberta all the way to Texas and this includes southern Saskatchewan, British Columbia and all the western states between Canada and Texas.

My fascination with Texas started when I was a youngster growing up in southern Saskatchewan. The well-known Matador Ranch was across the river from us. I heard many stories about the Texans who owned that ranch and the Texas cowboys who worked there. By the time I went there the Texans had long departed (they left in 1921), but the stories about them lingered on, so did the legacy and traditions. To a young boy like me this was like having a link to a bygone era. I loved it.

Now for a bit of ranching history in Texas. The cattle industry in Texas sprang from the Texas Longhorns, which roamed all over, especially in southern Texas. There were millions of them. In the mid-1870s, the relatively new state of Texas decided they should build a capitol building in Austin. The problem was that they had no money, but they did have a lot of unoccupied land. Some wise politician got the idea, why not trade some of that land to someone who had enough money to build the capitol building? After scouting around a bit they found some industrialists in Chicago, who were willing to build the capitol building. The deal they struck was that the state of Texas would deed over three million acres of land to them in exchange for the construction of the capitol building. The land was located in the panhandle area. It ran parallel with the New Mexico border. The ranch was twenty-five miles wide and two hundred miles long. They called it the XIT ranch. It covered the better part of ten counties.

They stocked the ranch with Texas longhorns, trailed up from southern Texas. At one time, the ranch had three hundred and fifty thousand cattle. That was way overstocked, so they cut back to between one hundred and fifty thousand to two hundred thousand head. The ranch was plagued by rustlers, prairie fires, drought, poor cattle prices and an odd blizzard called a Northerner. They persevered and gradually got it running as smooth as was possible with such a large operation.

Slowly they bred those cattle up with British-bred bulls and by 1910 the cattle on that ranch were pretty well all Black Angus. Over the years, they started to sell chunks of the ranch to other people including farmers. The historic Matador ranch bought a huge chunk of it. By 1950, they only had twenty thousand acres left. I am not sure what their status is today.

When I was feeding cattle in Texas and sometimes buying feeder cattle in Amarillo, I drove over large portions of the old XIT ranch. It is not too far from Hereford, Texas where I fed our cattle. The areas that were not broken up looked pretty much like it did a hundred years ago, around 1888.

Space will not permit me to write about all of the ranch's activity or of the cowboys who worked there. Suffice to say, there was lots of action such as getting bucked off ten miles or more from a cow camp, of which there were seven. Sometimes they roped a lobo (wolf); other times they had to move cattle into sheltered breaks during a snowstorm. What they hated most was fighting prairie fires, which occurred on a regular basis. In one big fire, they lost almost a million acres of grass and some cattle. They managed to move eighteen thousand head to the Canadian River area, which was not burned. (In case some of you are not aware of it, there is a river in Texas called the Canadian.) Sometimes they had to deal with rustlers who actually worked for the outfit. The managers and foremen always were seasoned cowmen who had to report to their bosses in Chicago.

There was also some British money involved. The XIT Ranch was often referred to as The Syndicate. Its actual business name was The Capitol Freehold Land and Investment Company Limited.

So you see, things south of the border were not that much different in the early days than in southern Alberta. Much of our early west practices and customs came from American cowboys who trailed cattle into this country from the United States. Those of you who enjoy western history will find many books on the subject in bookstores and libraries. As well you will find western history at the Glenbow Museum in Calgary, the Western Heritage Center in Cochrane and the Bar U Ranch historical site near Longview. I hope you all have a wonderful summer.

October 2000

In the depression of the 1930s, people suffered a great deal of hardship. There was no money, jobs were scarce and some people went hungry. This situation developed a hardy breed of young people. The depression affected young people differently than it did older people.

Older people who had worked hard as homesteaders and had experienced some good years in the 1920s suddenly found themselves in a tight financial corner. This caused them to become disillusioned and bitter. Some gave up, others persevered and eventually made a good comeback – saving the family farm or ranch in the process.

Those of us who were children or young people had not experienced the homesteading days or the roaring '20s and knew nothing but tough times. Kids are very resilient and adjust to their impoverished state. We learned to be frugal and work hard.

When the war came along in 1939, many young people joined the armed forces. Those of us who were too young stayed home and worked on the farm or ranch. When the war ended, thousands came home (a large number had died). In many cases those young veterans took over the family farm. Some started their own operations with some government assistance. They were the children and young people of the depression. The work ethic in most of them was very strong.

Consequently they did well in whatever profession they chose. They became the parents of the "baby boom" generation. The boomers became tradesmen and professionals and some stayed on the land. Most of the baby-boom generation is successful. I think the reason is that common sense and the work ethic rubbed off from their parents and grandparents.

Now we are into the generation of the baby-boomers offspring. The young people of today have been shaped and influenced by the affluence that surrounds them. Today, everything is high tech. Young people have high expectations. They read and hear of people who make huge salaries or some have started their own computer/Internet business and have become instant millionaires. This hope for fast riches puts a damper on their enthusiasm for more mundane ordinary work. Many young people are not fond of physical labor.

These days, high tech and sophisticated machinery and equipment have taken a lot of the drudgery away from many tasks. But there are certain jobs that still require manual labor. Each year it becomes more difficult to find people to take those kinds of jobs. Recently, I spoke to several farmers who could not find anyone to work on the farm. In the summer, some students did work for them. I also talked to a few businesses that said it is almost impossible to hire young people for jobs that require any labor.

One man told me they are trying to hire more older people, forty to fifty years of age. The reason he said was that his company found that young people, especially young men, expect big pay for very little work. But before some of you young people get mad at me, let me remind you that I was quoting what was said to me. I know there are still a lot of good young people who do a good job.

Our economy is a bit of a problem. Workers in service industry jobs and ordinary labor jobs often only get a minimum wage or slightly more. With the cost of living as high as it is, those people cannot make ends meet − many give up and become homeless. Each year the homeless population in the cities grows at an alarming rate.

My advice to young people is this:

1. Get an education, no matter how difficult it is to attain. I am not sure who will do the manual labor if everyone gets over qualified. I guess we will have to increase our immigration of less educated people − sounds kind of rednecked. The United States and Canada to a lessor extent have been doing this for the last two hundred years.

2. If you do have a job, always be at work ten minutes early rather than ten minutes late.

3. Wherever you work always do a job as though it is your business. This attitude and work ethic pays off big time when a job promotion comes along.

4. When looking for a job, try to select the type of work you enjoy. I know of people who have worked all of their life at a job that they really did not like.

5. Respect older people. If you do, they will respect you. Every once in a while ask for a little advice from an older person. Who knows, they may even give you a little financial assistance.

Now a little advice to employers. Treat your help well, but if you have someone working for you who does substandard performance, do not try to improve their quality of work by giving them a raise. It won't work. It might for a week or two, after that it's back to the old poor work habits. However, if you have an employee who does a good job, raise their salary – otherwise someone will hire them away from you.

Hope you don't get the idea that I am a know-it-all, but I have experienced and observed the things I write about – they are real!

CHAPTER SEVENTY-THREE

A COLUMN THAT NEVER GOT PUBLISHED

March 5, 2000

I am a bit of a news junkie. Every day I read newspapers and magazines. They consist of daily, weekly and monthly publications. I also watch TV news, listen to radio news (mostly when driving). I also have a lot of chats and visits with various men and women on the phone or in person. Our discussions usually consist of hashing over the latest news items. We very seldom solve anything.

I don't know if I'm losing it, or if the rest of the world is losing it. It seems to me that our society is going into a tailspin. It could end up in the crash that Y2K failed to deliver. Part of the problem may be an overload of information, provided by all the latest electronic communication gadgets. With the flick of a switch and a push of a few knobs, we can find out what the rest of the world is doing.

There are web sites for anything that exists in our global community. One we hear a lot about is on-line shopping (a glorified mail order catalogue service). We can also learn how to make bombs or other questionable projects or what the next Greenpeace goofballs' antics might be.

Another favorite pastime on the Internet is how and where to find a perfect mate (very few of them exist). I have read of a number of incidents where some older creep has become acquainted on the Internet with underage girls, culminating in the girl leaving home to secretly meet her Lothario. Last year in the United States, over eight hundred young girls, aged twelve to seventeen, and a few other people disappeared. The authorities have concrete evidence those girls were lured to whatever fate awaited them (rape, murder, or both). There are thousands more girls who disappear without Internet connections.

In North America, approximately half of those young runaway girls end up as prostitutes. In Southeast Asia, the figures are much higher. Many of those girls meet up with a smooth-talking pimp, who wines and dines them and even buys clothes and jewellery for them. His next move is to get them hooked on drugs, then he seduces them, and they then become virtual prisoners. The money they earn as prostitutes goes to the pimp. He often beats them. I had a city detective tell me of a case where a pimp put one of his girls out of commission for quite a while. What he did was take a wire coat hanger, insert it in her vagina, then twist it and pull it out. He probably did this several times. At any rate, she almost died from loss of blood.

In my opinion, these low-life pimps should be given much stiffer jail sentences. In fact, some of them should be executed. Over the years, worldwide, thousands of women have been injured or lost their lives at the hands of these monsters.

I got sidetracked, now back to our daily news.

The activists and demonstrators have gotten out of hand. Sure, there are things in our society that need correction, but the areas those wild-eyed protesters select as their targets are usually way off base from mainstream society's opinion. One example was on a website threatening to disrupt the World Petroleum Congress in Calgary in June 2000. In that release, they said Seattle was "just the warm-up." They also encouraged people to bring cheap musical instruments to the protest, along with pictures of aboriginal folks, rain forests, and endangered species to sacrifice to the "Gods of Oil."

I wonder what kind of material those musical instruments are made from? To the best of my knowledge they are made from wood, a no-no for tree huggers, or plastic derived from oil, or metal from mines, which is also a no-no. There may even be leather involved, that too is off limits by both the radical animal rights people and the endangered species lobby. In fact, those two gangs are often the same people.

I wonder how all those protesters from Canada and the United States and other parts of the world plan on getting to Calgary. Airplanes, ships, buses, and cars all use petroleum, so they are out.

Riding or driving horses and mules is cruel to animals, so that option disappears.

They can't hitchhike because whoever gives them a ride uses petroleum. If they decide to walk, they shouldn't use the highway pavement because that is made from petroleum products as well. If they walk in the ditch beside the road they might trample some endangered plants, or worse yet, accidentally step on an endangered bug or rodent.

So maybe not many will show up. That would give the police and authorities a much easier job of assuring the safety and security of those attending the congress.

I wonder what those protesters heat their homes with? Not many can afford solar energy heat. All other forms of heat require wood or fossil fuel.

Fortunately, the congress is held in June. At that time the temperature in Calgary is usually quite mild. The few that break the mode of travel and get here can sleep in the parks. It is a good thing grass is not on the endangered plant list yet. If it was, they might have to climb a tree for the night. Then again, that might be a problem as well. Maybe the tree they choose has a nest of an endangered bird, say a magpie (oops, I slipped up, magpies are not on the list yet.)

By now you must think I am a redneck. Well, I am, to some degree. I love animals and never mistreat them. I think there are a number of birds and animals that do need protection. I also like and enjoy trees (a renewable resource). I admire the logs in our house every day. I also like clean water.

The lumber, mining and petroleum industries did need some improvement in their operations. I think most normal people would agree that those industries are doing a good job these days in protecting the environment.

Of course, the activists and protesters claim credit for this improvement. I agree they had some influence. However, like everything else, small minorities of radicals go way overboard. People all want the good life, including the activists and protesters.

Without agriculture and domesticated animals and without lumber, mines, and petroleum our lifestyle would sink like a rock. In fact, in the Northern Hemisphere of the world, people could not exist. The moderate to hot climates of the world are already overpopulated. Unless we all wish to move to those poverty-stricken countries, we must keep the north functional.

June 20, 2000

The World Petroleum Congress has come and gone. It went off without a hitch, thanks in part to the $2,000,000 spent on beefing up security with fences and extra police. In the end, it appeared like dragging out a cannon to shoot a mouse. However, if precautions had not been taken it might have been a different story. If enough kooks and misfits who were bent on disruption and destruction, which was predicted on the Internet, had made their way to Calgary it could have happened.